without you

SIMON & SCHUSTER
new york
london
toronto
sydney

a memoir of
love, loss,
and the musical
RENT

ANTHONY
RAPP

SIMON & SCHUSTER
Rockefeller Center
1230 Avenue of the Americas
New York, NY 10020

For information about special discounts for bulk purchases,
please contact Simon & Schuster Special Sales at
1-800-456-6798 or business@simonandschuster.com

Designed by Jaime Putorti

Manufactured in the United States of America

10   9   8   7

Library of Congress Cataloging-in-Publication Data
Rapp, Anthony.
Without you: a memoir of love, loss, and the musical Rent / Anthony Rapp.
p. cm.
1. Rapp, Anthony. 2. Actors—United States—Biography. 3. Larson, Jonathan.
Rent. I. Title.
PN2287.R247A3 2006
792.02'8092—dc22   2005056318
ISBN-13: 978-0-7432-6976-6
ISBN-10:   0-7432-6976-4

The author gratefully acknowledges permission from the following sources to reprint
material in their control: EMI Blackwood Music, Inc. for lines from "A Long December,"
words and music by Adam F. Duritz, © 1996 EMI Blackwood Music, Inc. and Jones Falls
Music, administered by Hal Leonard Corporation; Gorno Music for lines from "Add It
Up," written by Gordon Gano, © 1980 Gorno Music (ASCAP), administered by Alan N.
Skiena, Esq., Epstein, Levinsohn, Bodine, Hurwitz &Weinstein, LLP; the Larson family
for lines from the musical Rent by Jonathan Larson, © 1992–1996 by Skeeziks, LLC and
Finster & Lucy, LLC; Night Garden Music for lines from "Losing My Religion," words
and music by William Berry, Peter Buck, Mike Mills, and Michael Stipe, © 1991 Night
Garden Music, administered by Warner-Tamerlane Music Publishing; Sony/ATV Songs
LLC for lines from "Waitin' for the Light to Shine," written by Roger Miller, © 1985 All
rights administered by Sony/ATV Music Publishing. Photos 1, 2, 7, 14, 15, and 17
courtesy of the author; 3 and 5: Douglas Rapp; 4 and 11: Mary Rapp; 6: Phyllis Wagner;
8: RR Best; 9: Touchstone Pictures/Disney; 10: Universal Studios Licensing, LLP; 12: The
White House; 13: Sony Pictures Entertainment; 16: Abbey Studios.

for

my

mother
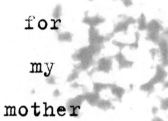

contents

vii

losing my religion

I sat down on the curb of Forty-fourth Street between Seventh and Eighth avenues, in front of the St. James Theatre, and glanced at my watch: no way was I going to be on time for my audition. *Fuck*. I raced to get my shoes off and my skates and helmet on, and launched myself into traffic, my skates gliding and buzzing, my arms pumping, my breath quickening, my skin relishing the balmy autumnal breeze that flowed around me. Rushing around New York City like this had always focused me: all my senses became more acute as I sped down Broadway, swerving among taxis and around jaywalkers, sprinting through yellow lights, avoiding at all costs any lethal car doors that threatened to spring open in my path. I hoped the *Rent* people would understand my reason for being late. They should. It wasn't as if I could've just up and left my friend Bill's memorial service early; that would have been unconscionable. I would just have to explain myself.

Ten minutes later, and twenty minutes after my scheduled appointment, I slid to a stop at the glass doors of the New York Theatre Workshop on East Fourth Street between Second Avenue and the

Bowery. Even though I lived only six blocks away, I had never actually been there. Still breathing heavily, I peered inside. Two actors, one male, one female, sat in the concrete-floored lobby on small wooden chairs between two sets of bright red wooden double doors. At least there were some people ahead of me. I rolled in and plopped myself on the ground, nodding hello to my fellow auditioners, unlatching my helmet, and wiping the sweat out of my eyes all at once. I quickly swapped my skates for shoes and reached in my backpack for my sheet music: R.E.M.'s "Losing My Religion." I hadn't had a chance to warm up my voice yet, and there wasn't going to be a chance to now. So I hummed some random notes at what I hoped was an imperceptible volume, just to get my chords working a little. If the others heard me, they thankfully didn't say anything; instead, their eyes alternately scoured their music and gazed vacantly out at East Fourth Street.

At least I now had time to settle my breath, to let my mind clear from what had been an emotionally draining and cathartic morning. I stared at my sheet music, even though I knew the song, in an attempt to zero in on something outside my head.

My fellow actors went in one at a time, and as much as I disliked listening to other people's auditions (I didn't want to disrespect them, but even more importantly I didn't want to psyche myself out if I caught the sound of someone who was really great), I couldn't help but hear the strains of Bonnie Raitt's "Something to Talk About" and Steve Perry's "Oh Sherrie" floating through the doors. Both of their voices were raw and strong and very rock and roll, and altogether intimidating. At least the three of us weren't all up for the same part, as far as I could tell; the guy looked older than I, and the girl was, well, a girl.

At last it was my turn to go in. I looked up from my music as the Steve Perry singer exited the theatre, and Wendy Ettinger, the casting director, poked her head out the door.

"Hi, Anthony, we're glad you could make it."

I gathered up my stuff and stood. "I'm sorry I was late."

She smiled. "Not a problem. We're running late too." Well, that was a relief.

Wendy opened the door for me, and I followed her into the theatre, feeling the familiar tinges of shyness and formality that often clouded over me when I headed into an audition room, at least during the introductory chitchat phase; once I got to read or sing, I was usually in good shape.

I had met Michael Greif, the director, a few months ago, when I auditioned for his production of *The Seagull* (he called me back, but didn't cast me), and I immediately recognized him sitting in the middle of the seats, his mop of black curls and dark, round, wire-framed glasses offsetting his pale, cherubic face. Having seen his production of *Machinal* a few years before, I was eager to work with him; I had been invigorated by the inventive, dark, and refreshingly theatrical vision he'd displayed. I always walked into an audition wanting to make a good impression, but the opportunity to get in front of Michael Greif again motivated me to try to make a great impression.

"Sorry I was late," I said, extending my hand for a shake. "I was at a memorial service for a friend." Had that been too formal of me to say? Too personal? A mistake?

"I'm sorry to hear that," Michael said. And right away, I was relieved; his tone was warm and gracious. "Well, we're glad you're here."

"Thanks." I glanced furtively at the other people spread out among the red velvet seats of the theatre: a young woman and two men, one younger than the other. I didn't recognize any of them. Well, that was no big deal; it was normal at an audition not to know who everyone was.

"So, are you ready?" Michael asked.

"Uh, sure." Good. I would get to do my thing right away.

"Great. Tim will play for you."

At the bottom of the aisle, in front of the stage, sat Tim at an upright piano. I made my way down to him.

"How you doing?" he asked amiably, a lot more amiably than most of the audition pianists I'd encountered over the years.

"Fine. How are you?"

"Oh, I'm great." He seemed like he really meant it, too, as he nodded and smiled. "What are we doing?" I handed him my music. "Oh, great tune."

"What are you singing?" a voice from the audience asked. I looked up to see that it belonged to the younger man, who was hunched down in his seat, a pencil in his mouth.

"'Losing My Religion,'" I said.

He nodded vigorously, also smiling. "Excellent." That response boded well.

I set the tempo with Tim, and jumped up onto the stage, glancing again at Michael, Wendy, the pencil chewer, and the two others I didn't know, all sitting there in the impassive yet attentive manner casting teams always displayed. I took a deep breath, and gave Tim the nod to begin.

The song's opening chords chimed. They were among my most favorite chords of any pop song ever, so simple and so hummable, and so *right* for the song. My body involuntarily pulsed in time with them, and I launched into my singing.

> *Ooooooooooh life*
> *Is bigger*
> *It's bigger than you,*
> *And you are not me*

I loved the way the song felt in my voice, right in the pocket, so I wasn't straining to hit any notes; I was just soaring on the melody and pouring myself into it. Images from the video of a twirling Michael Stipe danced in my head as I sang, my arms splayed out to my sides, my chest full.

> *That's me in the corner*
> *That's me in the spotlight*
> *Losing my religion*

I had read in an interview somewhere that this song was a love song, that in the South, where R.E.M. was from, losing your religion meant falling in love. I wasn't trying to sing it as a love song to anyone in particular; I was trying to sing it with as much heart and passion as I could muster, to anyone and everyone. I was singing it for the sheer joy of being able to sing it, and I could feel myself flying with it, grateful for the chance to open up my voice and fulfill some of my rock star fantasies, and to pay tribute to one of my all-time favorite bands.

I got so swept away that I lost the sense of where I was in the song, and jumped a verse:

> *Consider this*
> *Consider this*
> *The hint of the century*

Panicking, I peeked at Tim, but he was in the music and right with me. My panic subsided as quickly as it had come, and I charged on, building steam for the final chorus.

> *I thought that I heard you laughing*
> *I thought that I heard you sing*
> *I think I thought I saw you try*
> *But that was just a dream*

I flung my arms out to my sides, spreading them as far as they could go, my hands flaring open, the energy of the song shooting through me. My heart pounded as the final chords rang out, and just like that it was over. My fingers tingled.

"Thanks," Michael said. Was that it? Auditions always ended so quickly, and took so much out of me, like a sprint, leaving me spent, but also warmed up and hungry to keep going. Jazzed, I hopped off the stage and went to the piano, where Tim handed me my music.

"Good job," he said quietly, conspiratorially.

"Thanks." I knew that he was right. It had gone well, even with my fuckup. Not that an audition going well meant anything necessarily; I gave good auditions that led nowhere all the time. Cautiously satisfied, I started up the steps and encountered Michael standing in the aisle next to the young pencil chewer.

"I want to introduce you to Jonathan Larson," Michael said. "He's the writer of the show."

I took Jonathan's hand, shook it. "Nice to meet you."

"You too," Jonathan replied, smiling. He looked somewhat young to have written a show, but had what seemed like the right kind of intensity. His long body was all folded up in his plush red seat, and his large face, framed by ears that stuck out a bit too much, glowed pleasantly and openly under a mass of brown curls.

Michael handed me a cassette and some sheet music. "We would like you to come back and sing the title song," he said. "It's the first song on the tape."

"Cool," I said. I loved it when I got called back on the spot. It didn't happen that often, but when it did, it usually worked out that I got the part. I mentally crossed my fingers.

"Great," Michael said. "We'll see you in a couple of days."

The callback couldn't have come at a better moment. It was September 1994, and I had just begun my first-ever "real" job since moving to New York five years earlier: pouring lattes and cappuccinos and double-tall decaf skim no-whip mochas at a Starbucks up on Eighty-first and Second. I had been unusually lucky in getting enough acting work to sustain myself for the five years I'd lived in New York, but things had dried up over the last year or so, and I was now more broke than I'd ever been. If I were cast in *Rent*, the money would come in handy, and I would savor the creative fulfillment of working on a new show.

Back at my cramped but pleasant East Village apartment, which I shared with my older brother, Adam, and two other roommates, I sat on the floor of my living room and popped the tape in my boom box. All I knew about the show was from the description in the casting sheet on the desk of my agent, Paul, which had said, *"Rent* is a new rock opera about a group of friends in the East Village," and that my character, Mark, was a videographer. There was also a transvestite mentioned and a drug-addicted, HIV-positive S&M dancer and a rock musician and other characters. It seemed potentially interesting, but the phrase "rock opera" didn't fill me with a tremendous amount of hope; it could all turn out to be silly, with a lot of bad special effects and tacky makeup and big hair. Or it could be funky and hip. The only way to find out, though, was to listen to it, and see.

I pressed play, and a fake-sounding electric guitar solo wailed out a melody I recognized but couldn't place. Then, abruptly, it was cut off, and fake-sounding drums and more fake-sounding guitars kicked in, chugging along in a mid-tempo rock song. It all sounded sampled and computerized, and very '80s. I hoped the rock and roll vibe would get a little more authentic, but I reminded myself that the tape was probably a demo. I followed along with my sheet music as the guy playing Mark sang on the tape.

> *If I threw my body out the window,*
> *Brains all splattered, guts all steaming in the snow*
> *I wouldn't have to finish shooting videos*
> *No one wants to show*
> *RENT!*

Well, the melody was easy enough, pretty much staying on one note except for the end. The lyrics seemed extreme and vivid for an opening song, although there was a directness and an energy to them. I played on, as Roger sang next, with Mark joining him on the chorus. Its melody reminded me of the 007 theme.

> *How we gonna pay*
> *How we gonna pay*
> *How we gonna pay*
> *Last month's rent?*

It all seemed straightforward enough: obviously, Mark and Roger were frustrated and broke. I could identify with that. I rewound the tape back to the beginning and set about learning the song for my callback.

Ten in the morning was too early to be belting out anything, let alone the opening number of a rock opera, but two days later that's what I was about to be doing. Annoyingly, my contact lenses were blurring up, so I had to keep squinting to make out any of the tiny words printed on the sheet music I gripped in my hand. I hoped they wouldn't notice. I stood in the same spot onstage as my first audition, the same group of five sitting in the audience, and gave my eyes one last forceful rub, willing my vision to clear. Thankfully, it did. I nodded to Tim, he pounded out the opening chords, and I began to sing. On the wrong note.

"Uh, let's start again," Tim said.

"Sorry."

"No problem," Michael called out from the audience. I could feel myself blushing, but if Michael wasn't going to be overly fazed by my mistake, neither would I. So I concentrated on my breathing, trying to focus and channel the charge of my embarrassment into my performance; nervous energy was still energy, after all, and if I didn't let it fuel me, it would wind up spinning me out of myself and ruining my audition. I breathed steadily in and out, and Tim plunked the correct note and began the song again. Its drive infected me, and I sang, my voice edgy as I bit into the words, the spite and frustration of the lyrics erupting out of me. It felt good to vent, and good to sing.

"Thanks," Michael said when I was done. My heart pounded. He made his way down the steps of the theatre to the front of the stage, looking up at me as I crouched down to hear what he was saying. "That was fine, but I want you to try something." I waited as he found the words to articulate his thoughts, his eyebrows arching, his hands groping the air. "I want you to think of this less as just an expression of angst and frustration, and more of an attempt to entertain yourself and your friend. You guys are freezing, and you're dancing around to keep yourself warm. You're sort of laughing at your own plight. You're dancing on your grave. Does that make sense?"

I nodded and felt the twinge of wishing I had thought of that already. But at the same time I was grateful for the direction and the opportunity to try again. Too often at auditions directors say nothing at all, and I go home wondering if what I did was remotely close to what they were looking for. "Yeah," I said.

"Great. Also, really ask the question: how are you going to pay the rent? Really ask it. Don't just rant and complain about it."

I nodded. "Okay."

"Great. Let's start again."

He went back to his seat, and Tim played the opening chords. I sang, immediately feeling a lighter touch, and feeling how right that was. The whole song became more arch and sardonic, less nakedly angry, but without losing the inherent frustration that fueled it. I loved when good direction opened material up; it was always more interesting, more full, to have lots of layers to play with.

"Thanks," Michael said when I was finished. "That was great."

Flushed from my singing and sparked by Michael's response, I glanced over at Tim, who quietly but forcefully nodded, his eyes wide and knowing and happy. I jumped off the stage and headed up the aisle.

"Good job," Jonathan said as I passed him. He was also nodding and smiling, again folded up in his seat, a notepad in his lap, his eyes intense and delighted.

"Bye," I replied, waving to everyone as I opened the door and walked into the lobby. I stood there for a moment, chewing my lip. As exhilarated as I always was after a good audition, I also always wanted the casting people to tell me right then and there whether I had the job. That rarely happened, though. While I walked home, disappointment lurked around the edges of my excitement, but I did my best to push it aside and coast on my adrenaline for a little while longer. So I had to wait, as usual. That was okay. This one felt good. This one felt like it was going to happen.

II.

At ten in the morning a week later, I shuffled into the tiny, airless rehearsal room in the tiny, airless offices of the New York Theatre Workshop (surprisingly located in Times Square, the opposite end of the earth from the East Village) for my first day of rehearsal. A dozen or so other actors milled around, sipping coffee and murmuring hellos to one another, their faces bleary. First days of rehearsal were like that: a lot of sleepy people wandering around, not really expressing how happy they were to be there, especially when no one knew one another from previous jobs. In the center of the room a semicircle of metal folding chairs curved around a small upright piano, so I staked out one for myself on the end and sat, quietly watching everyone else. Michael and Tim and Jonathan stood off to the side, conversing.

The day after my callback, my agent, Paul, had phoned, his voice smooth and level and matter-of-fact. "You got it," he said. It was my first audition through his office—he had just become an agent—and he could barely disguise his pride.

"Great!"

"The contract is only for four weeks, it's a workshop. So the pay's not much."

"How much is not much?"

"Three hundred dollars a week."

That wasn't much. But it was better than nothing, and better than seven dollars an hour slinging coffee. And it was a show. It was *work*. "That's fine, I can handle that."

"So is this a yes?"

I was grinning so widely I could hardly move my mouth. I was thrilled that my gut had been right, and I was relieved that I finally had another paying gig, that I was a working actor once again. "Uh, yes, this is a yes."

"Great. Congratulations."

That day I steamed my last milk and called out my last order at Starbucks. I tried to be sensitive in sharing my good news with my

fellow out-of-work actors on the staff, downplaying my excitement—
"It's just a small show. No big deal."—but they all were happy for me.
One in particular, a many-freckled redhead named Steven, a devoted
musical theatre performer, kept sidling up to me as I worked the register. He asked me lots of questions about the show—the answers to
most of which I didn't know—and kept saying, "That's so cool.
That's so cool." I was grateful for the response and surprised at his
and the others' generosity. Maybe they now had that much more
hope for their own escape.

I called my mom and told her the good news. It had been a while
since I'd been able to call her on such a happy occasion.

"Oh, that's wonderful, Tonio," she said, her mellow, midwestern
voice brightened by a smile I could hear over the phone.

"Yeah, I'm very excited."

"I'm so happy you get to sing again." She had often told me over
the years how much she wanted me to do more musicals; it was how
I'd started performing when I was six, but I hadn't been in one since
getting out of high school. She had often flattered and embarrassed
me by waxing nostalgic about my "angelic" rendition of "Where Is
Love?" in the title role of *Oliver!* (a role I played in four different productions), and reminding me of the awards I had won in junior high
school for my singing.

"Yeah, I'm happy I get to sing again, too," I said. Although I was
unsure that my voice would hold up in a demanding rehearsal situation, especially one in which I was singing a rock score.

"You have such a beautiful voice."

"Well, I haven't really sung in a while, so we'll see."

"No, you *do*. I love when you sing—"

"Okay, Momma, I've gotta go. I'll talk to you soon. I love you."

"I love you, too. Break a leg. I'll be thinking of you."

In the rehearsal room, a young woman approached me, her arms full
of manuscripts. She handed me a thick rubber-banded libretto and a
tape, and then repeated this with the other actors, who by now were

making their way to their seats. They were all young, in their twenties, about half of them black and half white, with one young woman who looked like she could be a Latina. I hoped I could hold my own with them; it was beginning to scare me that it had been over six years since I'd sung this much. I had not been cast in a musical since my junior year of high school, eight years ago. I flipped through my libretto, happy (and intimidated) to see that there were many lines devoted to Mark.

"Okay, everybody, let's begin," a voice called out. I looked up from my libretto to see a bunch of new people filtering into the room. They stood by the door in a clump, most of them holding paper coffee cups. The last of the cast members took their seats, and the man who had been at my auditions stepped forward. He looked to be in his mid-30s, and his voice was mild and genial, his manner shy but friendly. He cleared his throat several times as he spoke.

"Hello, everybody, my name is Jim Nicola, and I'm the artistic director of the New York Theatre Workshop." Okay, that explained why he'd been at my audition. "We're all so glad you're here, and we're very excited to be doing this studio production of Jonathan Larson's wonderful piece." He put his hand on Jonathan's shoulder as he said this, and Jonathan grinned and bashfully lowered his gaze. "The other thing I wanted to say is that our offices are right across the hall, and if you ever need anything, if you ever have any questions, please don't hesitate to come in. We truly have an open-door policy here at the Workshop." I had worked at several nonprofit theatres in New York, and I had never heard an artistic director extend that kind of invitation.

He then had everybody go around the room and introduce themselves and announce their roles in the production or in the offices, a normal first-day-of-rehearsal custom. Of course, there were always far too many names uttered too quickly to possibly remember, but it was always done. As my turn approached, I felt a familiar pang of embarrassment looming around my throat, a leftover from grade school, and I concentrated on saying my name evenly and confidently and sweetly.

"Well," Jim said when the last name was announced, "we'll let you all get to work. Have fun." He and the rest of the artistic and administrative staff moseyed on out. Tim sat down at the piano, banged out a few chords, trilled some random notes, and Michael stepped out in front of the group of actors. Jonathan sat off to the side behind a table, his big eyes roaming expectantly around our faces, his hands folded in front of him.

"Welcome, everyone," Michael said. "I'm really looking forward, as I know Jonathan and Tim are, to getting to work. I don't want to say too much at this point, since you'll be hearing me talk a lot over the next couple of weeks. Because this is a musical, and really more accurately, an opera, I'd just like to start out by having you all sing together. So I'll give you over to Tim."

Tim poked his head over the top of his piano. "Hey everybody. Morning." He hit some chords and grinned. As in my auditions, he was preternaturally jovial and energetic. "Everybody awake yet?" We all murmured a version of "yes," and Tim chuckled. "Yeah, I thought so." He struck some more chords. "Tell you what. Let's do a little group warm-up, just to get a sense of ourselves, listen to each other, get ourselves all in the same room. Sound good?" More murmurs and another chuckle from Tim. "Great. All right. Here we go."

As he guided us through our warm-ups, I looked around at the other cast members, who in turn looked around at me and the others. The sound in the room, even with just mm's and ah's and oh's, was huge and resonant.

"You guys sound *great,*" Tim said when he had brought us through our final arpeggios. "Really great." He turned to Michael. "All yours."

"Thanks, Tim," Michael said and stood in front of the piano. "I want to start by learning a song. It's the song that opens the second act, and it's called 'Seasons of Love.'" Our stage manager got up from her seat and handed us all sheet music. "It's a beautiful song that Jonathan's written, and even though it essentially takes place at a funeral, it's very much about celebration. I just want you to bear that in mind as you're learning it and singing it. I think it's pretty self-evident what's going on in the song, but I just wanted to plant that seed, to let that inform you as you go."

"Okay," Tim said. "Cool cool cool. Check it out. This is the basic groove. I'm just gonna play this a couple of times through so you can feel it. And—" His head swung in time against the syncopation of the several simple, beautiful chords that descended and ascended, the pattern repeating and repeating. He played it through several times, and then spoke over the music. "Okay, now here we go. Here's the tune." And he sang:

> *Five hundred twenty-five thousand six hundred minutes*
> *Five hundred twenty-five thousand moments so dear*
> *Five hundred twenty-five thousand six hundred minutes*
> *How do you measure—measure a year?*

Chills shot up my arms and spine and the back of my head. I had never heard a song like it, especially in a musical; there was a direct-ness and a simplicity and a groove to it that were thrillingly new to my ears. I felt everyone in the room lean forward into the music.

"Okay, let's just loop that bit." And tentatively, we sang back what he had just sung for us, and then again, with more confidence, and then again, once more, nailing it. "Great," Tim said. "Moving on." He sang:

> *In daylights—in sunsets*
> *In midnights—in cups of coffee*
> *In inches—in miles*
> *In laughter—in strife*
> *In five hundred twenty-five thousand six hundred minutes*
> *How do you measure a year in the life?*

More chills tingled up my back. This song was so much more beautiful and evocative than the song I had heard on my audition tape. I couldn't believe it was written by the same person. I glanced over at Jonathan, who was listening with intense concentration and a pleased glint in his eye.

"Okay, let's loop that chunk," Tim said. And we did, stumbling on the rhythm of *"cups of coffee"* and *"in miles"* and *"in laughter—in strife."* Tim guided us through those bits a couple more times, until we had more or less gotten it, and then we sang through the whole section of the song.

"Great. Moving on. This is the chorus." And he sang:

> *How about love?*
> *How about love?*
> *How about love?*
> *Measure in love*
> *Seasons of love*
> *Seasons of love*

Even more chills spread themselves around my body. Everyone in the room nodded and grooved to the music, and to the gorgeous melody of the *love*s, suspended and rising and falling and ringing out.

"Okay, let's try that much." And we all dove into the chorus, our voices soaring and blending, the sound fantastic and full and exhilarating. "Wow. You guys sound *great*," Tim said. "I wish you could be sitting where I'm sitting. It's *enormous*." He jolted his head back as if he'd been hit with a giant splash of cold water, his eyes wide, his eyebrows just about reaching the ceiling. "*Really* great." He nodded decisively, and played the opening chords again. "Okay, let's put it all together. From the top."

And we sang, our bodies pulsing to the rhythm of the song, our voices hushed and rich. The progression of the song felt perfect, with the short, syncopated phrases of the verse releasing into the open, flying notes of the chorus. When we finished the chorus we all applauded.

"That's great," Tim said. "Really great."

I peeked back over at Jonathan, and he was now grinning one of the hugest, most delightful, satisfied grins I'd ever seen.

"So," Tim said, "that's the basic tune. There's another verse, and solo bits, and you break into parts in the chorus—the first verse is all in unison—but that's the gist of it." Well, if that was the basic gist of the song, it was already extraordinary. I could only imagine how amazing it would be with the rest of it in place.

That night after rehearsal I sat on my bed and played through my songs on the demo tape, reading along with the libretto. I didn't hear anything quite as stirringly beautiful as "Seasons of Love" in the rest of the music, but there was melody and heart in all of it. There was also the occasional lyrical clunker: in "Cool/Fool," a catchy, rhythmically inventive song between Roger and Mark, they needle each other by saying, *"For someone cool, you're a fool,"* and Mark berates Roger by calling him *"Mr. Negative 'cause he's HIV-positive."* I cringed when I heard those bits, but I played on.

I took an immediate interest in the relationship between Mark and Roger, which reminded me in some ways of my relationship with my brother, Adam: Mark is always trying to get Roger to open himself up (in this case by bringing him to an AIDS support group), and Roger adamantly resists, preferring to stay shut down. While the specifics were not the same (Adam is not HIV-positive, for one), Mark and Roger's dynamics were similar to those between Adam and me, and I was instantly able to hook myself into them, to begin to mesh myself with Mark.

In the next song, Mark and Roger's friend Collins shows up at their apartment with his new boyfriend, a drag queen named Angel, and they also invite Roger out to the support group. He declines, and an argument between Roger and Mark follows, which gets particularly heated, with Mark pushing and pushing and Roger resisting and resisting, until at last Roger hauls off and punches Mark in the stomach (I wondered if that punch would work onstage). Mark then sings a plaintive, elegantly melodic song, "He Says," which features this exchange:

Mark: *He says he doesn't need support groups*
Roger: *I say he'll bring his camera*
Mark: *He doesn't know why I go when I'm not sick or queer*
Roger: *Footage to make a career*

I loved the economy of the music and the fullness of the moment—it revealed so much about the mutual resentments that had been building up between two good friends and gave valid voice to both at once. Happy to have such a rich moment to play, encouraged by it, I plowed on through the score, listening to chunks of everyone else's songs, but mostly concentrating on my stuff.

Nothing else of mine jumped out at me until the end of the first act, when I discovered I got to lead the way in a rousing number called "La Vie Boheme." Mark starts it out by toasting:

To days of inspiration
Playing hooky, making something
Out of nothing

It was my kind of song: fast and fun and exuberant, the lyrics tumbling out almost faster than my ears could follow them, sometimes rhyming, sometimes not, all percolating above a funky bass line reminiscent of Vince Guaraldi's famous theme for the *Peanuts* cartoons. I leaned forward into the speakers to keep up.

After Mark's opening verse (a whole verse to myself!), the rest of the company joins in, escalating in intensity and harmony, throwing out lists of famous bohemians in cleverly rhymed couplets and triplets:

To Uta
To Buddha
Pablo Neruda, too

A true party atmosphere erupted out of my tiny boom box speakers, and I found myself bobbing my head in time to the music. I *loved* this line:

> *To faggots, lezzies, dykes, cross-dressers too*

This was a *musical*? You wouldn't hear that sentiment in Andrew Lloyd Webber's shows. Or Sondheim's, for that matter. Nor this:

> *To people living with, living with, living with*
> *Not dying from disease*

I had to shake my head a little to diffuse the jolt that hit me with that line. It was so joyful, so true, and it expressed *exactly* how I felt. In 1994 this was still a revolutionary idea—that it was possible to live a full life in the face of AIDS or cancer, that being ill didn't mean being dead. Jonathan proclaiming that in a musical, in a song that was all about celebrating life on the fringes, was unprecedented in my experience. I was thrilled to have the opportunity to express all of this myself; I couldn't wait to be in the rehearsal room with the rest of the cast and revel in the shouting out of those words.

Rehearsals soon moved from Times Square to East Fourth Street, to the top floor of the brownstone next door to the theatre. There was much more air and light in this room (it even featured a skylight), and it was much closer to my apartment, so I couldn't have been happier. The days zoomed by, crammed full of music learning and quick, inspired staging; we had to get the whole production on its feet in only two and a half weeks. Michael and Tim worked efficiently and improvisationally, giving us tons of room for input, while Jonathan silently soaked it all up, occasionally interjecting his support when Tim got stuck teaching one of Jonathan's particularly complex rhythmic or melodic phrases.

Toward the end of the first week, Jonathan brought in a new

song, "Over It," for me to sing with Sarah Knowlton, who played my ex-girlfriend-turned-lesbian, Maureen.

"This is great," Tim said as he handed us the music. "It's kind of Donnie-and-Marie-ish, but not in a bad way, just really fun, and very pop." Jonathan sat off to the side, beaming, as Tim set about teaching us the song.

The joke of the song was that I was telling Maureen she was going to get over being a lesbian (*"You never even wore flannel shirts"* was one of my arguments), and she was telling me that I was going to get over being in love with her. I was happy to have this whole other set of issues to bite into in Mark's story, and to get to come at Maureen with such fun lines as:

> Who's on top?
> Who wears the pants?
> Who leads when you dance?
> Give me one more chance, Maureen
> This is just a phase, like girls and horses

Sarah was trippy: tall and intense and dramatic, a chain-smoker with big brown eyes and full dark lips and a tangle of tight dark curls framing her pale skin. Her Maureen was dry, pretentious, and funny, a wannabe Laurie Anderson, with more attitude and more lipstick. I felt young and small next to her and wondered if our onstage relationship would be believable, but I tried not to worry about it; we just had to make sure our moments worked between us. This song was turning out to be strong enough that it didn't seem like it was going to be a problem.

On the break, I went up to Jonathan, who was poring over some music in the corner, counting it out in his head. We had spoken little since rehearsals started, mostly just exchanging hellos and goodbyes. I stood next to him and hesitated before saying something, not wanting to disturb him, until he looked up at me.

"Hey," he said, smiling.

"Hey," I said. "I just wanted to say that I think this song is great. It's very fun."

"Thanks," he said.

"No, thank *you.*"

I was at a loss as to what to say next, like I was a starstruck fan instead of a fellow artist and collaborator, and Jonathan looked away for a moment, down at his music, and then back at me.

"You know," he said a bit shyly himself, "I'm really glad you're doing this."

"Thanks." I didn't expect him to say *that.* "Me too."

"I got really excited when I saw that you were coming in. *Dazed and Confused* is one of my favorite movies."

"Really?"

"Yeah, I love that film. And then you came in, and I was so happy that you could sing."

"Wow. Thanks." I felt like I was saying "thanks" about a million times. But what else could I say? I was truly flattered.

"Yeah." He looked down at his music. "Anyway. This is all pretty exciting that it's happening."

"Yeah." I felt like I should say something more, but I wasn't sure exactly what. I didn't want to keep fawning, though; I wanted to get to know him better. Finally, I swallowed and said, "Well, it's exciting for me, too. This show is great."

He looked back up at me. "You think so?"

"Absolutely."

He nodded. "It's going well. I can't believe it."

I nodded too. "Yeah." We paused again for a few seconds, my jaw tightening and my cheeks burning as I searched for something else to say to break the silence. I hoped we could talk more freely and possibly even become friends, but I couldn't think of where to go from there. Jonathan seemed at a loss as well, and then Kristen, the stage manager, called out, "We're back!" Jonathan and I quickly shared a nervous smile, and returned to the comfort of work.

•　　　•　　　•

Work got more emotionally intense as we delved into Act Two. "Seasons of Love" had evolved into a full-on gospel number, complete with handclaps and the amazing soaring notes of our soloist's voice flying high above the final chorus. It was staged with absolute simplicity: all of us walked out during the elegantly simple piano introduction, took our places at the edge of the stage, standing in a straight line across the footlights, and sang the song from there.

As he was staging it, Michael told us, "I want to encourage you all to be yourselves in this song. To me, it's a very exciting opportunity in the show to sort of strip yourselves of your characters a bit, and let yourselves be exposed." I loved that notion, and it was one I had never heard expressed by a director. Michael had also spoken to us about his desire for the show to feel like the blending of a rock concert and a theatre piece, mixing straightforward storytelling with more presentational moments, and this last bit of direction seemed to fulfill that vision very well.

In working through the act we discovered that in context "Seasons" takes place at Angel's funeral, albeit abstractly, and the following scenes in Act Two occur in flashback, detailing the events of the year leading up to the funeral. Midway through the act, during "Contact," a desperately sexual song filled with chanted words and phrases (*"Please don't stop please / please don't stop stop"*), Angel's death suddenly rings out in a transcendent swirl of house beats, as he undulates and writhes and sings over and over:

> *Take me*
> *Take me*
> *I love you*
> *I love you*

Jonathan and Michael had imagined the death thrillingly: Angel becomes an ecstatic embodiment of release, the release that I imagined very ill people might experience when they're finally relieved of their pain and go on to whatever's next. Mark Setlock, the sweet-voiced, openhearted actor playing Angel, performed it beautifully, his body pulsing, his voice exploding out with tremendous love and heat and joy.

Then we are all at the funeral, where Collins comes to the front of the stage, clutching the coat that Angel had bought for him, and quietly and simply sings their love song, "I'll Cover You."

> *Live in my house*
> *I'll be your shelter*
> *Just pay me back with one thousand kisses*
> *Be my lover*
> *And I'll cover you*

As the song builds, the rest of us join in, our fourteen voices raised as one, wailing out our love and grief for our friend who is gone. The refrain of "Seasons of Love" mingles with the refrain of "I'll Cover You," the two songs weaving together, escalating and cascading over each other, our voices growing in passion and volume, the melodies and harmonies taking us to new notes and new heights of emotion, until all that is left at the end is Collins's wail ringing out. I was deeply moved by the singing of this song; we were all shaken by its enormous, bursting, aching heart. Once again, I was amazed that someone as young as Jonathan had written something so profoundly affecting.

After the funeral, "Goodbye Love" follows, in which the remaining seven central characters—Mimi and Roger; Maureen and her girlfriend, Joanne; Mark; Collins; and Roger and Mark's ex-friend-turned-landlord, Benny—begin to splinter apart in the wake of Angel's death. Roger is moving to Santa Fe to get away from everything, especially Mimi; Maureen and Joanne are in the middle of another of their frequent fights; and Mimi is tearing into Roger for giving up on her. (*"I'd be happy to die for a taste of what Angel had,"* Joanne and Mimi cruelly shout at their respective lovers, *"someone to live for / unafraid to say, 'I love you.'"*) Mark stands on the sidelines, feebly attempting to make peace between everybody (*"Come on, guys, chill!"* is one of his pathetic tries), a position I was familiar with in my own life; I tended to steer clear of direct confrontations and often wound up serving as a mediator in people's arguments. But Mark's attempts at peacemaking after the funeral appease no one, and ultimately a grief-stricken Collins intervenes: *"You all said you'd be cool tonight / so please, for my sake,"* he begs. After singing a plaintive and resigned *"I can't believe this is good-bye,"* everyone disperses, leaving Roger and Mark alone.

In tentative, delicately melodic dialogue, accompanied only by a piano gently spilling out a hypnotic arpeggio, Mark and Roger begin to talk. Mark begins, as usual, by nudging Roger, in this case to pursue Mimi. *"How could you let her go?"* he asks, to which Roger replies, *"You just don't know."* But before long, the tone shifts, and for the first time Mark turns his attack onto himself, expressing some of his fears to Roger:

> Mark: *"Mark has got his work,"*
> They say, *"Mark lives for his work,"*
> And, *"Mark's in love with his work"*
> *Mark hides in his work*
> Roger: *From what?*
> Mark: *From facing my failure*
> *Facing my loneliness*
> *Facing the fact I live a lie*

Once again, the correlation between myself and my character was remarkable: I sometimes wondered if my love of acting was an escape of sorts. I'd been doing it since I was a kid, and it felt natural for me to be onstage, inhabiting other characters' skins and souls, but offstage I often felt like a small, pale dork. I had always been comfortable while performing, never having to battle stage fright or getting overwhelmed by nerves, whereas offstage, I often retreated into the background. I enjoyed time by myself—I especially loved to read—but while I had a lot of friends and also loved hanging out with them, I often had a low-grade anxiety, a fear of doing or saying the wrong thing, of offending someone, of not being witty or sexy or cool enough, all buzzing in the background of my thoughts when I was in a social situation. My self-confidence grew enormously when I performed, probably because I had received nothing but flattering feedback from the first time I had set foot onstage (at the age of six, playing the Cowardly Lion at Island Lake Camp), while offstage I had often borne the brunt of teasing—from my brother, Adam, and sister, Anne, not to mention older kids all through junior high and high school. Like Mark, I hid behind my work; in my case, by transforming myself again and again into other people, funneling any of my own anxieties and fears and emotional chaos into my performances, rather than really experiencing and expressing it all offstage.

The scene between Mark and Roger continues with Roger's response:

> *You don't live a lie*
> *Tell you why*
> *You never finish your film*
> *'Cause the standards you set for yourself are too high*

Here was another aspect of Mark with which I could identify: I'd spent the last several years beginning various writing projects—short stories, a play, a screenplay—only to quickly abandon them out of frustration and insecurity.

Roger continues:

> *But the fact remains . . .*
> *You're the one to survive*

To which Mark responds:

> *I know*
> *I'm afraid the burden's gonna make me crack*

This line resounded with me, setting off bursts of insight and compassion. It was the first time Mark had expressed the crux of his dilemma: he was the only HIV-negative member of his circle of friends (even Maureen was positive in this version of the show), the only one with a wide-open future, and there was nothing he could really do for them. The only possibly meaningful response he had come up with was to make a film about all of them, to try to document their lives before they were gone. But of course he had been unable to finish it, and now Angel was dead, and who knew which one of his friends would be next. It would probably be Mimi, considering the way she looked—*"Mimi's gotten thin / Mimi's running out of time,"* Mark desperately tells Roger—and Roger was leaving, and *he* might be next, or Collins, or Maureen. And when they were all gone Mark would be truly, utterly, terribly alone. Although I didn't share his urgent circumstances, I empathized with his fear of losing loved ones and with the fear of being alone.

The scene ends with Mark and Roger quietly and awkwardly saying "love you" to each other, the only moment in the show in which they express any real warmth or affection for each other, a moment I was glad to have. As Roger walks away, a very weak Mimi emerges out of the shadows to intercept him.

Mark: *You heard?*
Mimi: *Every word.*

Then Mark stands off to the side and watches as Mimi sings to Roger:

I just came to say goodbye, love
Goodbye, love
Goodbye

Roger runs off, unable to face her, but Mimi keeps on singing after him, *"Goodbye, love,"* desperately wailing it out, until at last she quietly adds, *"Hello, disease,"* and runs off herself, leaving Mark alone onstage.

I found out later how much that last moment, as well as other moments in the show, paralleled scenes from Puccini's *La Bohème,* which was Jonathan's inspiration for *Rent.* But one of *Rent's* scenes veered very much from its source: the finale. In both Puccini's and Jonathan's versions, Mimi goes missing until she's finally found, near death, and is brought back to the loft. After a tender and heart-wrenching scene, in which all of her friends helplessly surround her, and her lover tries to reconnect before it's too late, Mimi dies in Puccini's version. But she only *almost* dies in Jonathan's, as she comes back from the brink after having a vision of Angel telling her it's not her time. I worried that Jonathan's ending might bother some people, that it would seem cheesy and contrived, but he was adamant that Mimi should live at the end of his story; he wanted for his show to end with life, not death. Besides, Angel had died, so it wasn't like there was an absence of loss and sorrow in his piece. I was ambivalent about his choice to let Mimi live, but Michael and Tim and all of us in the cast were able to find a way to make it feel real; we played it sincerely and fully; after all, near-death experiences did occur in the real world. We hoped our audiences would be moved in the end.

And after Mimi's unlikely revival, there was no denying the power of the very last moments of the show: the entire ensemble comes together to sing a full-voiced, passionate, soaring counterpoint of two of Jonathan's refrains from earlier songs: *"I die without you"* and *"no day but today,"* the latter phrase ringing out in gorgeous harmony as the lights fade.

III.

The days began tumbling into each other as I spent almost every waking hour at the theatre. A couple of days before our dress rehearsal, our overworked (and severely underbudgeted) costume and set designer, transplanted Berliner Angela Wendt, frantically pawed through racks of clothes during an impromptu costume fitting with me, both of us surrounded by shopping bags and tape measures in the cramped dressing room. After trying on and discarding several items and mixing and matching the remaining possibilities, we decided on a pair of dark blue sweatpants, a black-and-white zigzag-patterned rayon shirt, and my own red, plaid, zip-up wool jacket and pair of Blundstone boots.

"So what are we going to do about your hair?" she asked in her mild German accent, chewing her lip, one hand flitting around my head, the other hand rubbing her chin. "Hmmm. Something choppy, I think, like you could have cut it yourself."

"Sounds good to me." I usually surrendered to my costume designers' wishes, figuring that they knew much better than I did what would be best for the show.

"And how's your goatee coming?" She felt my scraggly chin and then took a step back to see it in the light. "Not bad. Maybe we have to put a little eyeliner in it or something. We'll see when you're onstage under the lights what it looks like."

"Sorry it's so light."

She laughed warmly, her mouth wide open. "It's not your fault you're so blond! It'll be fine."

Usually, technical rehearsals are *very* slow going, as all onstage work stops every few lines while lighting designers monkey with their cues and take many minutes on end to refocus a single light. But Blake Burba, our rail-thin, pale, focused, and quiet young lighting designer, miraculously didn't make us stop once. We went through the blocking onstage, and lights appeared where they should, occasionally delayed by only a few seconds. Blake always caught up with the action, his face aglow in the light of his computer screen out in the middle of the house, so we made quick progress through the scenes.

On the second day of tech, after the lunch break, Sue White, our sound designer and the technical coordinator of the New York Theatre Workshop, handed us all head mikes for the first time.

"Ooo, look, I'm Janet Jackson," Mark Setlock said as he put his on, performing a quick head-whipping music-video dance move to illustrate his point.

"Or Madonna," I added, laughing.

"Hey, don't play around with them, fellas," Sue said, stern but friendly. She was intense: sweet, but also *very* serious about her theatre. Her manner belied her tone; she would often touch people warmly on the arm or shoulder even when telling them off. "I know you know this," she continued, "but they're expensive. And they're all we've got. No replacements." She smiled benignly, and Mark and I shuffled away, chagrined, and made our way down to the stage. The rest of the cast was gathering there, watching the band set up.

Jonathan bopped around the theatre, more gleeful than I'd seen him yet. "Rock and roll!" he growled in his best Spinal Tap impression as he passed me. I gave him a little thumbs-up, and then Michael took center stage.

"Everybody," he said, "I'd like you to meet your band." Introductions went around the room, the band looking authentically rock and roll, complete with long hair and hip outfits. I wondered what it would be like for them to play in a musical. I hoped they'd be as into it as we were.

When introductions were complete, Michael resumed speaking. "The purpose of this rehearsal is just for you all in the cast, and you all in the band, to get a sense of what it's like to perform this music with each other. This isn't for blocking or lights. Just music. There's going to be a lot of trial and error as we finesse the sound mix—"

"You can say that again," Sue interjected.

"But for now, just allow yourselves to be informed by the power of a full-on rock band." He smiled. "Okay, Tim, whenever you're ready."

"*Oh*, sure," Tim said, clearly excited. "Let's start off with 'Rent,' shall we?" He bobbed his head up and down for a few counts, setting the tempo for himself, his whole body getting into it, and then, whipping his arms in rhythm, he called out, "A two three *four*!"

The explosive racket of the drums and guitar electrified the stage, and the entire cast looked around in amazement at one another, surprised and driven by the song's blazing kick. This didn't sound *anything* like Jonathan's demo tapes; this *rocked*. I suddenly began to worry whether my voice was jagged enough for this kind of music—singing these songs with just a piano was way different from singing them now. But I dove in, and did my best to bring out the edge in my voice. I could barely hear myself over the din of the music, but it didn't matter; I was too excited, feeling too much like a rock star, to care. During the guitar solo, I glanced over at Jonathan, who was beaming as he stood in the middle of the auditorium, awash in the huge, gorgeous clamor he'd created.

At the end of the number, we all whooped and cheered and applauded like crazy. My excitement shot to a new level, and the lift in everyone's adrenaline and spirit was palpable. Tim deferred all of our hollering—with a wave of his arms and vigorous pointing—to his band members, who looked overwhelmed and shocked that we were so psyched, but applauded right back at us, shyly grinning.

One of the joys of tech rehearsals is that it's the only time actors can sit out in the house and watch their fellow cast members' work from the audience's perspective. I took advantage of it every chance I got, which wasn't a lot because I was onstage during most of the show. But I did get to sit, captivated, and watch Daphne Rubin-Vega as Mimi cavort around the stage in her power-pop anthem, "Out Tonight," trying on and throwing off outfit after outfit like some coked-up runway model, blaring and growling out lines like, *"I've got an itch to be a bitch / I need to laugh like a child,"* each phrase full of fire and sex and abandon. I'd had no idea from the bits of her performance I'd seen in the rehearsal room that she was such a powerhouse. And she was *tiny* offstage, maybe five-four, but onstage she could have been six-four, there was that much energy and intensity blasting out of her.

I also sat out in the house, with the rest of the company, to watch Sarah's hilarious performance piece, "Over the Moon," for the first time. Accompanying herself on the cello, she deadpanned a pitch-perfect send-up of pretentious performance artists, complete with sudden fits of screaming that transformed instantly into robotic calm, non sequiturs galore, and the surprise bonus of several full-throated, manic "moooooooooooooos" to finish it all off. We all laughed like crazy during the piece, and then hooted and whistled and clapped for her when she was done.

On the night of our first performance, in the midst of all of the preshow backstage bustle, Michael thrust a piece of paper into my hands. "Do you mind reading this when you go on tonight?" he asked.

"Um, no," I replied. "What is it?"

"I just felt like we needed to set the scene a little bit. Let everyone in on the fact that we know it's just a workshop."

I glanced at the paper, skimming it. Lines like, "In the real production, there'll be lots of dancing, but we didn't have time for that this time around," jumped out at me.

"It's fun," I said, flattered to be asked to be the spokesman.

"Good. I'm glad you think so. Have a good show."

"Thanks." Michael went off to make his rounds, and I turned to my dressing room table to find that several cards had been placed there. One, a postcard, featured the campy black-and-white photograph of a young, bespectacled, exasperated man, his hair a mess, holding two silver film canisters, out of which the film had exploded, wrapping itself all around him, hanging off his neck and arms. On the reverse was the inscription, *"Your Mark is great. Especially in 'Goodbye Love.' Love, Jonathan."* I smiled to myself and placed the card in front of my mirror, making a mental note to thank him for it later.

The audience response during our ten-performance run varied from mildly respectful to extremely vocal and enthusiastic, and by the end of the run we were standing room only. The responses from my friends who were able to make it were mostly positive but occasionally critical; my agent, Paul, felt that the second act got too sentimental, but he loved the first act, while my friend Jay was completely blown away by the whole thing.

"I *loved* it," he gushed after the show, giving me a huge, warm hug in the back of the theatre. "Oh my god, it was incredible. Can I meet the guy who wrote it? He's a genius. I swear to god."

"Sure," I said, tickled by Jay's almost breathless glee. I brought him over to where Jonathan was receiving admirers and introduced him.

"Thank you so much for writing this," my friend said, pumping Jonathan's hand vigorously.

"You're welcome."

"How did you do it? It's amazing."

Jonathan shrugged, his grin sheepish and pleased. "I don't know. I just . . . wrote it."

"Well, it blew me away." I had never seen Jay so focused and hyped up. "Really. Totally."

"Thank you," Jonathan said, glancing at me with a grin. He then turned to meet another fan who was tapping him on the shoulder.

I escorted Jay out of the theatre, into the balmy, clear autumn night air and down East Fourth Street. He continued his gushing, and even started to sing bits and pieces of songs from the show.

"I love that theme—*And it's beginning to snow,*'" he trilled. "What a great melody. The whole show was great. I can't say it enough."

I couldn't help but smile; Jay's joy was so infectious, I felt like I was breathing it in. I had done many shows in New York, but it had been a few years since one had engendered such an undeniably exuberant response. I was proud and happy to be a part of this show for so many reasons, and I very much didn't want it to end.

grandpa

In November, right after *Rent* closed, my mom's father, Grandpa Baird, died. He'd been ill for a while, living, mostly bedridden, at home with Grandma Baird. I hadn't seen or talked to either of them in almost a year, but I had sent him a card a couple of months before his death, surprising myself; sending cards and letters was something I wasn't normally good about doing. *Dear Grandpa*, I'd written, *I wanted to wish you well and tell you I'm thinking about you. Love, Anthony.* It wasn't much, and I didn't know whether he was even cognizant enough to read it, or to understand it if it was read to him, but when Mom told me he'd died I was glad to have sent it.

Grandpa Baird had been a tiny man with big, sad eyes, a thatch of thick, close-cropped gray hair, and a perpetual salt-and-pepper bristle on his wrinkled cheeks. He'd always sat folded into himself at the corner of his and Grandma's huge dining room table when we visited their old house in Manteno, Illinois. He'd only speak to me when I spoke to him first, and with what seemed like a great deal of effort, his lips faintly trembling as they formed wavering words, his eyes roaming around or cast downward or occasionally meeting mine. Grandpa Baird had never read me bedtime stories when I was a kid or taken me to the zoo or told me jokes or ruffled my hair or pretended to discover quarters behind my ears or hugged me or told me he loved me. He had never been cruel to me either; he had just been a vaguely sweet, mostly silent, half-presence in the background of my life.

The only time we'd ever been alone together was in December of 1986 when I was fifteen and he spent two weeks with me as my guardian in Toronto while I rehearsed *Adventures in Babysitting*. He'd go with me to the rehearsal hall, sit and wait for me all day, and then shuffle silently through the snowy streets behind me as I impatiently slowed my pace, wishing I could be alone in the city so I could shop for CDs or see movies or play video games or simply explore Toronto and not have to worry about him. "What do you want to do, Grandpa?" I'd ask, and he'd reply in his barely audible, nasal, singsong voice, "Oh, I don't know." So we'd pretty much do nothing, or I'd go out and leave him in the hotel room by himself.

My mother told me later that he'd had a wonderful time. "He really enjoyed himself," she said.

"Really?"

"Yes. He thinks you're very sweet."

I didn't know what had given him that impression; I hadn't really treated him with much kindness during his visit.

Grandpa's dying meant that there would be a funeral, and that meant the Baird clan would assemble, which was always an epic undertaking: Grandma and Grandpa had produced thirteen children (twelve of them still living), who in turn had five spouses remaining among them (the rest having disappeared due to death or, like my father, divorce), and eighteen of their own children.

Mom was the eldest sibling. She could name all of her brothers and sisters in one breath, ticking them off with her fingers: "Tony-dianachrisrobertasheilajuliejoeamygraciakatrinalucieroman," she'd say, her voice calm and sweet and monotone, never betraying that some of them drove her crazy, or that she barely talked to others, or that, conversely, her sister Roberta was one of her closest friends.

Tony, her first brother, had died as an infant in his crib, from what was probably Sudden Infant Death Syndrome. "I sometimes think that's why Mom had so many kids," my mother said once. "Because Tony died. She just kept trying to replace him." That made sense, but I guessed Grandma's staunch Old World Catholicism had a lot to do with it, too.

Whenever I was around Grandma, images from the stories Mom had told me since I was an adolescent, about her experiences growing up, echoed through my mind like phantoms: Grandma grabbing my mother by the hair and banging her head against the wall while screaming at her, "I wish you were never born!" Grandma hitting my mother over the head with her hands and fists and brushes and hangers and pots and pans. Grandma telling my mother she was ugly and stupid and nasty. Grandma running away on several different occasions with whoever was the youngest baby, only to be found each time sitting in the same spot on a cliff at the local quarry, clutching her baby to her chest, weeping uncontrollably, threatening to jump. Grandma choking and shaking her youngest child, Roman, when he was a baby, because he wouldn't stop crying, almost killing him, until Grandpa was finally able to yank him away from her. Grandma following these episodes by holing herself up in her room for days on end, refusing food, leaving my mother to run the household and take care of all of her brothers and sisters.

I had never witnessed Grandma's violence—or even much of her temper—when we visited the old Manteno house, but I feared her all the same; I always imagined I could see something sinister in her open, pleasant, enthusiastic, frequent smiles. She was both vocally and physically more formidable than Grandpa, her strident voice and its throaty chuckles bouncing all around the house no matter what room she was in. Usually it'd be the tiny family room, where she'd plant herself in her oversized, cushioned rocking chair and hold forth, her eyes bright and clear and her strong jaw, broad shoulders, and large hands emblematic of the German heritage of which she was so proud. It seemed that the many years of struggles involved in managing such a large and troubled family had squashed Grandpa down while they had fortified Grandma. In fact, sometimes she could be downright jolly, and she was unusually lucid, not to mention hardy, for a woman her age.

"Has she still not ever acknowledged anything about the way she treated you?" I asked my mother from time to time.

"No," Mom always replied. "Never. She says she doesn't remember it that way at all."

Mom had pledged on more than one occasion to never treat my sister, my brother, and me the way Grandma had treated her, and except for a rare loss of composure when one of us was particularly ornery or sassy or obnoxious, she had kept her word remarkably well. I had always admired her for that, since I'd heard that very often children of abusers turned into abusers themselves. But not Mom.

The morning of Grandpa's funeral, Adam and I flew into Midway, the low-budget, smaller airport in Chicago, on a cheap airline, and shared a cheap limo straight to the funeral home, an hour away in Kankakee. We planned on zooming in and out of town; neither of us relished the thought of spending more than the minimal required time with Mom's family.

As we pulled in, there they all were, milling around the parking lot of the funeral home. Well, all but one: Julie, the seventh child of the clan, had fled to a Jesus cult in Vermont almost twenty years earlier and had lived there ever since. I remembered her only from a picture taken shortly before her getaway: a close-up of her grinning a sparkling, closed-mouth grin right into the camera, her face uplifted and triumphant and mischievous.

"Oh boy," Adam grumbled as we came to a stop. "Here we go." I chuckled and emerged into the bright, clear, breezy Indian summer morning, straightening my suit and steeling myself for the onslaught of our preadolescent male cousins, who were already crowding around the limo.

"Hey, guys," Adam muttered to them as he crawled out. "What's up?" Nathaniel and Matthew and Chris and Eric all played it as cool as ever, barely suppressing what I took to be their excitement at being around us, their older, exotic, New Yorker cousins. Adam casually slapped them all five, looking down on them from his towering, six-foot-three height, then scanned the horizon stoically, his jaw clenched. I greeted them with a wave and a hello, lacking, as usual, the offhand, austere style of my older brother, and feeling small and weak next to his bulky, athletic frame. Around these kids, I felt like a weirdo, interesting to them only because I was a teeny bit famous for having acted in *Adventures in Babysitting*. Adam was the much hipper, much more macho, much more compelling basketball star; they probably had no idea that he also had a career as a published novelist and burgeoning playwright.

Suddenly, the tiny, loose-limbed, explosively energetic, seven-year-old Rachel was sprinting toward us. "Anthoneeeeeee!" she cried. "Aaaaaaadam!" She leaped into my arms, tightly wrapping herself around me, giggling like crazy.

"Hi, Rachel," I said, also laughing. I squeezed her to me. "How are you doing?"

"Fine," she said, matter-of-fact as ever, and abruptly leaped down and lunged at Adam, who deftly deflected her by crouching down low enough to half hug her, his large hand patting her back.

"Hey, Rachel," he said. "Good to see you."

Rachel was technically our cousin, the little sister of Nathaniel and Matthew and the daughter of Lucie, Mom's youngest sister. But six years earlier, during my senior year of high school, she had become our little sister. Right after Rachel was born, Lucie's husband left her, and, since Lucie was out of work and in need of both emotional and financial support, Mom took Lucie and her three children in. It wasn't the first time Mom had helped out a sibling in such a way; in fact, she was famous in her family for offering endless amounts of support to whoever needed it. So for the next several months, Lucie and her kids lived with us, sleeping in the damp and chilly concrete basement of our small condominium, filling the house with chatter and fights and toys and a seemingly endless supply of crises large and small. I simply couldn't wait for them to move out and return some semblance of peace to the house.

"How much longer are they going to be here?" I'd whine to my mom.

"She's my sister, Anthony," she'd say. "They'll be gone soon. Just try to be patient."

Finally, Lucie got enough money together, and enough confidence, to move out on her own, to a small apartment a few minutes away. When she left, she took the boys with her but left Rachel behind; Lucie had agreed to allow Mom to continue to raise Rachel and become her foster mother. I couldn't believe that Mom was going to raise another child at her age—she was forty-six at the time, and had a full-time nursing job. On the other hand, her decision made some sense to me: the eldest of thirteen, she had raised children her whole life, and I was about ready to move out of the house, so why should she stop now?

Even though I questioned Mom's wisdom, I knew how loving and supportive she was going to be, and I also knew how insane and chaotic Rachel's life with Lucie and her two troublemaker brothers would have been. Matthew, the younger of the two, was especially diabolical: his beautiful, huge, ice-blue eyes, pale, prolifically freckled skin, and dark black hair and eyelashes reminded me of the young actor who had played Damien in *The Omen,* a movie that had given me many vivid nightmares as a child. When Lucie admonished Matthew for hitting Nathaniel or teasing Rachel or talking back to my mom, he never seemed remorseful or cowed; he usually just laughed or stared his mom down with cold fury, his lower lip jutting out, his arms folded, and spat out to her in his shrill whine, "You're *stupid*! I *hate* you!" Nathaniel, however, cried and sobbed copious, deeply tormented, repentant wails when he got in trouble, his chubby face contorting and turning various shades of magenta as he frantically paced around the living room, alternately clutching at his stomach or waving his arms as if he were on fire. While melodramatic, these displays of his conscience, of his little boy's heart breaking wide open, forever endeared him to me and gave me some hope for his future; Matthew was already a lost cause.

Unlike her brothers, Rachel was a happy baby, adorable and active and sweet, her crystal-blue eyes alight and eager, her smile infectious and almost constant. She found out early on in her childhood the truth of whose child she was (I was already out of the house by then), but decided to continue calling my mother "Mom" and her mom "Lucie." I didn't know if this was all going to confuse her later in life, but for now, she seemed perfectly at ease with it, and with the idea that Anne, Adam, and I were as much her siblings as Nathaniel and Matthew were. Having been the baby of my family before Rachel came along, I relished my role as her older brother, showering her with attention and love whenever I was around her.

"Hi, boys."

I looked around to see Mom walking up to us. I searched her pale, soft face for some signs of grief, but didn't really find any, and gave her a hug.

"Hi, Momma." She was a few inches shorter than I, and skinny, and her hugs were never firm—she wasn't strong enough to squeeze tightly—but they were always warm and open. Her large, comforting hands subtly pulsed into my back.

"Hey, Mom," Adam said when we broke apart, stooping down to her for his customary half-hug, which she met on tiptoe.

"So you guys made it," she said after their hug. "How was the flight?"

"Fine," I said.

"That's good."

A silent moment passed. I thought about saying something about Grandpa to Mom. *I'm sorry for your loss?* Too formal. *It's a shame, isn't it?* Same thing, only worse. She was my mom, not some stranger. Even though she and her dad weren't close, she must have been feeling sad about his death. I stared at the ground, and then Rachel suddenly broke the silence by clutching my hand tightly, spinning around on her heel, and flailing her free arm as if she were a spastic, errant, one-winged bird.

"Rachel, honey," Mom said, "calm down. We're going to go inside now, and I need you to behave, okay?"

"Okay," Rachel sighed, and forced herself to stop. I squeezed her hand and ruffled her hair.

"Come on, Rach," I said, "let's go say goodbye to Grandpa."

As we walked across the windswept parking lot, my sister, Anne, and her fiancé, Ken, emerged from their car and joined us. Anne had never been much of a hugger, so we just waved and muttered hello to each other and walked on in silence. Anne was so much not a hugger, in fact, that there was a time, not that long before, when Mom would ask Anne for a hug goodbye at the end of a visit, and Anne would simply extend her finger and poke it into the flesh of Mom's shoulder, giggling impishly. "Oh, Annie," Mom would say. "Give me a *real* hug." But Anne would just shake her head, still giggling, and turn to go. She'd gotten a little better at hugging since then, but not by much, and not with me—not yet, anyway.

We joined the procession of silent family members in the funeral home, no one meeting anyone else's gaze for longer than a second. I nodded to Grandma, who solemnly nodded back, and to Diana, Mom's oldest sister, who seemed to be always at Grandma's side. Adam and I glanced at each other, silently sharing our amusement at seeing her. Adam always sent Mom and Anne and me into hysterics when he joked about Mom's family, so I could guess what he was thinking now. In Diana's case, he loved to point out the fact that she looked way older than Mom, even though she was younger; in fact, she looked like she was way older than *Grandma,* with her frazzled gray hair and taut, deeply lined face. "And not only that," he'd say, "but she looks like she's got a dead Christmas tree plopped on top of her head." We'd all crack up at this, knowing that it was cruel, but at the same time so *true,* and Mom would laugh the hardest of all of us. Even though Mom had often advised us that "if you can't say something nice, don't say anything at all," when Adam joked like this, her face would screw up, her mouth open wide, and through her infectious, cathartic, almost silent guffaws, she'd start rubbing her eyes ferociously and sigh, "Oh, Adam, *stop*. You're going to give me a stomachache." Adam was brilliant at making Mom lose herself in laughter like that.

Soft, indistinct organ music droned in the background in the funeral home. Still holding Rachel's hand, I regarded Grandpa's coffin from where I stood, too far away to see inside it. I wondered what this whole event must seem like to Rachel; I had never been to a funeral home or a wake, only to my friend Bill Henry's memorial service on the day of my *Rent* audition, so this was strange for me, and I was almost twenty years older than Rachel. The only dead body I'd ever seen was at a distance: while walking along the Seine on a trip to Paris, I'd watched as several policemen recovered a bloated, pasty corpse from the river. But I'd turned away when they flipped over his body to reveal his face.

I wasn't sure what I should be feeling now. Death had visited me so little in my life: several pets had died since I was a young child, and a couple of actors I'd worked with had passed away, but they were only memories of people I'd once known when news of their deaths reached me. I had shed many chest-heaving tears over the passing of my pets, but my former coworkers' deaths were abstract, and I'd only felt a brief sadness for them.

When Bill died, I was for the first time faced with the loss of a friend, and what I initially felt when I read the news of his death in the *New York Times*—he had died suddenly of a heart attack—was numbness and shock. I kept thinking I should have felt more pain or sadness or grief or *something*. I kept trying to figure out how to grieve properly. While I was trying to sort out my response to Bill's death, I had a conversation over lunch with my ex-boyfriend Keith, who had remained a good friend after we'd split up. He'd always been a great sounding board and an uncommonly clearheaded source of wisdom and advice.

"I don't know what to do about all this," I told him. "I don't know how to process it."

"Well," he said, leaning forward intensely, as he always did when he talked, his right hand chopping the air, his boyish face bobbing up and down, "the thing is, the thing *is,* when you have someone you know who's died, you have to grieve, of course, but really, there are different things you have to grieve."

"What do you mean?"

"Well, you know, you have to grieve the loss of the *person,* you know, the fact that the actual *person* won't be there anymore to talk to, to laugh with, to share memories with, that sort of thing."

"Right."

"And then you have to, you have to mourn the loss of who that person held you to be. Because that dies with them. Their vision of you no longer exists. And a whole world of who *you* are is gone. So you have to mourn that, too."

I sat there and took that in, an electric current of recognition coursing through my body.

"That . . . makes sense," I said.

Keith nodded vigorously. "Yeah, it does. It does."

I shook my head. "How do you know all this stuff?" It was a question I often asked Keith; he and I were the same age, but his insight into profound human matters often outshined my own.

He laughed a high-pitched giggle. "I don't know." That was always his answer.

Standing in the funeral home at Grandpa's wake, I let go of Rachel's hand and swallowed—not out of horror or dread, but simply to prepare myself for this new, exotic experience of looking at a dead body—and approached the coffin. I peered in. There Grandpa lay, stiff as a wax figure and looking not at all how I remembered him; in life, his cheeks were not covered in blush, his hair was not so carefully combed and feathered back, and his face was not so gaunt or so smoothly shaven.

"Hi, Grandpa," I heard myself murmur, and felt foolish for saying it out loud. I considered reaching down and touching one of his hands that were laid across his chest, but then thought no, that was morbid. I didn't want to feel their cold stillness. So I just stood there and looked at him and waited for something transcendent to occur, for anything at all unusual or meaningful or unforgettable to happen. I breathed and I waited and I stared down at him lying there. I thought of what Keith had told me, that it was important when someone died to mourn different kinds of losses. But after a few long moments of standing and staring down at my grandfather, I started to feel absurd. And false. I hardly knew him. And he hardly knew me; he had even thought I was sweet to him when all I'd wanted to do was ditch him. Looking down at his inert, unfamiliar, costumed body touched nothing in me.

Finally, ashamed at myself for feeling so little, I stepped away from the coffin and sat down, talking to and looking at no one, until it was time to go on to the funeral.

Adam and I had been asked to join Nathaniel and a couple of other male cousins as pallbearers, so we all rode to the church together and then hoisted Grandpa's coffin out of the hearse. It was surprisingly heavy, and the smaller boys strained and stumbled under its weight, but fortunately we only had to carry it a couple of feet to deposit it onto a kind of gurney, which the grim, silent funeral directors used to transport Grandpa into the old stone cathedral.

Clenching my jaw, I entered the church and took my appointed seat in a pew near the front, next to Adam and Anne and Rachel. I couldn't remember the last church I'd entered or the last Catholic Mass I'd attended. I had never gone to church regularly, and I'd stopped going for good right after my confirmation; I'd designated that event as the last opportunity Catholicism had to reach inside my soul and truly mean something to me. When the priest of my confirmation had leaned over and anointed my forehead with sacred oil, intoning, "Do you accept the Holy Spirit?" I'd tried with everything I had to experience the Holy Spirit entering my body, to imagine a shimmering being floating in from above, enveloping me in light and warmth. But as much as I'd tried, nothing had happened. I'd said, "I do," anyway, and as I took my seat, I knew from that moment on I was no longer a

Catholic. And since that time, I began to take major exception to many of the teachings of the Catholic Church, most significantly its stance on queer lifestyles. So entering its places of worship had begun to feel like blatant acts of hypocrisy. But this day was not about me, I reminded myself, it was about Grandpa, and I wasn't about to make a scene at his funeral. As much as part of me wanted to.

During the service, I wrestled with whether I should participate; whether I should mumble the familiar prayers with the rest of my family or sing the hymns or kneel and stand and sit at the appropriate moments. I wound up joining in a little bit of the droning, lifeless mumbling, a little less of the off-pitch, thin, shrill singing, and all of the kneeling and standing and sitting, feeling silly and conflicted the whole time.

The priest was a remotely genial, slightly batty older Irishman, with a bulbous nose, thick, black-framed glasses, and silver hair. As all priests did when they performed a Mass, he resembled an extra from the set of an old Hollywood costume epic like *Ben-Hur* or *The Ten Commandments,* dressed as he was in his full regalia of blazingly white, gold-embroidered, floor-length vestments. He presided over the Mass as if by rote, absently muttering the prayers and shuffling around the altar. When the time came for his homily, the point in a Mass when priests extemporize on their chosen theme of the day— such as forgiveness or charity or rebirth—he ambled to the steps leading up to the altar and squinted down at all of us.

"Robert Baird," he said. "We are here to honor the life of Robert Baird." He folded his hands in front of his belly. "What can you say about Robert Baird?" I felt myself frowning. This wasn't going to be at all poetic, that was certain. "Well, Robert Baird was a very dear man to all of us in this room. He had a very large family, and he was a devoted father and lover of his wife." A devoted father? That was doubtful, if you asked my mom, but I guess it had to be said. "He loved music." He did? "In fact, Robert sang with the choir here." I was pretty sure that wasn't true. I began to get the uncomfortable impression that this priest didn't even know which member of his parish

Grandpa was. "He had a beautiful voice." Nope. Definitely not true.

"Robert accomplished much over the years he was on earth," the priest went on, "but I think the highlight of his life had to have been at the end. At the end, when he was so ill and unconscious and his devoted wife and so many of his loving children were there at his side, ushering him into heaven. Surrounded by so much love, Robert must have felt it was most certainly the highlight of his life." The highlight of his life occurred when he was unconscious? Shaking my head, deeply embarrassed for Grandpa, I had to stop myself from laughing out loud.

The priest rambled on for a little while longer, gesticulating expansively, intoning clichés about heaven and redemption and what lies in store for all of us on the other side. At last, when he was finished with that, he looked down at all of us sitting there and said, "Would anyone like to add any remarks?"

My body clenched up underneath the weight of the terrible silence that ensued. No one had prepared themselves to speak; it wasn't supposed to be part of the funeral's program. I frantically searched my brain for something that I might say, but then the thought of my getting up in front of everyone in the family to speak about a man I hardly knew struck me as ridiculous. I bowed my head and stared at my hands and waited for someone, anyone, to say something. But no one made a sound. I began to realize that everyone else was waiting for Grandma to be the first one to speak; that was the way things were done in this family. She called the shots. I resisted an urge to turn around and glance at her, to try to compel her to break the ice. Instead, I sat in my seat and stared at my hands and listened as the heavy silence stretched on and on.

Finally, Grandma's voice rang out from her seat, echoing against the stone walls of the cathedral. "No, Father, that's all right," she said.

My heart sank. That was it, then. No one else would have the guts to speak now, not after that. And as I and all of his children and grandchildren and friends sat mute in our seats, I shook my head and took in a deep, mournful breath. It was the first sorrow I'd felt all day.

wild bill

For as long as I could remember, my mom had always adored the esthetics, ideals, and mores of country life. Or at least what she perceived country life to be. Even though she'd settled down in suburban, mostly blue-collar Joliet, Illinois, she often expressed to me her wish to live out her years in New England, especially Vermont, in an old Victorian farmhouse with a huge, open porch. "I'd just love that," she'd say, and I'd fantasize about the day I would be able to buy her that house.

She collected large, impeccably framed prints by Charles Wysocki, a folk artist famed for his paintings of old-fashioned New England life; their prominence in her house was one of the only extravagances she afforded herself, and a modest one at that. Wysocki's primitive, autumnal-hued, cartoonish depictions of rosy-cheeked, bundled-up children playing in the snow; a village's frivolous Halloween festivities replete with white-sheeted ghost-children and snaggletoothed jack-o'-lanterns; or an immense, lazy, orange tabby cat perched smiling on a desk full of papers struck me as quaint and silly, but they seemed to inspire nostalgia in my mother for a life she'd never lived, except perhaps in her imagination. She loved his work so much that every Christmas, someone in the family made absolutely sure to buy her that year's edition of the Wysocki wall calendar; in fact, some Christmases she'd received more than one.

Her passion for country life was so renowned in her family that for Christmas 1994, right after Grandpa died, her brother Chris dreamed up a perfect gift for her: a week's vacation in a bona fide log cabin, situated in the middle of the woods in northern Wisconsin. Chris told her she could invite anyone from the family to join her, so Mom invited Chris and his wife, Bonnie; Mom's favorite sister, Roberta, and her husband, Bob (and their two mammoth English sheepdogs, Panda and Ollie); Rachel; and me. Anne and Adam were invited, too, but Anne was spending Christmas with her fiancé, Ken, and his family, and Adam couldn't afford the time off from work (even though he was a published author, he still had to hold down a day job to pay the bills). Mom was thrilled; she hardly ever took trips of any kind, and she had never stayed in a log cabin.

"You have to come," she said when she called to invite me, the excitement in her voice a rare treat. "It'll be so beautiful."

I was performing in a new off-Broadway play in New York—I hadn't stopped working since the *Rent* workshop, a complete turnaround from the year before—and had only Christmas Eve and Christmas Day off, so my trip was going to be extremely brief. But I figured it was worth it.

"Okay," I said. Even though I couldn't imagine myself sleeping in a log cabin in the middle of the Wisconsin woods.

"Oh, *good,*" she said.

With all the usual holiday delays and the early winter sunset, it was pitch-black out by the time I landed in Wisconsin. Chris picked me up at the airport. Long stretches of silence passed on our way to the cabin, as I stared out the window, straining to distinguish trees and houses and fields blurring past in the faint moonlight.

"So how are things going for you in New York, then?" he asked after a while in his soft, homey, midwestern twang, his eyes on the road.

"It's going well," I said. I thought about saying more, but didn't know how much I wanted to get into talking about the shows I'd been doing, since they all involved homosexuality. I wasn't sure what his opinion was on the subject, so I just said, "I love it there."

"Yeah, I bet."

Another silent moment passed. I searched for something else to say, my throat tightening. I really liked Chris, but I didn't know where to begin; we had spent so little time alone together. Finally, I asked feebly, "How about you? How's your work?"

"Oh, fine. Keeping busy."

I wasn't sure what he did for a living, just that he was powerful and influential in the field of reforming the juvenile criminal justice system. According to Mom, he was always flying to and from Washington, as well as giving lectures and presentations to governments and institutions all over the rest of the country. He was so soft-spoken around me that I had a hard time imagining him doing anything like that at all. On the other hand, he and his wife Bonnie often jetted around the globe to join various outdoors excursions—hundred-mile bicycle treks through the French countryside and white-water rafting expeditions down the Colorado River among them—that I knew there was a side to Chris that he didn't reveal to me.

Chris and Adam seemed to talk more freely than Chris and I did, bonding, as straight men so often do, on the subject of sports, especially basketball. Adam had been a star of his high school team, and had gone on to play in college on a partial basketball scholarship, and it seemed that Chris saw in Adam some of Chris's own missed opportunities. Chris had also played in high school, and very well apparently, until his senior year, when his mother forbade him to join the team. Defiantly, he'd tried out anyway and made it, and then lied to her about where he was after school. My mom and his other siblings covered for him, but Grandma eventually found out and, in a fit of rage, she immediately stormed over to his school, blasted into the gymnasium during the half-time of a game, and headed for the locker room, where she yanked out a stunned and deeply mortified Chris by the arm, all of his teammates watching the whole time. I figured that Chris's extreme shyness was a result of incidents like that.

Finally, we were driving through the thick of the woods, and before long, the log cabin loomed in our headlights. Its appearance surprised me; I'd expected a structure right out of *Little House on the Prairie*, all brown, rustic, and ramshackle, but this log cabin looked like a luxury condominium in comparison. Its walls were built of planks, not logs—although branches and small logs served as both the support beams for the front porch and its banisters—and the whole cabin was painted canary yellow.

"Well, here we are," Chris said.

We got out, trudged up the porch steps, opened the door—the handle of which was a branch—and stepped inside.

"Anthoneeeeeee!"

Rachel's patented squeal and mad dash toward me was right on cue. She launched herself into my arms. "You're here! I'm so happy you're here!"

I giggled as I always did. "Yeah, I'm here, honey."

"Did you just fly from New York today?"

"Yep."

"Coooool." She squeezed me tightly, wrapping her whole body around mine. "Come on," she said and jumped down, tugging my hand, leading me into the spacious living room where Roberta, Bob, Bonnie, and Mom all sat, situated around a gorgeous stone fireplace.

"Hey, Pete," Roberta said, rising up to give me a hug. Pete was a nickname she'd given me in my early childhood when she lived with us for a time. Not long before my second birthday, Dad left Mom, and soon after that Roberta, who needed a place to stay, moved in. She helped take care of Anne, Adam, and me, and, according to

Mom, Roberta and I bonded like crazy, clowning around with pup-pets and stuffed animals, and inventing all sorts of games. The most famous of these was "Movie Star and Peter Glamour," in which she was the Movie Star, and I was Peter Glamour. I don't remember how we played this game, but from an old color photo of Mom's that I loved, in which Roberta and I sat side by side on a sofa, sporting ridiculous, oversized sunglasses, I know we did our best to look as fabulous and, well, glamorous as possible. I had been Pete, or Petey, to Roberta ever since.

Roberta's hug was as strong as ever, and when we parted I waved hello to everyone else, Bonnie and Bob waving back from their seats, and Mom getting up for an embrace.

"Hi, Tonio."

And that's when I noticed how stiffly she was moving and that she was wearing a foam-rubber neck brace, and that her hug was even more delicate than usual and her small frame bonier than before. And my heart sank. She'd been doing so well; there hadn't been anything wrong with her in so long. I'd thought she was out of danger.

Two years earlier, right before Christmas, on December 22, 1992, Mom awoke in the middle of the night in agony, doubled over by terrible, blazing pains shooting through her abdomen. She'd suffered from unexplained episodes of internal abdominal bleeding before, so her nurse's training automatically kicked in, diagnosing that as what was wrong with her now. But as she continued to lie in bed in agony, she began to realize that the pain she was feeling this night was far worse than anything else she'd ever experienced. And she'd never felt so extraordinarily weak or lightheaded, either. She knew she must have been losing a *lot* of blood.

Only Rachel, five at the time, was in the house, asleep in the next room, and Mom didn't want to terrify her by waking her up, so Mom got out of bed, barely managing to roll herself over the edge of her mat-tress, and crawled along the floor, to a phone a few feet down the hall. Lying on the floor on her back, she called my sister, Anne, who lived nearby, and told her that she was feeling horrible, worse than she'd ever felt, and that Anne should call 911 and come over as quickly as possible. By the time Anne and the paramedics arrived, Mom was unconscious on the floor. All the commotion—the sirens, the paramedics' voices and bodies moving through the house—woke Rachel up, and Anne did her best to explain what was happening, as they both watched the paramedics hoist Mom up onto a stretcher and take her away.

The paramedics zoomed Mom over to St. Joseph's Medical Center, a large hospital a mile away where Mom had once worked as a nurse in the pediatrics ward, and they immediately brought her into the emergency room. Her vital signs were extremely low—she was in massive shock—and she'd been floating in and out of consciousness all the way to the hospital, muttering nonsensically about Rachel and Anne and Adam and me the whole time.

Dr. Allan Anderson performed the surgery, opening her up to discover massive internal bleeding ("It looked like a shotgun wound," he said later), which he found was the result of an adrenal gland that had inexplicably burst. She had lost so much blood by the time he got her on the table that he had to give her transfusions equaling twelve units of blood during the surgery—enough to refill her entire body one and a half times.

This all happened while I was asleep in New York City, and the next morning as I was eating breakfast, the phone rang. It was Anne, who normally never called me, not even on holidays or birthdays. We just weren't that close.

"Anthony?" she said, her voice tight and clipped. "Mom's in the hospital. You've gotta come home today."

A part of myself clamped firmly shut as she said these words, and I simply registered the information, not really reacting to it, just focusing on listening to my sister's voice, as if she'd just told me Mom had recently repainted the house or seen a good movie. "Okay," I said, as calmly and clearly as I could. "What happened?"

"I don't really know yet. She called me last night in the middle of the night, and I called an ambulance, and she's had surgery, and now she's in intensive care."

I breathed in and out and concentrated on her voice and on her words and tried to ignore all of the thousands of implications embedded in what she was saying. "Okay," I managed.

"Just come home."

"Okay."

And the rest of the day was simply one mercifully straightforward action after another: making a phone call to Adam at work to tell him what was happening and making a phone call to the airline to change our tickets home and packing our bags and hailing a taxi to the airport and sitting on the two-hour flight with Adam and getting picked up at the airport by Anne and riding with the two of them, mostly in silence, to the hospital.

And then walking down the corridor to Mom's room, not really noticing her mother and father and sisters and brothers who had gathered there, none of us doing much to greet each other. Pausing in the hallway before heading into her room, steeling myself. And then standing at the foot of her bed, watching her sleep, her face and body all milky white and swollen and puffed out. Standing there and absurdly thinking that in her current state she looked like a relative of the Michelin Man.

Standing there with Adam in silence as we waited for her to stir, listening to the steady droning rhythms of the machines that monitored her pulse and administered her pain medication and emptied her bowels and massaged her limbs. Staring at all the tubes in her nose and belly and arms.

Standing there and trying to absorb what I was seeing, as if I were at a museum gazing at an abstract painting. Trying to look at her misshapen, wracked, bloated body and face and still see Mom.

We had a meager Christmas celebration in the ICU a couple of days later, bringing our presents to the ward and opening Mom's for her.

Her swelling, which we found out later was a result of all of the fluids they had pumped into her, had gone down. Though she still looked horrible, she had begun to resemble her old self. But I saw in her eyes a new tinge of terror, which flashed around their edges as she adjusted her body ever so slightly to get more comfortable, or turned her head to stare at the wall.

Given the trauma her body had undergone, her recovery was incredible, and incredibly swift: within a few days she was out of intensive care, and within a few weeks she was back at work. She said later that Anne and Adam and Rachel and I had seen her through that horrible night; we had kept her there. "I wasn't ready to leave you guys," she said.

We soon learned that the whole incident was caused by a cancerous tumor that had been growing undetected on one of her adrenal glands; it was actually the tumor that had burst, not the gland itself as originally thought, although the gland was destroyed in the process. Dr. Anderson felt confident that the entire cancerous mass had been removed from Mom's abdomen in the surgery, but wanted her to continue getting tested every three months, just in case.

Mom had always named inanimate objects in her life—her homes, her cars—so it was only fitting that her tumor would have a name too: Wild Bill. She imagined Wild Bill as an out-of-control gunman who'd galloped in from nowhere and ripped a piece of her away. She visualized herself facing this gunman in the middle of the street and blowing him off the face of the earth.

For the next two years, we all thought she was out of danger. Every three months she went to the hospital for the afternoon and drank barium, a foul-tasting, radioactive dye, so her oncologist could scan her body for any growths that shouldn't be there. And every three months her oncologist found nothing. As time went on, and each scan resulted in good news, I buried the possibility that anything more would come of Wild Bill.

Adam and I lived together back in New York, and after a while we stopped speaking about what happened that night and about Wild Bill. We went about our lives in the city, Adam working on getting his novels published and his plays produced, and me auditioning and occasionally getting cast in something. I hardly thought about Mom's health scare until the Christmas following it when I went home for a visit, and saw taped to the side of the refrigerator a laminated copy of a notice she'd had printed in the Joliet *Herald-News:*

ON THIS WINTER SOLSTICE

It is a year since my near fatal encounter with "WILD BILL." There are so many people who helped in so many ways. I'll always be grateful & openly want to thank the following:

- The Paramedics
- Dr. Allan Anderson & Dr. Phil Meyer [Mom's anesthesiologist], who clearly saved my life.
- My dear sisters, especially Roberta & Gracia, who were there for me when I needed them most.
- All of my wonderful friends, especially Kathy, Marna, Gloria & Sarah.
- My Coworkers at Joliet Correctional Center, who continue to give me emotional support laced with humor, & all the people who donated blood which is truly the gift of life.
- And most of all I want to thank MY girls, Anne, who held my hand when I was terrified, and Little Rachel, who still thinks she dialed 911.

I made it for them.

MARY RAPP

I stood and read this ad over and over every time I opened the refrigerator during that visit, lingering at the kitchen counter with my orange juice or yogurt or peanut butter sandwich, trying to imagine once again what that horrible night must have felt like to her, and wondering what I would have done in her place, and feeling grateful that she had survived the ordeal. But as much as the ad touched me (especially the sweet line about Little Rachel thinking she dialed 911), it also left me ashamed. Ashamed that I wasn't mentioned. Ashamed that I hadn't been there for Mom in a way that merited her thanks. But the truth was I hadn't really been there for her, not in any way that mattered. Not only was I a thousand miles away, living an extremely hectic New York City life, but I didn't call her as much as she wanted me to—certainly not in the wake of Wild Bill—or go home for visits as often as she'd like. When I did call, I rarely asked her about Wild Bill, or talked to her about that night or her recovery or her prospects. I told her about my latest auditions and callbacks and all of the roles I wasn't getting, and spoke of little else. So she was right not to thank me.

As much as I believed that, though, I still wanted some credit. I could feel the insidious pull of that need lingering in my gut. I was her son, after all, and she had told me that she'd made it through that night for all of us kids, not just her girls. So why didn't she say that in print? Why did she strand Adam and me like that? It wasn't fair. But as I stood at the kitchen counter and read and reread the notice and thought all of this through and swallowed down my shame and pride and fear, I glanced over at Mom placidly sitting on the couch reading a magazine, her foot bobbing incessantly up and down as it always did, her head slightly cocked, enveloped in her usual aura of calm, and I decided that I could never bring it up.

A year later, in the log cabin in the woods of Wisconsin, I also didn't mention that I'd noticed her bones poking out of her already thin frame when I hugged her. I didn't tell her how that frightened me. Instead I chatted with her about my work and my life in New York.

"I brought home some reviews," I told her.

"Oh, good, let me see."

Reading my press clippings was one of her favorite activities. She was much better than I at cutting them out and saving them in scrapbooks, and I wasn't good at sending them in the mail to her, so I was glad to share them with her in person. And since she couldn't afford to fly out to New York to see everything I was in (and I couldn't afford to buy her plane tickets), showing her my reviews was the next best thing.

"It sounds very interesting," she said after reading one of the reviews of my current show, a dark, three-character, gay-themed play called *Trafficking in Broken Hearts*.

"I wear panties in it," I said, provocatively. Her eyes grew wide.

"Really? Panties?" Her brow furrowed. "Why?"

"I'm playing a sort of confused character."

"Well, I guess so."

"His brothers raped him as a kid, and this is one of the ways he's adapted."

"His brothers raped him? That's terrible."

"Yeah, it is. But it's a great part."

She started to read another review, peering down at it through her thickly-framed bifocals.

"Why can't you play a nice normal person sometimes?" she said after a moment without looking up from the paper.

This was a conversation we'd had before. And whenever we did, I always felt that she was still holding on to the memories of my childhood performances as Snoopy, Oliver, Tiny Tim, the Cowardly Lion, and the Little Prince—roles that were sweet and innocent and appealing, in shows that were wholesome and clean. "Everyone always loved you in those shows," she'd say, and that's what she wanted to see me do again.

"Well, I can play normal characters too," I said as she continued to read, "but this is what I was offered right now, and I'm having a great experience in it."

She put the paper down. "I just think it's funny that you play all of these strange characters, because to me you're such a regular guy."

"Well, I don't know. I think this is one of the best things I've ever done. I get to be so different from myself, and that's very exciting for me."

"I guess so." She nodded, almost imperceptibly frowning. "I'm sure you're wonderful in it, I think you always do a good job, but sometimes I just want you to, you know, play a nice, regular person."

"Well, maybe in the next thing I do I'll get to do that."

"I hope so."

What we weren't directly discussing was the homosexual content of the play. Mom and I had had a long history of talking—and not talking—about my sexuality, never to my full satisfaction, and I didn't know where she stood with regard to it now. But given her discomfort with the subject, I was fairly certain that my being in a gay play was an issue for her. I toyed with pressing the conversation further but decided against it. I didn't want to create friction during my short stay.

Later, as I was helping Mom do the dishes, I asked her about her neck brace.

"Oh, it's nothing," she said, the steam from the sink fogging her glasses. "My neck's been bothering me a little, is all."

I dried silverware in silence for a moment.

"Well, I hope it feels better."

"Oh, I'm sure it will."

I never knew how much to believe Mom when she talked about how she was feeling; she had a high tolerance for pain. When I was a tiny baby, she slipped and fell down a flight of stairs while clutching me to her chest, cushioning and protecting me from the pounding her body took. I wound up unhurt, but even though she was quite injured, she walked away from the fall without going to the hospital, and from that day forward she suffered from chronic flare-ups of back pain.

Over twenty years later, after one of the many sessions of scans for any traces of Wild Bill, her oncologist asked her if she'd ever broken her back.

"Not that I know of," she said.

"Well, if it had happened, I think it's something you'd probably know about."

"I had a bad fall once, a long time ago, but I walked away from it."

"Really? Well," he said, showing her the X-ray, "there is evidence here of a badly healed fracture."

"Huh," Mom said.

"So it would appear you did in fact break your back after all."

"Well, I guess I did."

Roberta and Chris and Bonnie and I took a walk that night, but Mom opted to stay in. "I'm a little tired," she said. "You guys go on without me."

"You sure?" Roberta said. "It's beautiful outside."

"No, I'm okay."

"All right then."

Mom was an avid walker. She took her dog Zelda out for frequent walks of over a mile almost every day, in any kind of weather. When she was in Toronto with me while I was filming *Adventures in Babysitting*, she'd often walked the several miles to the set. One day the cast and crew van was stuck in traffic during a heavy snowfall, and Mom beat us to the soundstage, impressing everybody in the van by chugging past us at a steady and implacable pace, her pale cheeks shining a rosy glow, her breath pluming out before her. So it was unusual for her not to join us.

"Have fun, guys," she said as we bundled up and shuffled out into the crisp, frigid, clear Wisconsin night. And as we made our way down the pitch-black road, our flashlights bobbing their irregular circles and ovals on the pavement, no one remarked on her absence, even though it was like a noisy flare trailing after us. We all knew what her staying behind probably meant. But we didn't discuss it. To discuss it would be to say that it was real, and no one wanted to say that it was real, no one wanted that at all.

getting
it all

In February 1995, while I was in rehearsals for an off-Broadway production of Nicky Silver's play *Raised in Captivity* (yet another show in which I was not a "nice, normal" character), I got a call from home.

"They've found another tumor," Mom said on the other end. "I'm going to have surgery so they can get it out."

I didn't want any more phone calls like this from home. I didn't want to have to keep flying there for emergencies; I couldn't afford the financial burden of these trips, and I didn't have an understudy. What if there were complications and I had to stay in Joliet for a long time? What would happen to the show then? I wouldn't want there to be cancellations because of me. But how could I even think about the future of the show when my mom was ill? Weren't there priorities? Shouldn't *she* be a priority?

Of course David Warren, my director, had no problem letting me go home. "You have to do what you have to do," he said, without laying on me a shred of guilt. So I packed for a quick day trip, hoping that would be all I'd need, and booked a flight with Adam. We arranged for our friend Anna, who'd directed me in *Trafficking in Broken Hearts,* to pick us up at the Chicago airport; her clear-headed strength and dry sense of humor would do us some good on our drive from the airport to the grim University of Chicago Medical Center.

But when we emerged from the jetway into the harsh fluorescence of O'Hare International Airport, all zombied out and cottonmouthed by our journey, we were greeted not by Anna, but by our father. My heart sank; I wasn't prepared to be the receptacle for his manic energy, and he and Adam didn't get along, so our trip into town was probably going to be much less calming than I'd hoped.

Even though our parents had been divorced since I was two years old, Dad had always been at least tangentially involved in our lives. He'd traveled down from Chicago to visit us in Joliet occasionally, and I'd done father-son stuff with him as a kid, like attending White Sox and Cubs games, and I'd spent time with him and his second wife and their children at their homes, and I'd enjoyed many holidays with his extended family. But overall, I considered his relationship with me to be more friendly than parental. Except for receiving Dad's minimal child support when it was due, Mom had truly been on her own when it had come to the daily grind of raising us kids. And maybe because I was so young when he left, I didn't resent him so much for the divorce. But Adam and Anne both begrudged him for it, and over the years, Dad had become a pariah in our family. So I didn't have any idea that he would have been alerted to Mom's condition, let alone taken it upon himself to pick Adam and me up at the airport.

"I was just at the hospital," he said to us, not even saying hello, his bright blue eyes more intensely focused behind his glasses than usual, his prematurely silver hair swept back from his pale face. "They didn't get it all."

Adam and I stopped and looked at each other, our bags weighing us down. "What do you mean?" I said.

"I don't know much more than that. They just said they weren't able to get it all."

This didn't make sense. It was supposed to have been a simple, routine surgery. They had to open up Mom's abdomen, isolate the tumor, and then cut it out. Easy. They did this sort of thing all the time. Didn't they? How much was the *all* of it that was so difficult to get? And what did it mean? Did it mean that this was the end, that Mom was going to die right now, or tomorrow, or in three months?

I didn't ask any of these questions out loud; I just let them kick their way through my head as Adam and I silently lumbered behind Dad, following him through the maze of O'Hare and into his dilapidated, cluttered car. On the way to the hospital Dad tried to make small talk, his chipper midwestern voice bright and lilting. "I'm glad we're getting to spend some time together," he said, and, "So, how are things going for you guys in New York?" Adam and I answered in monosyllables (what I really wanted to say instead of "yes" and "no" was *SHUT UP, THIS IS NOT THE TIME FOR THIS, SHUT UP SHUT UP SHUT UP,* but I didn't), and eventually Dad quieted down. In the ensuing silence I sat staring out the window at the spectacular Chicago skyline.

When we arrived at the hospital, we paused briefly in its vast lobby to pick up our absurdly large laminated guest passes before journeying endlessly through corridor after corridor just to get to the elevator that would take us to Mom's floor, where we then walked down even more corridors to get to her room. As we made our way through the garishly hued hallways, I began to think that I should memorize all of the details around me, in case I ever needed to act in a scene taking place in a hospital, or if I ever wanted to write a screenplay in which a character was dying. I imprinted on my memory the badly framed paintings by the masters (Matisse, Magritte, Cézanne, Monet) lining the walls; the insidious pall of the flickering fluorescents shining down from the ceiling; the generic, flat-out ugly, '70s-era modular furniture randomly strewn around rooms; the constant stream of stone-faced, badged doctors and orderlies and administrative assistants rushing around us. I staved off my anxiety, swallowing it down as I walked. In order to avoid thinking about Mom and how frightened and disoriented and doomed she must be feeling, I thought about how all of these mundane details surrounding me in this hospital might come in handy in my work someday.

Finally, we reached Mom's room, and walked in. Grandma Baird was there, and Roberta, and Anne, all slumping around in the semi-darkness, all with hollowed-out looks on their faces, no one moving or saying hello. In the center of the room was Mom, the white sheets of her bed glowing in the light of her bedside lamp, her face grim and spent amid the tubes snaking out of her nose, her eyes more drunken and exhausted and wild than I'd ever seen them.

"Hi, Tonio," she said, her voice ragged and dry. "Hi, Adam."

"Hi, Momma," I said, and sat down carefully on the bed, taking her hand in mine. Adam murmured hello and took a seat in a chair across the bed from me and gripped her other hand.

"What's going on?" I said, and immediately regretted it. What kind of a question was that at this moment? Mom's gaze in response was scared and stern and very very tired.

"I don't know." Her words slurred out of her mouth. "They said they couldn't get it all."

"But what does that mean?" Why was I so compelled to keep asking her these questions? Now was not the time. But then again, when would be the time?

"I don't know."

I could see out of the corner of my eye that Adam had put his head down, his free hand covering his eyes, and I wondered if he was crying, something I had never seen him do. And then I could tell that he was, silently.

"They can't tell me why," Mom continued.

"What do you mean?"

"No one will give me a straight answer."

Even though I sensed her exasperation, I kept going. "Why?"

"I don't *know,*" she whined, and I clenched my jaw and tried to resist asking her more questions. I didn't want to keep upsetting her, and I didn't want all the other eyes in the room burning into me, witnessing how much I was fucking up this moment with my mother. I could hear Dad jiggling his change in his pockets and attempting to make mumbled conversation with Grandma, who sat impassively in the corner. Roberta slumped in a chair, and Anne hovered near the foot of the bed, her eyes sharp and piercingly blue, her mouth set in a firm line. Mom, surrendering to the dope coursing through her body, closed her eyes and dozed off. I took the opportunity to slip out of the room, find a pay phone, and call Anna.

"Hello?" Anna said, her nasal midwestern twang strong and clear and an immediate comfort.

"Anna, it's Anthony."

"Hey, bubby." Her voice softened, becoming more intimate and gentle. "How you doing?"

"Well, they couldn't get it all."

"Yeah, hon, I know. Your father told me. That's how come he was there instead of me."

"I know."

"So how you doing?"

"Okay," I said, and my chest tightened and I tried to take a deep breath. "It's just weird. I don't understand. It doesn't make sense."

"I know, I know. These things don't make a whole lot of sense, generally speaking. You sure you're okay?"

"Yeah, I'm okay. I'm worried about Mom."

"Of course you are. That's an entirely appropriate response. You should be worried about her."

"Yeah."

"You need anything, anything at all, you call me. You know that, right? You call me."

"Okay, I will."

"How's your bro?"

"Fine, I guess. He doesn't say much."

"Don't I know it."

I looked down the hall at the doorway to Mom's room and wondered if they all minded my being gone for this long, if they resented my being on the phone.

"You need anything at all, you call me," Anna said again.

"I will."

"Love you, bubby."

"Love you, too."

I hung up and realized that I'd been pacing the entire time, as much as it's possible to pace while on a pay phone. I cracked my neck and all the knuckles in my fingers and swallowed and headed back to Mom.

There was so much silence in the room. Mom was asleep and none of us spoke to each other. I could feel Dad pace around and start to say something, then stop himself. At one point the silence was interrupted by a group of brusque interns on their rounds, dropping in just long enough to wake Mom, note her vital stats, and mutter medical jargon to each other. After their visit I went out into the hallway and tried to find Mom's oncologist, Dr. Barron, to get him to come to her room and explain what exactly was happening to her and why, but I just kept getting shunted off to his answering service. Finally, much later, he lumbered in, a tall, boxy man, his wild, gray, mad-scientist hair framing a huge, square head.

"How are you feeling, Mary?" he said, his voice mellow and mildly benevolent.

"Okay." She seemed much more alert now that he was there.

"Well, as you know, we couldn't get it all." That phrase again. "We're going to have to very seriously talk about all of the options now."

"Okay." I wondered if Dr. Barron knew that my mom was a nurse, and that she would see and hear through any verbal smoke screens he might attempt to put in her way.

"I want to very strongly recommend putting you on a course of chemotherapy, combined with radiation treatment. We want to shrink and kill that tumor." I hated chemotherapy, I couldn't stand the idea of it, I didn't want her to take it, it was poison. Why couldn't they get it all?

"Why couldn't you get it all?" Mom asked, weakly.

"We don't know yet. I haven't gotten the full report from your surgeon." Mom started to ask another question, but stopped. "Now," Dr. Barron continued, "I want to start you on the chemo as soon as possible. Time is of the essence. It will be rough, but I want to be aggressive. I want to beat this. I'll be in to check on you later."

"Okay . . ." Mom didn't watch him leave. She stared at the ceiling, and I saw slow tears drip down her cheeks. Anne, Adam, and I surrounded her, touching her legs and holding her hands.

"It's okay, Mom," Anne said. It was one of the only things she'd said since I got there. "You'll be okay."

"I want to see my grandchildren," Mom said, her voice cloudy from crying.

"You will, Mom, you will," Anne said. But I couldn't help thinking, *no, maybe you won't, maybe you will die from this, maybe you will die from it very very soon, and anything we might say to you now won't change that, why does everyone always think they have to pretend that nothing bad is happening, you are very very very sick, and that's the undeniable fact, you can't pretend that it's not.* But I remained silent.

Mom stared off at the wall, exhausted, and I said, "Mom, I don't know how much I'll be able to come home, because of the show."

She didn't look at me as she said, "I know . . ." Nothing I had said all day seemed to help or comfort or please her, and I hated my inability to help, but I had to talk to her. How many more chances would I have? I had to cram it all in now, because the next time might be too late. I couldn't bear to throw out empty false hope, because who really knew anything about what was going to happen?

And so I asked her, "What kind of chemotherapy are you going to have?" and she answered, "I don't know," and I asked her, "Why can't anyone tell you what went wrong in the surgery?" and she answered, "I don't know," and I asked her, "Are you going to be able to go back to work?" and she answered, "I don't know." And with each question I asked, she seemed to shrink deeper into her bed, and the lines around her eyes etched themselves more vividly into her skin, and yet I couldn't stop myself.

Finally, after a long silence passed between us all, it was time for me to return to the airport. I slowly stood and said, "Goodbye, Momma. I love you."

"I love you too, Tonio," she said, her weary eyes meeting mine for the first time in a while. I kissed her on the forehead and left.

saviors
and angels

Back in New York, back in the show, back in my life of running around to auditions and dinners and movies and plays, I barely called home. I kept thinking I should be doing more to help, or that I should *want* to do more to help, but the truth was that I was avoiding making contact with Mom, without ever admitting it to myself, for fear of what news might be on the other end.

From the little contact I did make, I learned that her recovery from her surgery was as swift as always, but that she wasn't going to be able to go back to work because of her debilitating chemo and radiation treatments. I tried imagining how she would look without her hair and thought that it would probably make her already large and prominent dark brown eyes all the more noticeable. I wondered what her scalp looked like. I didn't want to find out.

I could hardly stand the fact that at the end of the day, there was nothing I *could* do to help, not really. At least not from New York. I wondered if Mom resented my absence, if she wanted me to be home with her. I wondered if she still believed that I had always been the savior of our family, and therefore should try to do something to save us all once again; after all, she had credited me with literally saving all of our lives more than once. The first time was one night back in 1972 when I was a small baby.

Our tiny red Volkswagen Bug crawled down I-57. We were somewhere on the stretch of highway between Manteno and Glenview, Illinois, and it was dark, very dark; there were no lights alongside the road. We had just left Grandma's after our weekly visit; my dad was driving, my mom was in the passenger seat, Adam was curled up in the cubbyhole behind the back seat, Anne was slumped down in the back seat itself, and little one-year-old me was next to her, in my car seat. We three kids were asleep.

Mom and Dad weren't talking much, as usual, just watching the road speed beneath our car, relieved to be out of her mother's house, away from all of the noise that came from eleven brothers and sisters and several of their children running around all day.

I-57 was like most Illinois highways: completely straight for miles and miles, its four lanes separated by a grassy median, with the occasional dilapidated overpass thrown in. Cornfields and plains stretched out on either side. Every once in a while a barn or farmhouse or granary sprouted up on the horizon, usually accompanied by a huge oak tree or weeping willow. There were shoulders on the side of the highway, but if you pulled over, it might be a long time before anyone came along. Exits were few, and no towns were visible from the road.

It was late summer, but the night was cool. The steady *pat pat pat* of insects dotting the windshield and the sputter of the motor filled the silence between my parents. The radio wasn't playing, probably because they wouldn't have agreed on what station to listen to.

We passed a midnight blue Dodge Dart on the shoulder. Its door lay open, but no one was in sight. Mom thought that was odd. She looked at Dad, thought about saying something, and then decided there was nothing really to say; cars were often abandoned on the sides of highways.

Another couple of miles down the road, that same Dart passed our car on the left, moving at an incredibly fast speed. A young black man with an Afro and a goatee sat in the driver's seat. Again, Mom thought something was odd, but again, she didn't say anything. She looked back at me asleep, and at Anne, and then stared out the window at the barely visible cornfield whizzing by.

Soon after that, we passed two other cars on the shoulder: one a faded, rusty Gremlin; the other a clunky, army green Buick Elektra. In the Elektra was a group of three young men, two white, one black, and outside, between the two cars, stood a young white woman, talking animatedly to another young white man. Mom and Dad glanced over.

"Should we stop, Doug?" my mom asked.

"What? Why should we stop?"

"I don't know . . ."

He kept driving. My mom was growing more and more nervous, uncomfortably so. She reached back to me and adjusted my head in my car seat, rubbed Anne's hand for a second, and lifted herself up so she could peek over the back seat at Adam's sleeping, curled up, little-boy body.

Suddenly, the young woman's Gremlin zoomed by, going even faster than the Dart. Mom stared after it, her heart pounding. It didn't make sense, this many people doing this kind of driving, on this road, at night, she thought.

The headlights of the Buick Elektra splashed into the car, growing in intensity very quickly. Mom whipped her head around, staring into the beams. Recklessly, the Elektra changed lanes and drew up alongside our car. The three young men inside stared into our car.

"Doug, watch out, I think they're drunk," Mom said.

"Don't worry, I can handle it."

"Be careful. Slow down."

He slowed down, and the Buick Elektra slowed down. The guys

in the car were huddled together, talking to each other and pointing at us with their thumbs.

"What are they doing?" Mom said.

"Mary, don't worry, just don't look at them, and they'll leave us alone. They're just joyriding."

"I don't know . . ."

"Trust me."

Abruptly, their car slowed down, switched lanes so they were once again behind us, and bumped into our rear.

"Doug—"

"What the hell are they doing?"

"Doug—"

Another bump.

"I'm pulling over."

"No, why?"

"I'm not gonna let them just get away with that, who do they think they are? Jesus."

"No, Doug, don't, just keep driving."

Dad's face was getting all red. Another bump. Dad glared at the rearview mirror. The Elektra zipped back into the lane next to ours, and pulled up alongside us again. One of the white men, his hair a scraggly mane, a lit cigarette hanging from his mouth, made a motion for us to pull over.

"Wait," Dad said, "maybe they're trying to tell us something's wrong with our car."

"No, Doug, there isn't anything wrong with our car, now please, just slow down and they'll leave us alone."

Suddenly, there was the most aggressive bump yet, from the side, and with that, my head fell forward.

"That's it, I'm pulling over!" my dad barked.

"No, Doug." Mom reached back to right my head. As she did, she glanced in the window of the Elektra and saw the scraggly-haired young man watching her help me. Their eyes met. The red tip of his cigarette flared as he took a drag. He looked at me, then back at

Mom, then back at me. Another drag, and then he turned to his buddies in the car and said something to them. The driver craned his neck over to us, looked into our car once more, at Dad and Mom and me, and then sped away.

"Good riddance," Dad said. "Punks."

Before our arrival in Glenview, we passed two other cars on the side of the road, a station wagon and a VW bus, both abandoned. Once, we passed the Buick Elektra, which had one less passenger than earlier. Mom stared at each car as we passed by and tried to rub the gooseflesh out of her arms. She glanced over at Dad several times but didn't say anything more that night. When we got home, she put us all to bed and tried to put the whole incident out of her mind. But she couldn't; she lay in bed awake all night.

Many months later, Mom sat in a courtroom as an eyewitness, testifying against the young men in the Buick Elektra. That night on I-57, they had killed several people by bumping their cars off the road, taking them into the cornfield, shooting them point blank with a shotgun, and leaving them there to die. One member of the gang would then drive up ahead in the victim's stolen car and knock someone else off the road. Less than a minute after we passed the young woman in the Gremlin, she was murdered.

Mom told me this whole story one night when I was still young—about nine or so. On a rare evening off from her nursing job at St. Joseph's Hospital, Mom sat next to me on our couch and showed me old, yellowed newspaper clippings about the I-57 incident, including one in which she was interviewed, all of which were collected and saved in a flimsy scrapbook with a brown cardboard cover. When she was done, she closed the scrapbook and reached over to me, holding my hand in silence for a moment. I wasn't sure if I should say anything, so I just sat there, imagining those poor people being shoved into the mud in the cornfields, wondering if they felt any pain as they were shot, or if it was all over in an instant. I looked at Mom. She smoothed my hair and said, "If it weren't for you, we would have been killed that night." She smiled softly, gazing right into my eyes. "That guy saw you, and he couldn't kill a baby. Those terrible kids couldn't kill a baby. If you hadn't fallen forward, we would all be dead now. You saved our lives, Tonio." And I nodded solemnly, believing her to be right, believing that I should continue to do my best to take care of our family.

Years later, in 1990, a severe tornado ripped through Joliet and its surrounding towns, killing over sixty people, and wiping off the face of the earth two of our previous apartments. I was already living in New York by then, and our current house—a condominium that I'd helped Mom purchase by taking care of the down payment with money I'd made doing *Adventures in Babysitting*—sat within a half mile of the tornado's path. "If we didn't live here, we might be dead," Mom said to me at the time. "Thank you, Tonio. You saved our lives again."

And even though she was technically right, that there was a good chance our family had averted death twice because of me, it was strange to get credit for being a great savior since neither outcome had been my intention. I was a baby in a car seat in the one case, and I was a thousand miles away when a tornado randomly happened to miss our house in the other. But I knew that Mom still believed that I had been somehow endowed with protective powers, and she gave me full credit for our family's survival.

But now, as I was faced with this new reality of my mother's failing health and in a position to possibly do something to make a difference in the outcome, not just by default but by actions I could consciously take, I was consistently falling short.

In April 1995, a couple of weeks after *Raised in Captivity* closed (we were a critical and box office success, selling out our limited run, but, unable to move to a commercial off-Broadway house, we were forced to close), I got a call from my agent, Paul, about a job in the film *Twister,* and I promptly shipped out to Ponca City, Oklahoma, for the next couple of months. *Twister* turned out to be just a paycheck gig, with no creative fulfillment whatsoever—I was essentially an extra, on the "bad guy's" team. Although I was grateful for the boost in my income, I disliked being in the middle of Oklahoma and wished that I had more of an opportunity to work.

Several weeks into the shoot, my aunt Diana called me. "Your mom's not doing too well," she said. "Is there any way you can come home?"

"I don't know," I said, "I'll have to find out."

"Well, I hope you can. Your mother really wants to see you."

So here it was, another urgent phone call from home, and another moment I had to ask permission to leave work. I went right to our executive producers, Kathleen Kennedy and Ian Bryce, neither of whom I had seen since the first day of shooting, and explained to them my situation.

"Of course you can go," Kathleen said. She actually seemed concerned about Mom's well-being. "There's no reason why you can't spend time with your mother."

"Thank you," I said, flush with my newfound freedom and anxious about what I would find when I went home.

Melanie Hoopes, another fellow underused teammate, managed to get permission to leave with me (she had friends in Chicago and was as eager as all of us to get out of Ponca City), and so the two of us set off on a thirteen-hour drive up through Oklahoma, Kansas, Missouri, and Illinois, arriving in Joliet just after dawn. Her presence in the car was a gift, even though we weren't close friends at that time. When we started our journey, I said, "I don't know how talkative I'll be, or how I'll feel, you know, because of the circumstances," and without hesitation, and with complete sincerity, she replied, "I totally understand. You don't have to talk to me or entertain me at all. If you want to talk about anything, I'm here; otherwise, you don't have to worry."

Mom had always been thin and pale, but when I got to the house and saw her that morning after she awoke, she was far thinner and paler than usual, her skin milky and stretched over the bones of her face. I was relieved to see that she still had a full head of hair, although it was limper than I remembered. The many bumps dotting her skin stood out in a kind of relief, and her large eyes seemed even rounder and larger than normal. I hugged her gently, afraid that too much of a squeeze from me might snap her in two.

"I'm so glad you could come home, Tonio," she said.

"Me too." And I was, although I was already dreading my time in Joliet. In my excitement to get out of Ponca I had forgotten that, in many ways, Joliet was no better. And there was so much I wanted to say to Mom, especially regarding all of her unresolved issues with my sexuality, but would she want to talk about any of it? Wouldn't the barest mention depress her? Wasn't it selfish of me to want to force her to discuss my concerns with her when all she probably wanted from me was my kindness and care?

During my first couple of days home, I remained mostly silent and wandered from room to room, overwhelmed by the weight of my unspoken thoughts. Mom asked me to go to the store, and I went to the store. Mom asked me to cook a meal for us, and I cooked a meal for us. Mom asked me how the film was going, and I told her. During the day, I was numb and vacant, but as I lay in bed at night, staring at the ceiling, my mind chased after its reeling, swirling questions and panicky thoughts, until I finally drifted off to sleep.

Mom broached one of my concerns herself. We were sitting in the living room, watching TV at a low volume, when she turned it off and said, "I want you to start thinking about what you'll want from me when I'm gone."

The simplicity and clarity of her words instantly cleared the thick air of anxiety hanging over me. I was surprised that she was willing to deal with the truth of her possibly imminent death head-on. I looked right at her, took a deep breath, and said, "Well, Momma, I don't know. I'll have to think about it."

"Okay," she replied calmly. "Just think about it and let me know."

"I will."

And with that, she turned the TV back on.

The next day, I had to drive her up to the University of Chicago Medical Center for some tests, and because of our brief conversation the previous night, I was looking forward to the opportunity to sit and talk with her during the hour-long trip into the city.

Stuffed into Mom's tiny white Neon, a car she was so proud to own (she had only been able to afford used cars before her recent raise), we hit the road, and I wasted little time on I-55 before I said, "I was thinking about what you said last night, Momma, and I realized that there's really only one thing that I want."

"What's that?"

I couldn't tell if her voice held any tone of dread or suspicion, so I plowed on. "Well," I said, "I just want for there to be nothing between us. Nothing left unfinished. That's more important to me than anything else you could possibly give me." As I said this, I felt clear and cleansed and focused and true.

"Well, I want that too," she said. I glanced over at her and she looked small and delicate in the passenger seat, as she stared straight ahead out the windshield.

"Is there anything you want to talk to me about?" I said, feeling my pulse rise slightly as I did.

"Well . . ." she began. I glanced over at her again, to see a distinctly pained expression in her eyes. She frowned and then turned to me and said, "I just want to know that you've forgiven me about what happened with Zucchini."

This was the last thing I was expecting to hear; I almost laughed from surprise. But I was also touched by the sadness and fear in her voice. Zucchini had been an Australian shepherd I'd found in the Nevada desert a few years before while filming the movie *Far from Home*. She was an adorable, motley creature when I discovered her walking through town, but she was also almost dead from dehydration. I nursed her back to health, driving three hours to the nearest vet, and then three hours back, feeding her vitamin supplements from a tube, until she was as sprightly and joyful as any healthy puppy. When the filming was over, I brought her back to Joliet with me. I'd named her Zucchini after an eccentric Italian restaurant owner in Nevada offered Drew Barrymore, the star of the movie, a free plate of zucchini at dinner one night. It had been such a bizarre incident that it had become an inside joke among the cast and crew of the film, and thus an appropriate name for my new dog. Mom initially protested having another animal in the house—we already had a little dog, Scooter, as well as a couple of cats—but she quickly fell in love with Zucchini, and when I moved away from home the next winter, unable to bring Zucchini along, I was thrilled that Mom decided to keep her.

Because Zucchini had grown up in the desert, she loved to run, and Mom was always having to chase her down when she'd dash out of the house, which she'd do at the smallest opportunity. Mom and I had more than a few arguments about it—I was afraid that Zucchini would just disappear if she got on too much of a tear—but Mom always swore that she'd never let it happen, and we'd leave it at that.

The following Thanksgiving, however, while I was away at NYU, she called me, her voice choked with tears. "Anthony, I'm so sorry," she sobbed. "I'm so sorry. But Zucchini's dead."

I stopped breathing and moving and said, "What?"

"She's dead. She was hit by a car. It's my fault, I let her run, she got out, and I figured she'd come back, but she didn't, so I looked for her, and I couldn't find her, and then finally I found her, and she was lying by the side of the road, just lying there, and nobody had stopped or anything, and she's dead, and I'm so so sorry . . ."

"It's okay, Momma, it's okay," I said, but really it wasn't, it wasn't at all, it was terrible, and it was her fault, I'd *told* her that she couldn't let Zucchini run, it was so dangerous, it was her fault, it was, it *was*. After I reassured her some more and listened to her crying and calmed her down and then said goodbye and hung up the phone, I stood in my dorm room and wept and tried to remember what it felt like to hug my dog to me and to throw her favorite toy for her to chase and to take long walks with her at night. I had lost many pets over the years, but it never got any easier. I felt my grief over each loss keenly.

But in the years since, I had not given Zucchini's death much thought at all, and when I did think of it I bore Mom no ill will whatsoever, so to hear her ask me for my forgiveness almost six years later was totally surprising.

"Of *course* I forgive you, Momma," I said, and I really did mean it, absolutely. "I was always a little upset about her death, you know, because I loved her, but I really do forgive you."

"Well, you know," she said, her voice small and weak, "I just knew how much you loved her, and how disappointed you were in me."

"Well, yeah, I guess I was a little disappointed at the time, but that was years ago. It really is okay."

"I just didn't want to let you down. I know how much you loved her," she said again.

"Yeah, I did, but so did you, and I know it was very hard for you, too."

"Yeah. She was so sweet. Such a good dog." I heard Mom sniffle and glanced over to see that she was crying. I reached over and held her hand.

"Oh, Momma, it's okay. It's okay."

I was so relieved and happy that we were talking this way, and so touched by the depth of Mom's remorse, and so proud that I was finally able to bring her some comfort, that almost all of my fears of what we could and could not discuss immediately evaporated.

"Thank you, Tonio," Mom said.

"You're welcome, Momma."

At the hospital, Mom and I trundled through its endless, forbidding hallways from one appointment to another. I sat in each waiting room as she had blood drawn or received her final round of chemo or met with Dr. Kelly, the kindly female therapist the hospital had granted to help Mom cope with her cancer. Through it all, Mom methodically and quietly submitted herself to these rounds, talking little. I took her lead and kept silent myself, hoping that I was giving her support and strength by simply being there with her.

The only stop for which I joined her was the brief physical exam and interview she received from Dr. Barron in a cramped and drab corner room. I sat off to the side as he listened to her lungs with his stethoscope.

"How are you feeling, Mary?" he asked.

"Oh, *pretty* good," she said.

"Any pain anywhere?"

"Well, my back always bothers me. But that's nothing new. I'm just very tired."

"I understand."

He asked her to lie back, and tested the flexibility and strength of her legs. She inhaled sharply once or twice as he gently moved her feet up and down.

"That hurt?" he said.

"A little bit," Mom replied, but I could tell it had hurt much more than a little bit.

"Okay," Dr. Barron said, "you can sit up now." After Mom had settled into a more comfortable position, he sat down on the edge of the examination table and said, "As you know, Mary, we're going to stop your chemotherapy now and just concentrate on radiotherapy. But I'm going to need you to come back in tomorrow so we can perform an MRI. We need to do that so we can know exactly where your tumor is, and to see how much it's shrunk or grown."

"Okay," Mom said, her voice quiet, her eyes clear and strong. "That's fine."

Dr. Barron turned to me then. "We're doing our best to beat this for your mother."

I wasn't sure that I believed him, but I nodded and said, "Thank you," anyway.

• • •

By the end of the day, Mom was exhausted, and slept all the way home. I watched her periodically, in fleeting glances away from the traffic. Mom sleeping in the car was a turnabout from my childhood; she used to drive me into and out of the city for auditions and rehearsals and performances, and I usually fell asleep on the way back. Sometimes, our arrival home jarred me awake, but I never opened my eyes, and, night after night, Mom would reach into the back seat, cradle me in her arms, carry me up the two flights of stairs into our apartment, and lay me down on my bed, kissing me on the forehead and whispering "Good night" before leaving the room. It took all of my self-control to stifle my smiles and giggles on these nights as I feigned sleep. It was my little game. I didn't know if Mom realized I was awake, but if she did, she played along every time.

The next day as I sat and waited for Mom in the MRI waiting room, I called my friend Ben back in New York. I hadn't spoken to him in a while, but my being in a hospital had put him in my mind; he was very ill from AIDS.

Ben and I had gone to Interlochen Arts Camp together, when I was fourteen and he was sixteen, and we had kept in sporadic touch since then. He was a thin, pale, freckled, fey redhead from a farm town in Ohio, with an infectious, zany grin and a rare sweetness. He and I hadn't talked openly about sex or sexuality back at Interlochen, but we gravitated to each other as young queer people tend to do, hanging out with the other undeclared queer kids on the lawn outside our rehearsal rooms, chatting and telling jokes and sharing our love of Kate Bush and the Eurythmics and Peter Gabriel. For some strange reason, we called each other "Worm." I'm not sure who coined it, but the nickname stuck to all of us in our little group, and even after camp was over, Ben signed off every postcard or letter to me as "Worm." Three years later, he and I both moved to New York, and we saw each other fairly often at first, but then lost touch for a few years after that.

Then one day as I was leaving the Vineyard Theatre after a performance of *Raised in Captivity*, there he was, his orangey-red hair shining above his bespectacled face, his body shrouded in a dark wool overcoat.

"Anthony?"

"Ben? Oh my god, how good to see you!" And as I said this I could see right away that there was something wrong; his hair was thin, his face was wan and bony, and I felt a tremor in his hand as I took it in mine and gave him a hug.

"Hi," he said, giggling, his smile as bright as ever.

"Thank you for coming," I said. "It's so nice that you came."

"Oh, the play was very good, but I have to admit, I had a little trouble staying with it in the second act; I had a little trouble concentrating, because of my medication."

I took a breath and nodded before I said, "Are you—?"

"Yeah," he said, quick and unapologetic, nodding boyishly, and still smiling, although a little ruefully now.

"I'm sorry," I said, pathetically.

"It's okay, it's okay." He shrugged, still smiling, his hands wide open before him. "We have a lot to talk about. I kind of have to go, I have to lie down, it's this medication. Can we get together?"

"Sure, sure," I said. "Absolutely."

"Great. I'd love that."

"Me too."

And we exchanged numbers and said goodbye, and then just like that he was gone. I stood in the lobby for a long while after he left, as if I were coming down off a very intense, very brief drug trip, and tried to fit my memories of the Ben that I knew onto this strangely happy but very, very ill young, young, *young* man I had just seen.

We got together for lunch at an East Village café a couple of days later.

"So, how are you doing?" I asked.

"I have to tell you," he said over his salad, his eyes bright and his face beatific, "getting sick has been in some ways the best thing that's ever happened to me."

"What do you mean?"

"I don't know," he said. "I don't want you to think I'm crazy."

"I won't think you're crazy," I said, and I meant it.

"Well, I went through a *very* rough time a little while ago. I moved back home to Ohio and I went back to school and I was miserable, I hated it, and I got into some very bad scenes. I was really unhappy."

"Bad scenes?"

"Where people were having a lot of unprotected sex."

"Oh."

"And I joined in. I knew exactly what I was doing. I did it on purpose. I wanted to die."

All I could muster in response was, "Wow."

"But my life has totally changed. Seriously, I'm the happiest I've ever been. Even though I'm sick. Or maybe because I'm sick. I have a boyfriend now, who's been so supportive. I'm very lucky, I feel."

"That's wonderful," I said, and again, I really did mean it. Sitting across from him, I was convinced he wasn't just in denial or something; I was completely bathed in his glow.

"Now here's the part where I don't want you to think I'm crazy," he said.

"Okay."

"You saw *Angels in America,* right?"

"Of course. Four times. I loved it."

"Me too, I loved it, too." He leaned forward in his seat, his hands clasped in front of him. "Well, you see, I had a vision recently. I saw an angel. I did. An angel came to me, but it wasn't like an angel from the Bible or anything, it was like the angel from that play. And it told me that I was, well, that my illness was a gift, and that because of that gift I was now a healer. I can help to heal people's fears and prejudices through my being sick." He grinned. "And, I don't know, that's how I feel. That whatever time I have left I'm going to get to do a lot of good for people."

I felt myself nodding. "That's . . . kind of amazing."

"You don't think I'm crazy, right?"

"No, I don't, I really don't."

"Well, I'm glad. I mean it. I've never felt better about my life before. I'm very, very lucky."

The next time I saw him he was less animated but still cheerful.

"I want to show you something," he said, and he pulled a large manila envelope out of his bag. "I just got this today." Out of the envelope he drew a large X-ray, its plastic surface making a kind of music with its wobbles. He laid it on the table between us.

"What is it?" I asked.

"It's of my throat." He indicated a fuzzy white oblong shape at the center of what I could now make out was his esophagus. "This is a tumor they just found. It's a kind of lymphoma."

I knew that couldn't be good news, and yet he was inexplicably chipper. But as surreal as our conversations were, I was grateful to get the chance to talk to Ben so easily and openly about his condition. Ben didn't flinch or shy away from my questions as Mom did, so I asked him more. "Is it big?" I asked. "Can you feel it?"

"It's moderate, apparently, and I can feel it a little bit when I swallow. It feels like something's caught in my throat. And in a way, something is."

"Is it treatable?"

"Yeah, absolutely. They can do a lot of stuff to lymphoma now." He gestured to the X-ray. "But do you know what? I understand why I got this. It's because I've locked up so many of my emotions over the years. I've stopped myself from saying so many things. So of course I'm going to get something that affects me in the throat. But now that I'm really speaking my mind about how I feel about things, now that I'm really living my life, I know I'm winning half the battle. I know I can beat it."

I believed in what he was saying to a certain degree. But I was still worried about him.

"Well, I hope you do," I said.

•　　　•　　　•

The next time I saw Ben, a few weeks later, was the last time I saw him before I left for Oklahoma. We went to a small Chelsea restaurant, where we were joined by his boyfriend, Calvin. Right away I saw that Ben had worsened, although he still occasionally glowed with a force that belied his weak, slightly spaced-out condition.

"Isn't he doing great?" Calvin said, rubbing Ben's back. Ben smiled wanly, his eyes wandering, seemingly of their own will.

"Yeah," I said, although I really didn't think so. Throughout the meal I kept watching Ben not eat. I listened to him start sentences that he didn't finish and waited for him to register and then respond to things Calvin and I said to him. My stomach clenched up throughout the meal until I had little appetite, but I ate everything on my plate, and when it was time to go, I gave Ben a huge hug and told him, "You look wonderful. Keep it up. I'll talk to you soon."

He dazedly waved goodbye, smiling, and said, "Okay," and then slowly walked down Eighth Avenue, Calvin supporting him with a strong arm around his thin shoulders.

I didn't talk to Ben again until I called him from the pay phone in the University of Chicago MRI waiting room. The other end rang several times before it was picked up.

"Hello?" Ben said, his voice as meager as I'd ever heard it.

"Hi, Ben? It's Anthony."

There was a slight, strange pause before he replied, "Oh, *hi!*"

"I just wanted to call and say hello and see how you're doing."

Again there was a little pause. "Well, I'm okay." Another pause. "I was just resting a little."

"Is this a good time to talk?"

"Oh, yeah," he said, and then paused. "How are you?"

"Well, I'm okay. I'm at the hospital with my mom. She's not doing too well at the moment."

"Oh," he said. And then a pause. "I'm sorry to hear that."

"Me too," I said. "She's very strong, though."

"Yeah," he said. "I bet."

I listened to him breathe for a second and then asked, "How are you doing?"

"Well, my throat is very sore." A pause. "It's the radiation. It kind of burns." A pause. "I have to keep swallowing all the time." A pause. "Or else it hurts too much." A pause. "But I'm okay."

"I hope so."

"Yeah." A pause. "Calvin left me, though. I need to find a new place to live."

"What? Really?"

"Yeah. It's okay." A pause. "I'll be okay. I have a couple of options."

"Jesus, Ben. That's terrible. I wish I could help you out," I said.

"I'll be fine," he said. And paused. "Don't worry."

"You're sure?"

"Yeah," he said. A pause. "I'm sure."

"Well, if you need my help, you let me know, okay?"

"Okay," he said. "I will."

I rubbed my forehead and stared at the floor and searched for something else I could say, but the enormity of what he was going through stymied me. I came up with nothing, and I finally bailed out of the conversation with, "Well, I should let you go rest. I don't want you to hurt your throat anymore."

"Okay," he said. "Thanks for calling me."

"You're welcome. I love you," I said.

"I love you, too."

"Bye."

"Bye."

I hung up and stood there holding on to the phone for a few long minutes, clenching and unclenching my jaw, a pit opening up in my stomach, wishing there was something I could do for him, but knowing there wasn't anything, at least from where I was. What kind of boyfriend was Calvin that he would leave his dying lover? I couldn't get my head around it. But then I remembered that when I saw Louis, a character from *Angels in America,* leave his ill lover, Prior, in the course of the play, I had deeply empathized with Louis. I'd recognized myself in his fears—of facing death, of watching his lover fade away, of his own inadequacy to be the kind of caretaker his lover wanted and needed him to be. If I had been in Calvin's position, I wasn't sure that I would have been able to have the guts to stay with Ben either—I'd had enough trouble finding words of comfort and support for Ben on the phone just now, and I was having enough trouble being around my own mother's illness in this past week. And that thought, that realization of the depths of my cowardice, flooded me with a terrible, overwhelming shame.

Mom's MRI did not yield good news; the tumor had not shrunk at all. The previous several months of chemo had been ineffective and had in fact probably worsened Mom's overall health; chemo was poisonous, after all. I was furious, but I didn't air any of my frustrations to Mom. She took the news stoically.

"I think the radiation will be easier," she said. "The chemo just wiped me out."

"I know, Momma," I said. "I hope you're right."

Soon after that day, the *Twister* production company called me; it was time for me to return to Ponca City. Melanie had already made her way back, so I set off on the road alone in my rental car, blasting my CDs all the way, happy to be speeding down I-55, and truly more than a little relieved to be getting away from the day-to-day pressures of witnessing Mom's illness.

Little had changed on the set of *Twister* in my absence, and by the end of the shoot, after almost three months of being on location, I'd spent only five days in front of any camera. It was the least fulfilling job I'd ever had, including my brief stint at Starbucks. At least at Starbucks I'd felt myself to be of some real value. But on the set of *Twister*, my teammates and I were the tiniest cogs in a huge, unwieldy machine of a production. Creatively speaking, my experience on *Twister* was the antithesis of why I wanted to be an actor; there wasn't even a shred of an opportunity for self-expression possible in what I was given to do. At least my bank account had been helped out, which was no small thing.

And luckily, I knew artistic fulfillment was only a few months away, when I'd get to do *Rent* again. Jonathan had called me while I was on location to tell me everything was moving forward for a full off-Broadway production at the New York Theatre Workshop in the fall. He even played a tape recording of a new song he'd written for me: a driving, rock and roll duet with Roger called "What You Own." Jonathan told me he'd written it with my voice in mind, an incredibly flattering statement, and the first time any composer had ever paid me such a compliment.

I could hardly contain my anticipation to do *Rent* again, but I tried not to brag when my fellow actors on the set of *Twister* would ask me, "So what are you doing next?" and I'd reply, "Well, I'll be doing a show in New York in a couple of months. I'm excited about it. I think it's going to make quite a splash." "That's cool," they'd say, or something like it, and then we'd go off to the craft services table for a snack or hang out in Helen Hunt's trailer playing card games, biding our time before we could all be sent home again without having really worked at all.

A couple of weeks before my time on the *Twister* shoot was over, I got a call from my friend Leslie Smith, who'd offered me the title role in his ultra-low-budget film *David Searching* before I'd left for Oklahoma, although he'd been waiting for financing to come through before we could actually make the film. It turned out the financing was now in place, and we would start shooting about a month after I got home.

So my string of work that had begun with the workshop of *Rent* continued unabated; for the first time in years I hadn't gone more than a couple of weeks without employment. I was always happiest when I was working, but even more so now, when all this work was helping me keep my mind off my mother's illness.

Even sooner than I thought, I was going to be able to get the empty taste of *Twister* out of my mouth. As a surprise bonus, soon after I returned to New York from Oklahoma, I was cast as the lead in yet another low-budget film, this one a screwball comedy called *The Mantis Murder.* On-screen I played a dim-bulb cop, a deliciously silly, inept hero who saves the day in spite of himself, and offscreen I became good friends with Christina Haag, the film's femme fatale. Christina was the only person in my life I allowed to call me "Tony," because she sounded so refined and sexy when she said it. We spent five goofy weeks up in beautiful Greenwich, Connecticut, making splendid fools of ourselves in front of the camera, enjoying the late-summer heat, and appreciating each other's comic gifts on and off the set. The experience was a perfect antidote to the difficulties of the last three months.

The only professional downer of that time was the news that Paul, my agent at ICM, had been fired suddenly, for not being "aggressive" enough. This was ridiculous to me, and if the powers-that-be at ICM couldn't value the kind of dedicated and resourceful agent that Paul was, there was no way I wanted to stick around. I resolved to leave the agency where I'd been represented for the past nine and a half years, and promptly called my friend Sarah Fargo, who'd been an assistant at ICM years before, and who was now an agent herself at a much smaller but still very reputable agency. She was feisty and fun, her trademark red ringlets framing her pale, pretty face. I'd always loved Sarah.

"I don't want to be presumptuous or anything," I said to her over the phone from Connecticut, "but I'd love to work with you."

"Oh, are you kidding? I'd love to work with you, too!"

"Great," I said, genuinely flattered. "That's great. Thanks."

When I went into her office a few days later to sign my papers, I told her about *Rent.*

"I haven't heard anything about that," she said. "What is it?"

"Well, it's a rock opera based on *La Bohème,*" I said.

"Uh huh." She was clearly skeptical, but she nodded and smiled politely. "Sounds intriguing."

"It is. I think it's going to be great."

"Well, cool. Can't wait to see it." I could tell that I hadn't convinced her, that she was simply behaving as both a good friend and a good agent by being supportive, but I didn't press the issue; I'd let the show speak for itself. I happily signed my agency contracts with her lucky, green-sequined pen, shook her hand, and left, glad to be entering into this new partnership with my old friend.

After the shoot for *The Mantis Murder* ended, I had a few days off and then started work right away again, this time on *David Searching*. Even with our tiny budget (we had a crew of three on most days) and all of its inherent constraints (no real meals to speak of, the need to quickly film scenes guerrilla-style on the streets, hoping no cops would ask for our nonexistent permits, Leslie having to pay a real New York City cab driver to drive back and forth on East Fourth Street just so we could get a shot done), the filming went off without a hitch. I was honored that Leslie had entrusted the lead in his film to me (he told me he had written the role with me in mind), and I had the pleasure of working with a couple of old friends for the first time, Camryn Manheim and Julie Halston, as well as a great cast of wonderful New York actors, including Stephen Spinella, Craig Chester, John Cameron Mitchell, Joseph Fuqua, and David Courier.

One night toward the end of the shoot, Julie and I were filming an intense scene in which my character, David, meets a man who is very ill from AIDS. He is the lover of Julie's character (whose name in the film was—intentionally, of course—Julie Halston), and he is the first person with AIDS David has ever met. As we rehearsed the scene, I began to think about Ben. I wondered where he was, I wondered if he'd found a place to live; I had called his ex-boyfriend upon my return to New York from Oklahoma, but he'd never called me back. I didn't know how to find Ben after that; he wasn't listed in information, and we had no mutual friends. I had thought of him on and off since, but this night he was very much on my mind.

There was a hush, a respect for the power of a sickroom, that had fallen over the set as we worked that night. Conversation was at a minimum, but after we did a couple of takes of the master shot, and while John, the cinematographer, lit the room for my close-up, I turned to Julie and said quietly, "You know, I've been thinking a lot about a friend I have who's very sick right now, and I'm really frustrated because I have no idea how to get in touch with him. I just wonder how he is."

"Ouch, that's a tough one. What's his name, dear?" Julie asked, her usually manic energy greatly subdued, and a rich, lovely serenity taking its place.

"Ben. Ben Wackerman."

"Ben?" She frowned for a moment. "Wait. Was he very young? Did he have red hair?"

I was absolutely shocked. "Uh, yeah. You know him?"

"Yes, yes, he worked for a friend of mine."

"Wow. Do you know where he is?"

"Oh, sweetie," Julie said, and took my hand into her own. "Ben died. He died a few weeks ago."

"Oh . . ." I managed. I took a deep, shuddering breath. "Yeah, I was afraid of that."

"Oh, honey, I'm sorry. He was very, very sick at the end. It was his time to go."

"Yeah . . ."

"I'm sorry, sweetie. I really am. He was so young. And very sweet. A very, very nice young man."

"Yeah, he was . . ."

We fell silent after that, as we waited for the call to do our scene again. I just stared at the ground and concentrated on my breathing and railed in my mind against that asshole who hadn't ever called me back. I thought of Ben and his joy and radiance even in his illness, and I thought of his mom, whom I'd never met, but who must have felt enormously lost right now. I thought of my mom and wondered how much longer she had left. I looked up to the ceiling, beyond which I thought maybe, just maybe, Ben might be able to see me or hear me or feel my thoughts, and I sent him—or his spirit or my idea of his spirit or whatever it was, even if it was nothing—I sent it or him all of my love and all of my wishes for his peace and comfort. I said a silent goodbye to him and then I went back to work, pouring all of my shock and love and sorrow into the scene, in no small way grateful that I had the chance to channel it all somewhere, hoping that I could perhaps, by doing so, pay my friend Ben some tribute.

mr. and mrs. smith

My sister Anne's wedding to Ken Smith, her boyfriend of a couple of years, was scheduled for the day after Thanksgiving 1995, and Adam and I flew out to Joliet a couple of days before to be a part of it.

"I want you guys to be ushers," Anne said over the phone when she told us of her plans for the wedding. I had never been in anybody's wedding, so I was happy to be included, although it was strange to participate in a wedding for two people I hadn't spent time getting to know deeply. Of course I had more than a passing relationship with my sister, having grown up with her, but Anne and I hadn't talked that often as adults, and when we did, it was not about intimate issues. Instead, we discussed the movies we'd seen (she liked *The Joy Luck Club*, which I hadn't caught, while I liked *The Piano*, which she thought was good but not great), and the music we were listening to (we shared an affection for Sheryl Crow, among others), but beyond that our tastes diverged. We never talked about how either of us was feeling about Mom's illness. Nor did we ever discuss the remarkable fact that Mom had rebounded significantly from her tough summer of chemotherapy and radiation and was now well enough to walk down the aisle and give Anne away at her wedding.

In the ten months since Mom's surgery, many of us in the family would not have predicted that Mom would have been able to do that. But none of us brought it up directly with one another, perhaps because none of us wanted to tempt fate. Instead, we allowed Mom's strength to speak for itself, and we allowed the happy moment of Anne's wedding to carry the day.

"I'm going to be the flower girl," Rachel announced, eager and joyful, when Adam and I walked into Mom's house with our bags.

"That's what I heard," I said. "Congratulations."

"I wanted to wear a tux, but Mom wouldn't let me."

"Oh, Rachel," Mom said. "You're going to look very pretty."

"I know," Rachel sighed. And then she gave me one of her customary, supertight hugs around my legs.

As Adam and I said our hellos, I didn't press the wardrobe issue with Mom, even though I thought Rachel should have been able to wear whatever she wanted to Anne's wedding; there was no reason for Mom to perpetuate gender stereotypes. Besides, Rachel would have been totally adorable in a suit. But it wasn't my place to say anything, and even if it had been, I didn't want to have an argument with Mom in my first moments home.

Mom looked better than when I'd last seen her over the summer, which was a relief, although she was still far too thin for her frame. Her hair was as thick and glossy as ever, though, and her excitement for Anne's wedding sparkled in her big brown eyes as I kissed her hello on the cheek.

The next day felt almost like summer, not like late November at all, with a bright, cozy sun blazing the worst of the autumn chill out of the air. Buoyed by the weather, and finally starting to feel the excitement of Anne's big moment, I threw on my tux and unpacked my camera, bringing it over to Anne and Ken's house so I could document everyone's final preparations.

Mom had spent the night at Anne and Ken's so she could get up early for her beauty treatment in the morning, and when I arrived, she was sitting serenely at the kitchen table, her hair poofed up like Elizabeth Taylor's, her face tilted up to one of Anne's friends, who was applying her makeup.

"Mom, you look great," I said, although I preferred her usual plain and simple look to this new, foreign, glamorous one. She glanced over to me and made a silly face, sucking in her cheeks, puckering her lips, and bugging her eyes out.

"You think so?" she said.

"You do," her makeup artist chimed. "Mary, you look gorgeous. Doesn't she look gorgeous?" she asked the roomful of bridesmaids.

"Yes, absolutely," one of them said.

"*Definitely,*" another agreed.

"Wow, I've never been told I look *gorgeous* before," Mom replied in a slight English accent, goofily wiggling her eyebrows.

"Now hold still there, Mary," the makeup artist said, gently taking Mom's chin in her hand. "We're almost done."

I snapped a couple of pictures of Mom sitting there, and then a couple of pictures of Adam and Rachel (who looked adorable after all in her velvet sailor dress, white stockings, and buckled patent leather shoes), and then as I was looking for some fresh angles and new ideas for shots, Anne appeared from upstairs.

Anne had always been a cute girl, with her absolutely stunning, cloudy, blue-gray eyes shining under her auburn hair, but I had never seen her more beautiful than she looked that morning in her wedding gown. Her skin, peppered with light freckles, had been tanned to an exquisite golden brown, which glowed against the pure white lace of her dress; the combination of light and dark made her amazing eyes shine even brighter than usual, and her perky, sweet face sat perfectly framed underneath girlishly elegant bangs.

"Anne," I said, "you look beautiful."

Anne giggled bashfully. "Thanks," she said. Her friends ooohed and ahhhed, sending Anne into more giggles. "Okay," she finally said to her friend the makeup artist, "when you're done with Mom, you have to check me."

"Oh, Anne, I don't think I have to touch you. Look at you!"

Anne giggled yet again, sheepishly looking around the room. I couldn't remember ever seeing so much joy in her face, so much light, and then I turned to Mom, and my heart burst when I saw the same joy and light mirrored there.

I drove to the church with Adam and our friends Walt and Ross, blasting Smashing Pumpkins all the way. We were all originally from the Midwest, but none of us felt at home there, each of us having scurried away to New York City at our first opportunity. So in a way, on our short trip from Anne and Ken's to the church, our little car, crammed with midwestern expatriates and filled to bursting with the raucously beautiful sounds of Billy Corgan and his band mates, became the locus of our own tiny rebellion against the silence and blandness of the monotonous towns and villages and suburban sprawl stretching out all around us.

At the church, Adam and I took to our tasks, quietly leading everyone to their seats and handing them xeroxed programs. The room remained virtually silent, except for the subtle tones of organ music hanging in the air like fog. The congregation simply sat, staring straight ahead, as if they were under a spell or transfixed by some distant television program.

Suddenly, the familiar tones of the "Wedding March" resounded through the room. Dad and his mother, Grandma Doris, hadn't yet arrived. This was no big surprise, though; Dad was almost always late, and usually by a wide margin. And even though Mom, not Dad, had been designated by Anne to be the one giving her away, I was pretty sure that Dad's absence wouldn't please my sister. But if Anne was bothered, I couldn't tell from looking at her as she slowly walked down the aisle, holding on to Mom's arm, both of them keeping their eyes front, their proud faces poised and serene. And I doubted that anyone who didn't know my mother was ill would have known by looking at her that her body was locked in a battle for its survival; there was that much life force glowing out of her.

Rachel followed behind, struggling in vain to hold her head up in a similar fashion as Anne and Mom, which struck me as odd at first, until I looked closer at her face and saw that she was crying. I wouldn't have thought that an eight-year-old would be prone to such adult behavior, but there she was, methodically and seriously placing one foot in front of the other in time with the music, as her lower lip quivered and her big blue eyes spilled over with tears.

Right after the procession ended, I checked to see if Dad had arrived, just in time to watch him and Grandma Doris enter the lobby. I popped out of the main room and helped them with their coats.

"Has it started?" Dad said.

"Yeah," I said, "but only just."

"Oh, well at least we made it in one piece," Grandma Doris said with a big grin, as jolly and vital and spirited as ever.

Anne and Ken had their backs to the congregation by now, so they couldn't see us come in, but I hoped that she would somehow sense Dad's entrance; there had been so much bad blood between them over the years, and I didn't want for there to be any more spilled on Anne's big day.

After the wedding, Walt, Ross, Adam, and I parked far away from all the other cars in the reception hall's lot so we could smoke some pot before heading inside. I felt childishly naughty; I rarely smoked pot in the first place, and I had never, ever smoked pot right before I was about to spend time around Mom and my family. When I was sixteen, Mom had lectured me about drugs, leaning against the door to my room, her arms folded across her chest.

"I want you to *promise* me you'll never do any drugs," she said.

"I don't think pot's all that bad, Mom," I replied.

"Yes, it *is*. It's terrible."

"Why?"

"It kills *so* many brain cells, and you're just too smart to do that to yourself. You take such good care of yourself, why would you want to do damage to your brain? Please promise me you won't do it. *Please.*"

"Mom—"

"I mean it. I want you to promise me you won't ever smoke pot or do any other drugs at all, ever."

I stood there and considered her for a long moment, trying to think of some way to say no to her and get away without an argument, but her steady, intense, wounded gaze melted my resolve, and at last I said, sighing, "Okay, I promise."

"Thank you."

And for at least a couple of years, I had kept that promise. When people would offer me a joint, I always refused. Until I finally decided that what Mom didn't know wouldn't hurt her, and besides, I was too old to be living my life under her rules and expectations. So I casually, and only occasionally, smoked a little pot with a few of my friends, breathing in and trying to swallow the twinge of guilt that crept around the edges of my mind.

Even as I inhaled in our car at Anne's reception, trying not to cough out the harsh, hot smoke from Ross's pipe, I wasn't sure why I was so boldly smoking up right then and there. Maybe I was simply succumbing to peer pressure, or maybe I really did want to tempt fate and flaunt my drug use, as sporadic as it was, in my mother's face. More likely, though, I just wanted to relieve the tension that had insinuated itself through my body that day, as it always did when I was around my family for long periods of time.

The four of us quietly and quickly shared our pipe, and then just as quietly and nonchalantly strolled into the reception. I felt giddy as I feigned sobriety, not just because I was stoned, but also because I suddenly saw myself as some kind of ridiculous suburban outlaw, packing heat and on the lam from the local authorities. Real, scary paranoia, a common byproduct of pot, thankfully stayed at bay, though, as I greeted Mom in the foyer, wondering if she'd notice if my eyes were already red, or if she could smell the residue of cannabis on my tux as I hugged her. If she did, though, she didn't say anything, and she hooked her arm into mine and allowed me to escort her inside.

By the time dancing came around after the meal, my high had fallen a little and I was mellowing out, but that didn't stop me from jumping up out of my seat so I could boogie to the middle-of-the-road, Top 40 hits the deejay spun. I didn't care that I didn't dig the music he was playing; it had been a while since I'd cut loose on the dance floor, and I sorely needed the sweat and release that spazzing out in public gave me. Anne and Ken jumped into the fray, too, surprising me with their enthusiasm, their grins enormous and infectious, Anne surprisingly letting herself go, spinning around and hugging her new husband, and even planting a few kisses on him every now and then.

Midway through the dancing, the deejay slowed everything down and announced over the PA, "Now we'd like to ask the parents of the bride and groom to join each other in a dance." I whipped my head around to see Mom's reaction, but she was unreadable, although she did rise out of her chair a little stiffly. I stood off to the side and watched as Dad met Mom on the dance floor, his shock of gray hair, his handsome and youthful face, his bowed legs, and his distended gut all combining to make him look old and young at the same time. He looked odd and small and awkward. And yet he approached Mom evenly and directly, with what felt to me like true openness and warmth, which she didn't quite return. She remained stoic throughout their brief dance, her back and arms tight, her head down, keeping her distance from him as much as she could while still dancing in his arms. They exchanged a few words, which I couldn't hear from where I was, and as I watched them dance, I wondered if they'd ever danced together when they were dating or married. I didn't think so, although I couldn't be sure; the stories Mom had handed down left me feeling that their abbreviated married life was hectic, leaving little or no time for nights on the town. I watched them and wondered if they'd ever really known or loved each other. I wondered what Anne and Adam were thinking as they watched the dance. I wondered how it felt to Mom and Dad to touch each other more intimately than they had in years and years, and how it felt to them to be doing so in public. I wondered if they would perhaps attempt to resolve any of their unfinished business before Mom died, if in fact she was as close to death as we all feared.

And then the dance was over, and they parted quickly, without a hug or even an acknowledgment of any kind. As Mom walked away I saw her roll her eyes at her sister Roberta, who rolled her eyes back, and I saw Dad furtively glance around and rub his neck, looking scared and lost. I was amazed that they had ever been together, that they had ever made love together, that they had ever stood in front of each other and their families and their friends and their God and declared their undying love and devotion to each other, that they had embarked on living their lives together, only for it to end a few years and three children later. As I watched them find their way back to their seats, I wished for Anne and Ken a happier and healthier and fuller road together.

we begin

Rehearsals for the off-Broadway production of *Rent* were scheduled to begin on December 19, 1995, more than a year since we'd finished the studio production. I had kept in sporadic touch with Jonathan over that year, periodically checking in on the progress of the show. He'd told me that there were now a couple of producers associated with it who were helping to pay for the New York Theatre Workshop production and were eager to move the show to a commercial off-Broadway run if it was a hit. "They're young and hip and they believe in the show. They're looking at this cool space," Jonathan said, his voice full of its usual gleeful energy. "They're talking about converting an old club, to try to make it site-specific." I was grateful that Jonathan was keeping me in the loop, that we were beginning to forge a friendship.

He'd also called me soon after I'd gotten home from *Twister*. "I got invited to present a couple of songs from *Rent* as a part of this evening of presentations by local opera companies," he said.

"That sounds interesting."

"Yeah, I think I'll be the only rock opera."

I smiled. "Probably."

"And there will also be a lot of people there who really know *La Bohème* inside and out. It'll be fun."

"Cool."

"Now I know you're playing Mark and everything, but would you be willing to sing a couple of Roger's songs for it? We haven't found a Roger yet, and I didn't want to get any of my friends' hopes up, you know, by asking them."

"Yeah, sure, of course I'll do it." Again, Jonathan had flattered me. I felt that he was beginning to consider me a true member of his ensemble, an important collaborator. I had heard of composers working with actors in this way, but had never experienced anything like it.

I skated over to his apartment on the West Side, waited on the sidewalk outside his building for him to toss down his keys (he had no buzzer that let people in), and then climbed the five flights up to his railroad flat. I'd been there once before, during the studio production, and I was struck once again by the charming but decrepit environment in which he lived: the bathtub sat in the kitchen, the walls were painted various colors that didn't match, and the furniture was makeshift and threadbare. His workstation, however, seemed very well appointed and organized, situated in the corner of the living room in front of his big windows: computers and keyboards and speakers surrounded him, while framed posters and programs and awards climbed up the walls on either side.

We worked up the songs ("Light My Candle" and "Another Day," the latter a tad high for me, but manageable), and the next night I met him down in SoHo for our little performance. We sat through some mild-mannered art songs and excerpts from new folk operas, and then it was our turn. I had no idea what this crowd was going to make of our noisier version of opera music. But before I could find out, Jonathan got up in front of the small audience and spoke, his head tilted to one side like a puppy, his hands animated, his voice mellow and clear.

"I've always loved *La Bohème* and Puccini's other work, and I've also always loved Billy Joel and Elton John and the Who, and I've also always loved Stephen Sondheim and the medium of musical theatre. And I wanted to write something that could incorporate all of those influences.

"Well, a few years ago, several of my friends came to me and told me that they were HIV-positive. And then a couple of them died. And as I was coming to terms with this, I realized I had to write something in response. And so I began to work on *Rent*.

"*La Bohème* was the perfect starting point. Instead of Puccini's artists' garret in Paris, I placed my characters in a loft in the East Village. Instead of consumption, my characters became infected with AIDS. Rodolfo, the poet, became Roger, the lead singer of a failed rock band called the Well Hungarians." Jonathan smiled as the audience laughed. "Marcello, the painter, became Mark, the documentary filmmaker. And Puccini's Mimi became my Mimi Marquez, a heroin-addicted S&M dancer." More laughter.

"I'm very honored to be asked to be a part of tonight's presentation," he continued. "I dedicate this work to my friends that I've lost. Thank you."

There was a smattering of applause, and we began. I had never heard Jonathan speak at such length about the origins of his show, and as I sang, the power of his words resonated through me.

I invited Jonathan to my birthday party at the end of October, and I was happy that he showed up and stayed a long time, socializing and drinking and laughing. I didn't get to talk to him much that night, but after he left, my friend Kevin came up to me and said, "Who was that guy?"

"Who, Jonathan?"

"Yeah. What's with him?"

"What do you mean?"

"Well, we were talking, right? And I asked him what he did for a living, and he said to me, with a perfectly straight face, he said, 'I'm the future of musical theatre.'"

I guffawed. "Really?"

"Yeah, dude. Totally. I mean, what is *that* about?"

I chuckled some more. It was a crazy, bold, wild thing to say. "Well, maybe he's right," I said.

Kevin took a swig of his beer. "Yeah, but still. Would anyone want to *admit* that? I mean, come *on*."

On December 18th, the night before rehearsals began, Jonathan hosted what he called a "Peasant's Feast," a potluck dinner for the cast and crew, at his apartment. I put together a salad and headed west, running a little late as usual. When I got there, the apartment was bustling with people, although the only ones I knew were Jonathan; our director, Michael Greif; our artistic director, Jim Nicola; and Daphne Rubin-Vega, who was going to be reprising her role of Mimi. I said my hellos, giving Daphne a huge hug, and then Jonathan pulled me aside.

"I want you to meet the guy playing Roger. His name's Adam Pascal. We're really excited about him. He's never done anything on stage before, but he's got an amazing voice. He can really *sing*."

"Great," I said, and Jonathan took me to him. Never done anything? Not *anything*? This should be interesting, I thought.

"Adam," Jonathan said, "this is Anthony. Anthony, Adam."

"Hey, nice to meet you," Adam said, and grabbed and shook my hand vigorously.

"You, too," I said. If Jonathan hadn't told me that this guy was playing Roger, I never would have predicted it. His disposition was too outgoing and friendly, and the combination of his dyed blonde hair, in a caesar cut; his close-cropped, dirty-blond beard; and his outfit—a forest green sweatshirt with a medieval-style lace-up collar, underneath denim overalls—made him seem to me more like one of Robin Hood's Merrie Men than an ex-junkie wannabe rock star. But

I trusted Jonathan; I knew how long they'd sought a good Roger. I looked forward to hearing him sing.

When it was time for dinner, we took our seats in mismatched chairs along two long tables that had been set up, and Jonathan rose, clinking his glass so he could make a toast. His head was tilted like it had been at the opera event, but his voice was much softer and his body much more still as he spoke.

"I invited you all here because every year at Christmastime, I have what I call a Peasants' Feast. Since a lot of my friends and I don't have very much money, it's hard for some of us to go home and be with our families at the holidays. So we began this tradition of feeding each other and bringing each other a little holiday cheer.

"Well," he continued, "this year, I wasn't sure what I was going to do, because the show was about to go into rehearsals, and I wanted to do something to mark that occasion, but I also didn't want to break tradition and not have a Peasants' Feast."

He paused, took a deep breath, and then continued, his voice beginning to waver. "I am so grateful to the New York Theatre Workshop, and to all of you who are a part of this show. This is one of the greatest things that's ever happened to me, getting this production together. It's been a very long time coming." He paused again. "I wrote this show about my life. About the lives of my friends. And some of my friends are gone. And I really miss them." He paused again and wiped tears off his cheeks. "I guess I just wanted to say that you all are going to bring my friends to life, and I wanted to thank you for that. I wanted to thank you all for being my new friends."

The next morning, I rolled out of bed and walked through the snow and the cold to East Fourth Street, happy that our first day of rehearsal had finally come. The cast and crew milled about the skylit, airy rehearsal room, munching on doughnuts and slurping coffee and murmuring conversations with one another. On one wall, a collage had been put up featuring articles about grunge rock and Nirvana, pictures of the East Village sculpture gardens, and a makeshift placard that declared in a scrawl, STOP ARRESTING ARTISTS. Michael Greif was standing alone in front of the collage, and I wandered up to him, a little bit nervous about talking to him, but emboldened by my excitement for the work we were about to do.

"I didn't get a chance to say this last night, but I'm really happy that I'm getting to do this show again. Thanks for bringing me back."

Michael smiled politely. "Well, I'm happy to have you back."

"I've been so looking forward to it."

"Yes, well, hopefully we'll be able to make the show even better than it was last year. We'll see how we do." I didn't say anything more, but it seemed that I was a bit more confident about our show's prospects than Michael was. It would be interesting to see if his caution would prove to be well-founded.

Only three of us from the studio production were returning: myself, Daphne, and Gilles Chiasson, an ensemble member with an exceptionally strong, beautifully piercing tenor voice. I sat next to Daphne throughout the first days of rehearsal, intoxicated by the giddiness of being in on a big secret that the rest of the cast was only beginning to learn. When we began the first day's rehearsal by singing through "Seasons of Love," just as we had a year before, I felt a powerful rush as our fifteen voices blended together, with our same musical director, Tim Weil, guiding us expertly through the song's syncopations and harmonies. The sound and feel of this cast was already stronger and tighter than the previous year's, and we made fast and vigorous progress through our rehearsals.

I started to bring my camera to some rehearsals, snapping pictures when I could, which wasn't as often as I'd like because I was onstage so much. A small price to pay for being one of the leads. One day, I sat on the floor clicking away while Michael worked with Adam on the staging of "One Song Glory." Jonathan had not been remotely hyperbolic when he'd told me that Adam could sing; the boy could really *sing*. His rich, throaty, raspy, rock and roll voice exploded out of him with a force and passion that completely belied his affable, somewhat naïve demeanor. And even though he had no previous acting experience, he sang from a very instinctual, deeply rooted, emotionally expressive place.

While Adam sang through the song, Michael leaned down to where I hunkered with my camera underneath his table and whispered, "Isn't he fantastic?" I nodded vehemently in agreement and snapped some more pictures.

Jonathan also leaned down to me at one point, a gleam in his eye, while Michael talked privately with Adam. "It's perfect that you're taking these pictures," he said. "You're like Mark with his camera. It's great."

That hadn't been my goal; I'd wanted to document the rehearsal process for my own sake, rather than as research for my character, but I was happy that once again I'd done something of which Jonathan approved.

Jonathan had made extensive changes to the text of the show since the studio production, cutting out several songs, writing new ones in their place, and rewriting lyrics to already existing songs. The embittered, self-abusive rants in the title number had been transformed into a series of urgent, driving questions that expressed the themes of the show, such as *"How do you document real life / when real life's getting more like fiction each day?"* and *"How do you leave the past behind / when it keeps finding ways / to get to your heart?"* All the revisions felt like giant steps forward.

One of the biggest transformations in my character's journey occurred late in the second act, during the conversation between Mark and Roger in "Goodbye Love." Instead of a sensitive, bonding, soul-searching, more passive scene, Jonathan had fashioned a true confrontation between the two old friends. Mark no longer confessed his weaknesses to Roger; instead, Roger told Mark what his weaknesses were:

Yes, you live a lie—tell you why
You're always preaching not to be numb
When that's how you thrive
You pretend to create and observe
When you really detach from feeling alive

To which Mark responded, *"Perhaps it's because I'm the one of us to survive!"*

The exchange ended without any real resolution, and all in all it felt much more potent and fraught with conflict and truth than what had been there before.

The song that Jonathan had played for me over the phone while I was working on *Twister,* "What You Own," came next, replacing the light musical-comedy number "Real Estate" that had appeared in the same spot a year before. Incredibly challenging to sing, with its long phrases—all belted at the top of my range and the top of my lungs—and its intricate, weaving harmonies, "What You Own" quickly became my favorite song to sing in the show. I loved blasting myself out of my skin as I sang, riding on its propulsive beat, soaring over and through and alongside Adam's amazing voice. And I found Mark's opening lyrics to be reflective of my own struggles to come to terms with Mom's illness and its implications:

Don't breathe too deep
Don't think all day
Dive into work
Drive the other way
That drip of hurt
That pint of shame
Goes away
Just play the game

As I sang the song, I knew once again that I shared Mark's ability to avoid dealing with pain in his personal life by pouring himself into his work. I'd been doing the same thing for the past year as I jumped from one job to the next, hardly calling home, while Mom suffered through her scans and surgery and chemo and radiation treatments and MRIs. I was grateful, however, for this new opportunity to tap into my detachment and fear and put it to use on stage.

Even though we only had two nights and one day off from rehearsal for Christmas, my brother and I flew home. Mom seemed to be continuing her rebound, although she spent most of Christmas Day lying on the couch in the living room, her new favorite spot.

Every year, Mom asked Adam for the same Christmas gift: to draw one of his loony cartoons of our family. Mom treasured the several satirical family portraits he'd made for her over the years, saving them all in a folder and pulling them out once in a while so she could lose herself in laughter. In one, Adam depicted me with the body of a tortoise (for some bizarre, unknown private joke of a reason, he and Anne had taken to calling me "Turtle Boy" that year) but with my own oversized, human head. Adam and Anne had also taken to calling me "Pumpkin Head" that year, in honor of my larger-than-normal cranium, so out of the top of my cartoon head sprouted a pumpkin stalk. (It was far from flattering.) In another portrait, Anne stood in her bra, curling her hair, a goofy, ditzy expression on her face, surrounded by thought balloons filled with crazy images of the various boys on whom she had crushes. Inevitably, Adam's cartoon versions of himself were flawlessly rugged and muscular and dashing, a detail that made Mom laugh all the more.

For the past several years, however, Adam had stubbornly refused to draw a new portrait for Mom, for no particular reason that I could discern. She'd beg him again and again, but he'd always say no, and he'd always mean it. But this Christmas he came home and holed himself up in his room for a while, finally emerging with a new portrait. Maybe he'd done it now because he knew that he might not have another chance to give Mom what she so deeply wanted.

I was sitting in the living room with Mom when Adam strolled out of his room and handed her the new portrait. I pulled out my camera so I could capture her reaction.

"Oh, Adam, *thank* you," Mom said, clutching the piece of paper to her chest before looking at it. "Thank you, thank you, *thank* you."

"You're welcome," Adam said. He looked sheepish, like he was stifling a bigger smile underneath the small one he'd permitted to cross his face. He leaned down to Mom and gave her a brief hug. "Now look at it," he said.

Mom laid back down, a bright shaft of sunlight crossing her face, and raised up the portrait to study it. She immediately started laughing her quiet, high-pitched, breathy laugh, her mouth wide open, the force of her laughter squinting up her eyes. I clicked away with my camera.

"Oh, Adam," she said. "Oh, Adam, you're a *riot.*"

"Let me see!" Rachel said, and leaned over the arm of the couch so she could get a look as well. She started giggling with Mom. "That's *funny,*" she said. "Adam, you're *funny.*"

"You are, Adam," Mom said. "You're so *good* at this." And then a fresh wave of laughter overtook her. I clicked some more shots. I didn't even need to look at the portrait myself; I knew it would be brilliant, and I was content to capture her reaction. I loved watching her laugh; it happened so rarely anymore.

My brief visit home ended, and I headed back to New York for more *Rent* rehearsals, which continued at a productive and wonderful pace. The show was already taking shape, the ensemble blending together beautifully. I was elated by our progress.

At about the midway point in our rehearsals, Michael announced that we were going to come back from our lunch break that day and meet with a guest speaker, a woman named Cy O'Neal, who ran an organization called Friends In Deed. I pricked up my ears at this news; I had heard of Friends In Deed the year before, when I attended their gala benefit, a tenth-anniversary concert performance of *Sunday in the Park with George.* Since then, I'd been on their mailing list, receiving newsletters that informed me that Friends In Deed was an organization dedicated to offering free counseling and services to anyone faced with a life-threatening illness. This included the caretakers and loved ones of people who were ill, so I'd considered going to a meeting or workshop but had stayed away. I wasn't sure why. Maybe because I was afraid of really talking to anyone about how I felt about Mom's cancer. Maybe because I wasn't sure I was able to articulate to myself how I felt about it, let alone anyone else, and if I started to open my mouth and express my chaotic, unpredictable, confusing, upsetting feelings, it seemed likely there would be no end to them. Maybe I didn't go because I thought that most everybody at Friends In Deed was dealing with AIDS and had much more urgent concerns than I. Or maybe it was all simple procrastination on my part. But from the little I knew about Friends In Deed, their work seemed potentially life-changing, so I was happy to be getting the chance to listen to Cy O'Neal speak.

When we got back from our break, our chairs were arranged in a semicircle. I sat across the room from Jonathan and a few seats down from Cy, a straight-backed, tall, thin, elegant, and earthy middle-aged woman who had floated into the room and quietly taken her seat. She wore a dark turtleneck, dark jeans, and dark glasses, all of which were offset by her several silver rings, a large silver bracelet, and a pair of silver earrings. Her salt-and-pepper hair was cut short, to about a schoolboy's length, with a side part. In some ways she looked like my mom, albeit much more refined and with a lot more silver jewelry. My mom had always cut her hair short, often took to wearing turtlenecks and jeans, and had worn tinted glasses at different points in her life. I sat and watched Cy as she intently and eagerly looked around the room while we slowly filtered in and took our seats. She sat perfectly straight, almost on the edge of her chair, her hands folded in her lap, her feet planted firmly, her legs uncrossed. She immediately struck me as possessing an odd combination of monk-like serenity and old-school New York City glamour.

When we were all assembled, Michael handed the proceedings over to Jonathan.

"Everybody," Jonathan began, his tone mild-mannered and re-spectful, "I'm very happy that Cy agreed to come here today. It was important to me that you all would get a chance to meet her and hear what she had to say. I don't know how much you know about Friends In Deed, but they're an amazing organization. When my friends Gor-don and Pam and Matt all became HIV-positive, they asked me to go to meetings at Friends In Deed with them, and I did, and it really helped us all deal with everything. I just responded to how they viewed life and death and illness and all of it. And so it's really in-formed what I've written. I wrote the Life Support scene as an at-tempt to capture what goes on at Friends In Deed.

"So, anyway, I asked Cy if she'd be willing to come to our re-hearsal, because I felt it was important for all of us to hear her speak, and she said she would, and here she is, and here we are."

"Yes, here we are," Cy said, her voice husky and refined and warm all at the same time.

"So," Jonathan continued, turning to Cy, "I thought I'd start everything off by asking you some questions. I wrote up a list of what I thought was important for everyone to know." He flashed a sheet of notebook paper he'd been holding in his lap.

"Okay," Cy said, smiling. "Sounds good."

First, Jonathan asked her to explain what Friends In Deed was and the organization's philosophy.

"Well," Cy began, "at Friends, we come from the point of view that, in life, there are no accidents. It's all okay. There is nothing really ever *wrong*. Everything in life is exactly the way that it should be, very simply because that's the way that it is. There is no other way that it *can* be." She paused, letting us mull these ideas over to our-selves. She continued:

"Another very important aspect of our work at Friends is our point of view that the quality of our lives is not determined by the circumstances. So if you have AIDS, for instance, while your physical body may very well be under attack from a terrible virus, and while this circumstance may make the business of living much more difficult in many ways, we suggest that the presence of AIDS in your life does not mean that the quality of your relationships, or the amount of love you experience, or even your sense of yourself, none of it has to suffer. This is not necessarily easy stuff for people to consider sometimes, as you can imagine."

Intrigued and stirred up, I raised my hand and asked, "If you're saying you come from the point of view that nothing's ever wrong, that everything's always okay, what do you do with anger and sadness and grief when something bad happens?"

Cy regarded me for a tiny moment and then replied, "Well, try to think of it this way: there are two realities. On the one hand, you have this idea that I've been talking about, this reality, that it's all all right." She held up her right hand as she said this. "And on the other hand," she continued, holding up her left hand in opposition to her right, "you have all of your opinions, and all of your feelings, and all of your notions about it. Like 'it's terrible,' or 'it hurts,' or 'I don't like it,' or 'it's painful,' or 'it's sad.' And the goal is to be able to live with both realities." And with that she brought her hands together. "Neither one is more true than the other. Neither one is better than the other." She leaned forward, resting her elbows on her knees. "I lost my husband, Patrick, to cancer a couple of years ago, and believe me, when it was happening, I was absolutely devastated. It was incredibly painful. I missed him terribly when he died. I still miss him terribly. And, at the same time, while he was dying, and in the years since he's died, I can also see that it's all okay. It's all happened exactly the way that it should have happened, because that's the way that it happened. There's no other way that it *could* have happened. It's simple." She leaned back. "But sometimes I could no longer see that, and I would feel overwhelmed by grief and sadness, and I would feel terrible, and I would cry, and miss him, and then with time, all of that would pass, and once again I'd see that everything was okay. That my grief was just as much a part of my life as everything else. There's nothing wrong with grief. It's an entirely appropriate response. Of course we feel grief. The trouble is, in our culture, there isn't always a lot of permission for people to grieve. And so we think that we shouldn't go through it, and we stifle it down, because it's not allowed. And that's when we get ourselves in trouble. But grief is absolutely real, and there's absolutely nothing wrong with feeling it. Quite the opposite." She paused again and regarded me with her clear and open gaze. "Does that answer your question?"

"Yes," I said. "Yes, it does. Thank you." I resolved to try to incorporate all that she'd just said into my life, not very confident that I'd be able to, but already feeling comforted.

A couple of weeks later, we moved into our technical rehearsals, the last stage in our process before opening the New York Theatre Workshop's doors to the public. I wondered how Jonathan was feeling; I hadn't seen much of him lately, except for the day he'd dashed into the rehearsal room, waving a ream of papers, and promptly sat down at the piano. He'd started pounding out his new song for Maureen and Joanne, "Take Me or Leave Me." Its groove and chord progression reminded me of the classic R&B song "Lean on Me," but that's where the comparison stopped. Instead of composing something that was blindly derivative, Jonathan had written a truly original, supremely catchy, sublimely raucous pop tune, giving Idina Menzel and Fredi Walker, who played Maureen and Joanne, the opportunity to blow the roof off the theatre. Idina is an outrageously gifted rock and roll singer, very different from Sarah, who'd played Maureen in the workshop production. Idina's Maureen was all sex appeal and eagerness, while Sarah's had been all restraint and pretension. I had been fond of Sarah's rendition, but I was thrilled by Idina's. Listening to her and Fredi learning and rehearsing their new song, their voices bursting with fire and energy, their sound contrasting and blending flawlessly, both of them trying to top each other without turning it into a ridiculous *Star Search* contest, was one of the most exciting aspects of the last two weeks of rehearsal.

Other than that day, Jonathan had been lying low; there wasn't a whole lot he could have contributed to rehearsal after we learned his music. We all needed to get the chance to try our stuff out, and sometimes fall on our faces, without Jonathan's protective eyes and ears in the room.

He popped up again, though, when we moved into the theatre and started singing with the band, so he could help refine the sound mix in the house. As the cast and band gathered onstage, Jonathan stood in the midst of the theatre's red velvet seats, thrust his hands in the air in the infamous devil's horns gesture, and shouted, *"ROCK AND ROLL!"* in his best Pete Townshend imitation, grinning like an idiot. I laughed, and Tim counted us in for the title song—"A two three *four*," and we charged our way through the score, filling the intimate theatre with the sounds of Jonathan's sometimes beautifully noisy and other times quietly stirring music.

The only time I talked one-on-one with Jonathan during those days was on a quick break in rehearsals. Clutching a coffee cup, looking both hyper and exhausted, he approached me in the lobby.

"Hey, can I talk to you for a second?"

"Sure," I said.

"It's not about the show," he said, smiling. "It's about Christina Haag." My costar from *The Mantis Murder.*

"What about her?"

"Well, I met her at your birthday party, and we've been hanging out a lot since then, and, well—" he paused, grinning bashfully and shrugging his shoulders. "I really like her."

I smiled. "That's great," I said.

"But I don't know what to do about it. I don't know if she feels the same way about me."

I found his schoolboy's crush, and its attendant uncertainties, to be completely charming. "Well, why don't you tell her how you feel?"

"I don't know. I can't tell if she just thinks of me as a friend. I really, really like her. A lot."

"Well, the only way to find out is to let her know."

"You're right. You're right." He took a sip of coffee. "But the thing is, you know, with her ex-boyfriend being so famous, it's a little intimidating. It just makes me feel like she'd probably never be interested in me."

Christina had dated John Kennedy Jr., one of the world's most desired bachelors, for several years, so I could understand Jonathan's intimidation. "Yeah, that is kind of a big deal," I said. "Do you want me to say something to her for you?"

"No, no, no, you don't have to do that. No, that wouldn't be good, I don't think." He shook his head emphatically.

"Well, like I said, you'll never know what could happen unless you say something. She's a very cool woman. I think she'd be honest with you."

"Yeah, you're right. You're right." He nodded somberly, staring into his coffee cup. "Maybe I will say something. But I'll probably wait until we're up and running. It's not like I could really do anything about it now anyway."

"That sounds like a plan to me."

"Hey, thanks for talking to me," Jonathan said. He smiled ruefully. "Sorry I'm so high-schoolish about this."

"No problem," I said, smiling and giving him a little pat on the shoulder. And with that, I went inside the theatre, back to rehearsal.

A couple of days later, Adam Pascal and I were gathered around the piano with Tim and Michael, cleaning up the harmonies in "What You Own," when I noticed some commotion at the back of the theatre. I saw Michael notice it as well, but he didn't stop us, so, unsure of what was happening, Adam and I continued singing.

We're dying in America
At the end of the millennium
We're dying in America
To come into our own
And when you're dying in America

At the end of the millennium
You're not alone

Sue White, our efficient, intense, motherly production manager, made her way down the aisle to the stage, motioning us to stop our work. In a low, calm voice, she said, "Nothing to worry about, but Jonathan just collapsed in the back of the theatre. The paramedics are on their way."

"Wait a minute, what happened?" Adam said.

"We're not sure. He just collapsed. It doesn't seem too serious. He's up again right now, but he's very pale and disoriented, and we're going to take him to the hospital, just to make sure that he's all right. It's probably nothing. He's just stressed out and exhausted."

"Wow," I said.

"We'll let you know what's going on," Sue said. "But I'm sure everything is fine."

I looked up at the back of the theatre, but couldn't really see anything: just a clump of people that had gathered around, talking quietly to each other. I could see Jonathan leaning against the wall, his head down, with someone's hand resting on his arm. Tim, Adam, and Michael stood next to me on the edge of the stage for a moment, all of us silently trying to figure out what to make of this.

Finally, Michael said, "Well, I guess we should probably continue working. We don't want to freak Jonathan out."

"Sounds good," Tim said, sitting back down at his keyboard. "Let's take it back from the top."

Adam and I started the song again, and as we sang, Jonathan left with Sue and the paramedics, and the strange, unexpected chill that had descended over the room gradually dissipated, until we were all firmly back in the groove of our work, trusting that Jonathan would be all right.

Over the next couple of days—our final days of tech—we first got a progress report from Sue that Jonathan was still suffering from flu-like symptoms, most likely from a combination of stress and exhaustion, and possibly the result of a bad turkey sandwich he'd eaten at the Cooper Square Diner. His stomach had been pumped at the hospital, just in case, and they had sent him home to recuperate. Then Sue told us a day later that Jonathan had gone to a different hospital because he was still feeling terrible, and that after some tests he was sent home with the news that he probably had the flu. I thought about calling him to check up on how he was feeling, but then thought better of it; he needed to relax, and phone calls weren't necessarily the best medicine, especially from a cast member who would remind him of what he was missing at the theatre.

Meanwhile, we all continued our long, long days, singing and teching from noon till midnight, putting together all of the final elements of the show, so we could finally perform it for our first audience on dress rehearsal night.

That night finally came, and thankfully Jonathan was feeling well enough to return to the theatre, joining Michael and the cast onstage before the performance for a brief photo shoot with a *New York Times* photographer. The *Times* had sent the photographer with a writer—not a critic—who was doing a story on the one hundredth anniversary of Puccini's *La Bohème* and thought it might be interesting to include our modern-day, rock opera version in his piece. Jonathan still looked wan and ashen, but his nervous excitement for his big night shone through as the flashes went off.

After a few minutes the shoot ended, and it was time for us to go backstage and ready ourselves. Jonathan stood at the edge of the stage and said, smiling and waving, "Have a good show, everybody. I'll be watching!"

For a dress rehearsal, it was a great show. The audience was with us from the first moment, cheering each number, and leaping to its collective feet at the end of the night. Their response reminded me of the response that *Six Degrees of Separation* had received on its dress rehearsal night when I appeared in it at Lincoln Center. For *Six*

Degrees, our audience had laughed so uproariously that the actors in *Some Americans Abroad,* the play upstairs from us, could hear every thunderous outburst, even through the concrete floor that separated our theatres. *Six Degrees* wound up a huge critical and popular hit, with a real and lasting cultural impact, so if responses at dress rehearsals were any indication, *Rent*'s future suddenly seemed assured. Of course, we needed to get a great review in the *Times* to really make us a hit; many an audience's favorite show had been hurt by bad press in the *Times.* But the critic from the *Times* wasn't coming for another couple of weeks, giving us plenty of time to continue refining and cleaning up the show, so it wasn't worth worrying about right now. For the moment, I reveled in the immediate joy that was bouncing around the theatre.

I emerged from backstage to see most of the audience still milling around, another good sign. From the stage, I could see a large group of admirers clamoring around Jonathan in the far aisle, shaking his hand and talking his ear off. I was so happy and I wanted to go over to him as well and give him a congratulatory hug, but then I decided that I should let him savor his glory—I could talk to him later—and I headed over to my friends who'd been in the audience.

One of them, an East Village playwright named Dan, rushed up to me and gave me a crushing hug. "Oh, Anthony," he said, his words pouring out of him, "it's so *beautiful.* I can't tell you. I can't. It's a beautiful, beautiful thing. Thank you, thank you."

I grinned hugely. "I'm so glad you liked it."

"Oh, my god, I *loved* it. I mean it. I *loved* it."

Still grinning, I asked, "Have you met Jonathan?"

"Oh my god, yes. I had to. I had to just go up to him and tell him how amazing he is. He's like a hero. You don't understand. He's created something so gorgeous and important, and I can't really keep talking about it because I'm going to explode. Really. I've got to go, I've got to just go off and not talk anymore. Oh my god, thank you so much."

Giddy from his thrilling response, I said, "You're welcome."

Dan dashed off, and behind him was my agent, Sarah. Her eyes were wide open, brimming over, and she was trembling as she gave me a warm, firm hug.

"Rappy, it's amazing," she said, holding onto my shoulders and looking right into my eyes.

"See?" I said, beaming affectionately. "I told you so."

"Oh my god, you were so right. Rappy, it's *amazing*. I had to go up to Jonathan at intermission and tell him. And then the second act just blew me away even more. I can't believe it. It really is beautiful."

My face was starting to hurt from all of the grinning I was doing. "Thank you," I said.

"I can't believe it," Sarah said again, shaking her head, her eyes bright. "I can't believe it."

After I said good night to Sarah, I glanced over to see if I could finally get a chance to talk to Jonathan, but he wasn't there. There was so much I'd been saving up to tell him on this night, so many thanks I'd wanted to give him: for jump-starting my career; for giving me the chance to sing onstage again; for asking me back after the studio production; for expanding my role so fully in the past year; for writing me new songs to sing with my voice in mind (in addition to "What You Own" I'd also been given a lovely, haunting soliloquy following Angel's funeral, called "Halloween"); for sharing his process with me; for entrusting me with the role of narrator; for writing this amazing show in the first place; for writing a musical that featured such richly developed queer characters; for writing a show that was so incredibly fulfilling to perform, and so moving for its audiences; and, most important, for becoming both my new, supportive friend and a true, enthusiastic collaborator. I usually stored up these kinds of sentiments for my coworkers, writing them down in little cards, which I delivered on opening nights, but I wanted to tell Jonathan all of these things to his face, especially now that the night had gone so phenomenally well. But I looked around the theatre and couldn't find him.

"Have you seen Jonathan?" I asked Linda, NYTW's associate

artistic director, who was calmly sitting in the back of the theatre, drinking in the intoxicating buzz that was flying around.

"He's in the box office, talking to the *New York Times*," she said, more than a little portentously. That was a good sign; if the reporter from the *Times* writing the piece on *La Bohème* was actually talking to Jonathan, he had to think there was something to our show. Hopefully his colleagues at the paper would follow suit.

"That's exciting," I said. Linda smiled knowingly.

"We'll see," she said.

Michael came up to me just then and gave me a hug. He had spent the performance pacing around the back of the theatre by the sound booth, obsessively twisting his dark black curly hair into fright-wig proportions, but now he seemed genuinely happy.

"Thank you for your work tonight," he said.

"It went pretty well, huh?" I said, aware that Michael responded positively to understatement.

"Yes, it went very well, but we have a long day tomorrow, so you should go home and get your rest."

"Okay, I will," I said. "I don't know if I'll be able to sleep, though."

"Well, do your best. We've got a lot of work to do." He flashed me his legal pad full of notes, and I nodded and said good night. When I got into the lobby, I peered in the box office window, where Jonathan was still talking to the *Times* reporter, his head bobbing up and down, as it always did when he talked about his work, his hands working overtime to keep up with his words. I watched him for a few moments, and thought about knocking on the window so I could at least wave good night to him, but decided not to disturb them. This was Jonathan's moment, his first real interview. I would have plenty more opportunities to tell him all of the things I wanted to tell him. Even though I'd wanted to say it all tonight, it didn't matter *when* it was said; it only mattered *that* it was said. And so I turned and walked out of the theatre, heading home, floating along on the knowledge that tonight had been only the beginning of what was probably going to be an amazing run.

Mom and Rachel at Mom's house in July 1996.

Anne, Mom, Adam, and me, circa 1983.

3

Mom and Dad in 1971. That's me in Mom's belly.

4

Mom with our pseudo-aunt Gloria, back in the day.

5

Dad with his current (and third) wife, Sandra, after they saw *Rent* in Chicago.

6

Family members in the lobby of the Nederlander Theatre on opening night, before the performance: Roberta, me, Mom, Chris, and Bonnie.

7

Me, Anne, and Rachel at dinner after they saw *Rent* for the first time, in Chicago.

That's me singing "Where Is Love?" in *Oliver!* at the Little Theater on the Square.

8

Me as Daryl Coopersmith in *Adventures in Babysitting,* up to no good as usual. Ya think?

9

Me as Tony Olson in *Dazed and Confused.* Don't try this haircut at home.

10

11

Mom at Anne's wedding.

12

Here we are, the original Broadway cast, with the Clintons. Missing from the picture is OBC member Kristen Lee Kelly.

13

A shot of me from the movie version of *Rent*.

14

Jonathan in the cozy New York Theatre Workshop rehearsal room.

15

This was taken right after Daphne's last performance. That's her husband, Tommy, in the mirror with us.

Mom's glamour shot, taken on the day of Anne's wedding and used at her funeral.

The cover of the program for Mom's memorial service.

Mary Lee Rapp

October 19, 1941 to May 22, 1997

"God has given us our memories that we
might have roses in December."

--J. M. Barrie

jonathan

I woke up the next morning, January 25th, earlier than my alarm, sweating, having been cooked by the sunlight that was streaming through the window above my bed. I sat up, threw the covers off, and rubbed my eyes. The triumph of the previous night washed over me again. I reached for my phone, hoping that there would be some congratulatory messages waiting for me on my voice mail, and dialed. The only message was from Jim Nicola, NYTW's artistic director.

"Anthony," Jim said, his quiet, mellow voice sounding more than a little weary, "this is Jim over at the Workshop. Please call me as soon as you get this message." And then he abruptly hung up.

I had no idea what could be so important, but it didn't sound like it was something good. I didn't understand; last night had gone so well, everyone should be thrilled. Maybe somebody had been fired, I thought. Maybe previews were being postponed for technical reasons. I was thinking about this, about to call Jim back, when the phone rang.

"Hello?"

"Anthony, it's Sarah."

"Hi, good morning."

"Did I wake you?"

"No, no, not at all. What's up?"

"Well, Anthony," Sarah said, and then paused. "I don't know how to tell you this."

"What?"

"Jonathan's dead."

My chest froze in an instant. "What?"

"He is, he's dead. He died last night. His agent works with me, and he got the call this morning. It's unbelievable."

"What happened?" My entire body felt electrified. My heart began to pound, my face began to heat up, and I tried to simply focus on Sarah's words, to bear down on myself and keep my head clear as she talked.

"They don't really know yet what happened. He just collapsed last night after he got home. His roommate found him on the floor. Oh, Anthony, I'm so sorry to have to tell you this."

"I don't know what to say . . ." My heart still thundering in my chest, I sat very, very still and noticed I wasn't breathing, and forced myself to inhale and exhale.

"It's unbelievable. He was so alive last night when I talked to him, so happy."

I considered this, seeing in my mind the images of all of the people surrounding him, the images of him sitting in the box office. "What does this mean for the show?" I asked.

"Well, no one knows for sure. I think it will continue. It has to."

"Yeah, yeah, it does." It *had* to continue, for Jonathan.

"Oh, Rappy, I'm so sorry."

"Yeah," I said. "This is crazy. I'd better go, I guess. I've got to make some phone calls."

"All right. If you need anything, call me."

"I will. Thanks, Sarah."

"Bye, Rappy."

I hung up and sat staring at the phone. Everything was shifting in me so quickly: I felt wildly crazy and perfectly calm at once. Jonathan's death made bizarre sense; he'd not been well, he'd gotten this show out of him, which was the most important thing he'd ever done, the biggest expression of himself he could ever put out into the world, and when he was done, he'd died. Shaking my head to get these thoughts away from myself, I picked up the phone again and dialed the Workshop.

"Hello, New York Theatre Workshop, this is Sue." Her voice was unusually subdued and strained.

"Sue? It's Anthony." I could hear Sue breathe in sharply on the other end. "I just heard the news."

"Yeah," Sue said. "Yeah." She sighed. "Well, whenever you can get down here, we're all gathering together, to try to figure out what to do about this."

"Okay," I said. "I'll be there soon."

"All right, honey." I could hear her trying to keep her voice from quavering. "See you soon."

I hung up and stared at the phone again, feeling myself suddenly click more completely into a protective, efficient, practical mode, a much easier state to be in than actually dealing with all that was roiling in me. There were tasks that needed to be accomplished, after all: phone calls needed to be made, people needed to be notified, arrangements needed to be coordinated. And if I was available to do them, I should. So, almost as if I were being compelled by an unseen force, I reached over to my address book and flipped through its pages, trying to think of who I should tell. I felt like I had been thrust into a made-for-TV movie. As I flipped through my pages, wondering who should know, it hit me: as far as I was aware, I was the only person who knew of Jonathan's friendship with Christina Haag, so chances were she wouldn't be on anybody's list of people to notify. So I called her, steeling myself as the phone rang.

"Hello?"

"Christina, it's Anthony."

"Tony! Hi! How are you?"

"Well, I'm okay, but I'm calling to tell you some terrible news." I just had to come right out with it; there was no other way.

"What?"

"Jonathan's dead."

Christina's shriek was instantaneous and terrifying and seemingly endless. "What?!?" she finally managed, breathless, almost hyperventilating. I clamped down on myself, to keep my stomach from leaping up into my throat as I listened to her sobs. "What—what do you mean?!?" she cried.

"He died last night, they don't know why yet. He just collapsed."

"This—this can't be. Oh my god, no, it can't be!"

"I'm sorry, Christina. I'm sorry."

"Oh my god, oh my god." She sobbed again.

"I'm sorry to be the one to tell you."

"No, no, you had to. Thank you for calling me. I've got to go, I'm sorry, I've got to go."

"I'm sorry."

I heard her gulp down a sob as she hung up. Shaken, I sat for a moment, slowly breathing in and out, and then I abruptly dialed the number for Friends In Deed. Cy wasn't in, so I left her a message that Jonathan had died, and hung up, and then kept going through my address book, making calls, telling people that Jonathan had died, each time feeling strangely outside of myself and at the same time very much in control of myself, dialing number after number, because it felt like the only thing to do, saying it again and again, "Jonathan's dead," until there were no more people to call. And then I numbly got myself ready to go to the theatre, and made my way outside into the bright, harsh winter morning, and slowly walked down to East Fourth Street.

On the corner of Second Avenue and Fourth Street, I ran into Byron Utley, one of my fellow cast members, and even though we didn't know each other well, we immediately fell into a wordless hug. Byron was tall, so I pressed my face into his comforting, puffy down coat and squeezed him tightly for a moment. We pulled apart, silently shaking our heads, and then he went inside the corner deli and I continued on into the theatre.

The theatre was quiet, even with all of the people who were wandering and sitting around. Sue was the first person I saw, and we shared a silent, firm hug. Then I saw Daphne, and we both rushed into each other's arms, and that's when at last I started to cry, pressing Daphne to me, Daphne saying, "Oh, honey, oh, honey," and tenderly rubbing my back, soothing me while she cried as well. It was as if I'd been waiting for her embrace to allow me to unleash my sadness; now I could let go and weep, my tears impossibly hot and fast, my throat closing up, my face burning, my chest beginning to heave. I held Daphne and she held me, and finally my breathing eased and my tears slowed, and then we parted, holding each other's hands and looking into each other's eyes.

"Jonathan, man," Daphne said, her voice thick and low, her eyes still moist with tears. "That fucker. What does he think he's doing, leaving us like this? That motherfucker."

"Yeah," I said.

"But, I don't know," Daphne continued. "I don't know. I guess he was done, you know? I guess he did what he had to do, and just split. Asshole."

"I guess," I said.

And then there wasn't anything else that either of us could say, and we found ourselves slowly joining the rest of our fellow cast members onstage, where they either sat, their eyes cast down, or stood, embracing each other. Michael, Tim, and the band were there too, everyone's chairs arranged in a circle, and Daphne and I walked up onstage and silently hugged each person, everyone's face looking wasted and surprised and puffed out and grim. I took my seat, looking searchingly at everybody, overwhelmed by the intensity of feeling swirling around me.

We sat together, mostly in silence, for a very long time, the silence occasionally interrupted by someone's halting words, such as, "I can't believe it," or "It's terrible." I felt that, for me, no words could do this situation the remotest justice, so I remained silent. Suddenly, Tim, who'd been sitting slumped in his chair, shaking his head ruefully, began to sob violently, burying his horribly contorted face in his hands. We all just watched him, allowing him his grief, and Taye Diggs, sitting to Tim's right, placed his hand on Tim's shoulder, steadying him, until at last his agonized sobs faded.

Gradually, our circle dissipated, and people broke off into smaller groups, or continued sitting quietly by themselves. I suddenly needed to leave; I was feeling both cleansed and oppressed by the grief all around me; and so I stepped outside, breathing in the bracingly cool air, and made my way to the corner deli. As I wandered up and down the aisles, unsure of what I wanted, just certain that something would bring me some comfort, I slowly realized that the music piping in through the store's tinny stereo sounded naggingly familiar. I opened my ears to it, and it was then that I heard Michael Stipe and R.E.M. chiming their way through "Losing My Religion," and even though I wasn't sure whether I believed in ghosts or spirits or messages from the Great Beyond, I found myself standing perfectly still in the middle of that deli, closing my eyes, letting the song wash over me, feeling that Jonathan was somehow there. He had to be; this song was several years old, and it wasn't played on the radio anymore, so what was the likelihood that at that exact moment I would just happen to hear it? Maybe it was Jonathan's way of saying hello, I thought, maybe it was his way of saying that he was there, that he was okay, that he was at peace. But even as I thought all of this, I realized I was reaching desperately for something to hold on to, something that might make sense out of a senseless situation. But whatever the truth of the matter was, hearing that song in that deli in that moment made me feel almost blessed.

Back in the theatre, Michael approached me, his brow furrowed, his pale face flushed red. "Can I talk to you?" he said.

"Sure."

He pulled me over into a corner of the room, away from every-body else. "I've been talking to Jim," he said, "and we've been going back and forth about what we should do about tonight's preview, and I wanted to ask you what you thought about it."

I was flattered to be asked, and glad to have something practical to focus on. "Well, we have to do something, don't we?"

"Yes, we do, we both agree about that, but we're just not sure what."

"What are the options?"

"Well, Jonathan's family is flying here right now from Albu-querque and they're going to come to the theatre, and I think we should just cancel the preview but invite Jonathan's friends here and perform the show for his friends and family."

I felt myself nodding emphatically. "That sounds right."

"But I wouldn't want the evening to be about all of the technical issues, you know, I wouldn't want to get caught up in quick changes and lighting cues. I'd want it to be about the songs."

"So what should we do?"

"I think we should just have you all sit up there at the tables and sing through the score."

This felt absolutely correct to me. "Yeah, that sounds good."

Michael looked relieved. "Good, I'm glad you agree. I wasn't sure if it made sense or not, but I'm glad you agree."

So we talked to Jim, and solidified our plans, and then Michael told the cast, who all agreed that it was the right thing to do, and suddenly we all had a purpose. The energy in the theatre gathered steam as we all took part in the preparations for that evening's per-formance.

Hours later, shortly before our performance was scheduled to begin, I returned from our dinner break to find the lobby teeming with shocked, disoriented people, some standing alone, some huddled to-gether. I saw Christina, and we shared a tight, clinging hug—"Thank you for calling me," she said in my ear as we embraced—and then I went inside the theatre. Michael came right up to me, fresh tears streaming down his face.

"His parents are here," he said. I breathed in deeply, my jaw set. "I just can't stand it. I can't stand seeing so many parents lose their children. It shouldn't be this way." I just nodded and squeezed Michael's shoulder.

"Where are they?" I asked.

"Right there." He indicated a short, gray-haired couple, standing off to the side, quietly greeting well-wishers. "I can't imagine how they must feel," Michael said.

"Yeah," I managed to say, my chest tight. I approached them. "Mr. and Mrs. Larson? My name is Anthony."

Mr. Larson gripped my hand firmly, his eyes both soft and a little wild, his voice quiet, almost a whisper. "Oh, yes, yes, of course. I'm Al. Jonathan told me a lot about you."

I shook his hand for a moment, unsure of what to say. Finally, I said, simply, "I'm very sorry."

"Yes, yes," Mr. Larson replied. He released my hand, looking lost for a moment, and then gestured to his wife. "Oh, this is my wife, Nan."

"Hi there," Nan said, her voice a little stronger than her husband's, her eyes moist, her hand shaking slightly as she took mine in hers. "So nice to meet you. So nice to meet you."

"We're, uh, we're very sorry, and we're glad that you're here," I said.

"Well, we had to come," Al said. "We had to."

I stood there for a moment longer, chewing my lip, and then said, "Well, I'll see you afterwards."

"Okay, okay, we'll be seeing you," Al said vaguely, and then turned to the next person who waited to speak to him. I stepped away, concentrating on my breathing as I headed backstage, my head churning, unable to fathom the depths of Al and Nan's grief and shock.

•   •   •

Backstage, we wandered around in a semidaze, occasionally clutching each other's hands or hugging one another. Some people warmed up their voices, others sat quietly. Our only costume pieces were our headset microphones.

Finally, it was time to begin, and we headed out onstage. The set's three long metal tables were placed end to end across the edge of the stage, with bowls of Ricola lozenges and boxes of tissues spaced evenly across them. As we took our seats, I gazed out at the audience. The house was entirely full, with many people spilling out onto the aisles' floors, and many others standing in a crowd in the back of the theatre. I spotted Christina and the Larsons and Michael, as well as cast members from the studio production. They looked expectant and exhausted, and no one spoke.

Jim made his way down to the floor in front of the stage, holding on to a crumpled piece of paper. He cleared his throat.

"I'm, uh, I'm not used to making speeches in public," he said, his gentle voice wavering. "And this morning when I woke up, I certainly never thought I would have to make a speech like this. But." He cleared his throat again, glancing down at his notes. "As you know, Jonathan Larson died last night, after he went home after our dress rehearsal. We have found out that his death was the result of an aortic aneurysm, a freakish cause of death for a young, thirty-five-year-old man. I think it goes without saying that this doesn't seem fair at all. I can think of a lot of people I'd like to see die of an aneurysm right now. Certainly not Jonathan Larson." He paused, clearing his throat once again.

"As we came together at the theatre today, trying to make some sense of this horrible turn of events, we decided that all there was for us to do was to continue the work that we and Jonathan had begun together. We owe it to Jonathan. Even though he's gone, this beautiful, loving, courageous piece that he created lives on, and we will do our utmost to honor his memory by bringing it to life every night here at our theatre.

"When we were trying to figure out what we were going to do

about tonight's scheduled preview, we knew that what we couldn't do was keep our theatre silent. We knew that much for certain. But we also didn't want tonight to be about anything other than Jonathan's words and music. So we asked our amazing cast if they would simply sing through Jonathan's score for us, and they agreed, and I'll stop talking now, so we can all listen to them, and listen to Jonathan. Thank you."

Jim abruptly sat down, and the house lights dimmed. I centered myself as best as I could, silently pledging to get through it, thinking that if we could all just get through it, we'd be giving Jonathan's friends and family an incredible gift.

I had the first lines, and so I took a deep breath and glanced over at Tim, who stood at the ready in front of his keyboard. I nodded, and Tim cued our guitarist, Kenny Brescia, to begin. He plucked the opening notes on his guitar, and I dove in.

"December 24th, nine P.M.," I sang, my voice stronger and clearer than I'd thought it would be, *"Eastern Standard time / From here on in, I shoot without a script / See if anything comes of it / instead of my old shit."* As I continued singing, I gained momentum, clicking into a real performance, embodying this character that I knew so well and so loved to play, and I focused all of my energy and sent it out to the audience. I was owning the story, driving it forward, sharing it.

As we continued, the audience laughed at all the right jokes (especially Kristen Lee Kelly's "Voice Mail" as Mrs. Cohen), and when the band kicked in with a blast of energy on "Rent," I could feel the voltage in the room rise enormously. By the song's climax, when all fifteen of us defiantly raised our voices in climbing, flying harmonies—*"Rent, rent, rent, rent / We're not gonna pay rent!"*—the hairs on the back of my neck stood on end. And when Adam and I screamed out our last line at the top of our lungs—*"'Cause everything is reeeeeeeeeeeeeeeeeeeeeeeent!"*—holding out that last note for what felt like forever until Tim and the band crashed themselves into a huge, crazy, rock-and-roll finish, the entire audience instantaneously erupted in thunderous, joyful, cacophonous cheers.

We plunged forward, the first act continuing on with Jesse Martin and Wilson Heredia's tender "You Okay Honey?" and Adam's heartbreaking "One Song Glory." A hush descended over the theatre as Adam sang, his voice tentative at first and then explosive, his eyes cast down at the index cards he still needed to remember his lyrics.

One song
Glory
One song
Before I go
Glory
One song to leave behind

I couldn't believe the strength and clarity with which Adam was singing, and to Jonathan's parents, who must have been in agony as they listened to this song evoke their lost son. I sat still and watched intently as Adam leaned into the chorus, his voice a gorgeous howl.

Time flies
Time dies
Glory
One blaze of glory
One blaze of glory
Glory

And then he came back into himself, quieting down, the song ending in a surprising, suspended chord, not resolving itself. And even though it was over, the riveted, awestruck audience didn't move a muscle, didn't even seem to breathe, and then Tim cued the band, and Daphne and Adam went right on into the sweet, sexy, seductive "Light My Candle."

We were doing more than a simple sing-through. Sure, we weren't moving around, and there were no lights or costumes or sets, but the undeniable electricity of a full performance positively sizzled through the air. We all felt it onstage, too, playing off each other, warming up as we went, letting loose, singing our hearts out.

By the time we got to "La Vie Boheme," it was clear that the time for sitting down was over, and as I began my opening verse, I climbed right up onto the table, just as I did in the show, and sang out to the crowd Jonathan's joyful valentine to all things bohemian. Soon, everybody else in the cast was joining me up on the tables, and we danced and spun and wailed our way through the song, its energy and drive overtaking us, its propulsive percolating beat sending us flying. As I led the group in our final *"Viva la vie boheme!"* I knew that there would be no going back to our seats when we came back from intermission. We'd have to get up and really do the show; its power was too great. And the audience seemed to agree, their cheers and applause enormous and full and overwhelming.

And, true to form, when the house lights came up, Michael rushed to the stage, delighted and exuberant. "That was fantastic," he said to us all. "We have to do Act Two for real now." We all immediately agreed to continue on with full staging and props and lights, but no costumes; we didn't want to get snagged up by Angel's quick change into Pussy Galore in the middle of "Happy New Year," or the ensemble members' quick changes into the finale.

The intermission zoomed by, and soon the opening chords of "Seasons of Love" rang out, and we made our way to the edge of the stage, looking right out at the audience. Some of them held tightly to each other, and, even before we began singing, I knew that it was going to take every last shred of control and strength in my being to just get through these songs in Act Two. They were all too terribly appropriate to the occasion.

Singing requires an open, clear throat; it's the only way pure, melodic sound can come out. But as we sang "Seasons," its lyrics resonating through me in a thousand new ways, I began to cry, and my throat began to close up, and then I could hear others in the cast crying as they sang, which made my tears run even faster and hotter. But somehow we all managed to keep singing, we all managed to open our throats back up, and let our hearts up and out through our voices, as we sang about love and joy and remembrance. Gwen Stewart miraculously led us through the final chorus, her voice wailing up to heaven for Jonathan and his friends and family and God and everyone, her tone as clear and powerful and acrobatic as ever, her amazing, soaring notes sending Michael's hands into the air as he sat in the back of the theatre, tears streaming down his face, which sent even more tears streaming down mine. And when Gwen and the rest of us were finished with the song, the audience raised their voices in a clamorous, seemingly endless cheer.

During their applause, I swallowed down the last of my tears, wiping my face and abruptly switching gears into my narration for "Happy New Year." The show had its own incredible, undeniable motor at this point, and I was doing my best to keep driving it, staying as focused and true as possible.

"Happy New Year" gave way to "Take Me or Leave Me," and Fredi and Idina might as well have literally burst into flames during their number, that's how on fire they were. I luxuriated in Michael's staging during their song; he had me sitting off to the side so I could just sit and watch the action. It was thrilling to be onstage with them when they resoundingly brought the house crashing down all around them at the end of the number. Tim and the band held for what felt like several minutes while the audience screamed and whistled and cheered, and I thought that Jonathan could surely hear all of this glorious noise. It was all for him, after all, and he had to be out there somewhere. My chest burst with joy and pride for him, and for all of us, in that moment.

Finally the audience calmed down, and then came the "Seasons of Love" reprise, and immediately the tone shifted from jubilation to sorrow, and I steeled myself through that brief song, fighting my closing-up throat once again as we sang, *"How do you measure a last year on earth?"*

The segue from the final chords of the "Seasons of Love" reprise into the acoustic guitar intro of "Without You" was one of my favorite musical moments in the show, and Tim led Kenny into it perfectly. I settled myself into my chair so I could let Daphne's voice wash over me and watch Michael's beautifully simple and eloquent staging. I had no idea how Daphne was going to be able to sing this song; its lyrics were so directly about why we were all there tonight:

> *Without you*
> *The ground thaws*
> *The rain falls*
> *The grass grows . . .*
> *But I die*
> *Without you*

Yet she managed, her eyes burning with concentration, her arms and hands splayed out to her sides in a kind of reaching surrender, her voice raspy and grief-stricken and lost.

More tears rolled down my cheeks as I sat there listening to Daphne sing and watching Jesse's Collins gently tend to Wilson's Angel in his sickbed. It was a rare moment in the show in which I could just let go, in which I didn't have to hold anything together or move anything forward, and I released into it as much as I could without falling apart completely.

Then came "Contact," which provided a brief respite from the intensity of "Without You," at least until Wilson started to sing. I bowed my head, holding myself together as Wilson sang over and over again, *"Take me, take me, take me."* It was all the more difficult to stand because I knew what was coming next in the show—Angel's funeral—and I did not know how any of us were ever going to get through that without losing control.

But, again, we managed, beginning with our eulogies, the words of which could so easily have been said about Jonathan. "You always said you were so lucky that we were all friends," Idina said, her voice

cracking. Then she looked right up to the sky and said, "But it was us, baby, who were the lucky ones."

And at last, Jesse slowly took his place at the edge of the stage, clutching his coat. His kind, handsome face illuminated only by a pin spot, his big brown eyes deeply mournful and loving and humane, he began his song to Angel and, tonight at least, to Jonathan.

> *Live in my house*
> *I'll be your shelter*
> *Just pay me back with one thousand kisses*
> *Be my lover*
> *And I'll cover you*

The room was completely silent and still, except for Jesse's resonant, heartbreaking voice and Tim's accompanying, soulful piano. More and more tears fell down my face, and I could feel my fellow cast members crying too, which again made me cry all the more. I couldn't even bear to look out at the house, because I knew what I'd find there, and before I knew it, it was my turn to sing with the rest of the ensemble, and I joined the line at the edge of the stage and did my utmost to produce some kind of sound. But no sound wanted to come out, my throat was choked. I saw the sorrow in the faces of the audience members in front of me and my heart broke all the more—I could not believe that we were here right now singing this song for such a terrible reason—and I tried to sing through my sobs, but I could only manage a few notes, my voice croaking through the climax of the song:

> *Oh lover I'll cover you*
> *Oh lover I'll cover you*

Jesse amazingly held us all together, never wavering, and ending with a wrenching wail that echoed through the theatre, until the light on him faded to black, and the audience exploded once again with an extraordinary, cathartic cheer.

I gulped down my grief as much as I could in the transition into "Halloween," and actually regained the power of my voice just enough, as I sang the questions we were all asking ourselves that night:

> *How did I get here?*
> *How the hell?*

Even though I was shaking as I sang alone onstage, I was finally able to channel everything I was feeling into the song, rather than be overpowered by it, although it was definitely a struggle. But I made it through to the end:

> *Why am I the witness?*
> *And when I capture it on film*
> *Will it mean that it's the end*
> *And I'm alone?*

And then we were into "Goodbye Love," with its explosive fights between Daphne and Adam, and Idina and Fredi, which Jesse broke up with another set of lyrics that absolutely could have been about what we were all experiencing that night:

> *I can't believe he's gone . . .*
> *I can't believe this family must die*
> *Angel helped us believe in love*
> *I can't believe you disagree*

And we all joined in on the final line, singing through our tears:

> *I can't believe this is goodbye*

Adam was a rock during our fight, and we were able to hold it to-gether through the end of the scene. But when Daphne began wailing out, *"Goodbye, love, goodbye,"* I wished I weren't standing off to the side all alone, that I had someone to steady me before my knees gave out from all of their shaking.

But then I had "What You Own," and I attacked it ferociously, pouring my exhaustion and grief into every note, letting the fierce propulsion of the band launch me into my angry, sad howls.

The audience cheered again at the end of that song, and I flowed, spent, into the finale with the rest of the cast, helplessly standing off to the side once again as Adam sang his love song "Your Eyes" to Daphne, and then joining in with everyone else in the final chorus. Again, we were singing about Jonathan:

> *There's only now*
> *There's only here . . .*
> *No other path*
> *No other way*
> *No day but today*

Again and again, the men repeated that refrain, *"No day but today,"* while the women repeated over and over, *"I die without you."* We were singing for ourselves and Jonathan and his friends and his parents, and when the song ended, his friends and his parents leaped to their feet, raising their hands above their heads, their faces both released and terribly sad. We bowed, and bowed again, and then made our way backstage, where we silently embraced each other, exhausted but uplifted. As we quietly busied ourselves with taking off our headsets and gathering our things together, I realized there was no sound coming from anywhere in the theatre, and I opened the backstage door to find the entire audience sitting in absolute, perfect stillness and silence. No one moved, no one spoke. They all just sat, some staring straight ahead, others sitting with their heads in their hands, still others sitting huddled together. Afraid to move myself, afraid to disrupt this moment, I walked across the stage as quietly as I could and found a group of actors from the studio production and sat with them, looking down at my hands, feeling the crushing, enormous silence of over one hundred fifty people bearing down on me. I have no idea how long we all sat together saying absolutely nothing, but it felt like forever. Finally, a male voice from the back of the theatre called out, "Thank you, Jonathan Larson," and with that utterance the spell was broken, and the group began to move and breathe again.

Christina found me then, her face alight and pained. "I don't know how you all did that," she said. "That was . . . that was incredible."

"I don't know how we did it either," I replied. "We had to."

"Well, I won't ever forget this night."

We said goodbye, and I found Al and Nan, standing somewhat dazedly in the middle of the house. Al's eyes were surprisingly clear, his manner intense, as he firmly took my hand in his.

"You all were amazing," he said. "Now we've got to make this show a hit. We've got to make this show a hit."

"We'll do our best," I said, and I knew that all that was now left of his son was this show, and I resolved to honor that. I think we all did from that night forward.

Our work over the next two weeks of previews was urgent and intense. Michael and Tim had the unenviable task of second-guessing what cuts Jonathan would have been willing to make (there was no question in anyone's mind that Jonathan had been looking forward to revising the show during previews), and they presented each proposed cut with respect and sensitivity. And, inevitably, every cut they proposed made sense. We had to believe that Jonathan would have been pleased.

Our subsequent audiences were never as responsive as the one on the night of the sing-through, but they seemed to love the show nonetheless, and I remained cautiously optimistic about our prospects with the critics. My greatest fear was that they might not be willing to open themselves up to the show's enormous heart, which was the source of most of its power. But I did my best to leave those anxieties at a low murmur so I could concentrate on the work.

Jonathan's memorial service was scheduled for a Sunday morning a week and a half after his death, and I arrived early, along with the rest of the cast, Michael, and Tim. We assembled at the off-Broadway Minetta Lane Theatre, coincidentally situated next to a restaurant called La Bohème, on a small street in the West Village. Jonathan's memorial had been announced the day before in the *Times,* so the Workshop had been deemed too tiny to contain the crowds that were expected to attend.

Our job as a cast was to sing "Seasons of Love," the reprise of "I'll Cover You," and "La Vie Boheme," and Adam was to sing "One Song Glory." We quickly ran through the numbers for a sound check, and then milled around as we waited for everyone to arrive.

I didn't recognize most of the somber faces that poured into the theatre, and as I sat and watched them come in and quietly take their seats, I realized that their grief was thicker and fresher, somehow, than ours. It struck me that those of us involved in the show had actually benefited from the nightly catharsis our performances had afforded us. We had been able to be active with Jonathan's memory in a way that allowed us to process our grief, while his friends and family and acquaintances had been left to their own devices. The show had become a healing conduit for us, and this memorial service would serve that purpose for everyone else.

One by one, Jonathan's friends stood on the stage, in front of a series of slides of Jonathan, and introduced one of his songs, or shared stories of their lives with him. I sat next to Daphne, holding her hand. I had cried so much over the past week and a half, onstage and off, that my tears felt dried up, but when I heard Jonathan's song "Destination Sky"—written for a children's video entitled *Away We Go!* and sung by a young boy in a pure, sweet, angelic voice—I was instantly shattered by its simple, delicate melody and lyrics:

So auf wiedersehn
Gotta catch the plane
So don't be sad or cry . . .
Destination sky
Destination sky

I squeezed Daphne's hand tightly as I wept. I couldn't stand such a light in the world as Jonathan being gone, I couldn't stand all of the songs he hadn't yet written never being heard, I couldn't stand that only now I felt like I was really getting to know him as a full human being, now when it was too late. I couldn't stand that I would never be able to tell him how much I loved being a part of his show, how much it had already given to me, how much the people who witnessed his work embraced it. As much as I'd tried to make peace with his absence, as much as all of us in the cast told each other and ourselves that he lived on in the words and music he'd left behind, the truth was that he was dead, he was *dead,* and there was no denying how fucked that was, how wrong.

And then the song ended, and the fresh, intense wave of grief and anger that had washed over me began to fade, and my head began to clear, and I felt once again a moment of peace, of acceptance. Grief was, after all, just as Cy had told us it would be: unpredictable and frightening and cathartic, sometimes all at once. But as painful as this time had been, in some ways I had never felt more engaged with my life, more receptive to and appreciative of the people around me, or more exposed to the complexities and depths of my own emotional core. Life had suddenly become incontestably immediate to me, necessary and vital, and that was something for which I was profoundly grateful.

glory

Opening night was on February 13, 1996, ten days after Jonathan's memorial service. I was still feeling cautiously optimistic about our prospects with the critics, who had all attended the last few preview performances so their reviews could appear promptly after opening night. My friends' reactions to the show were encouraging, and the audience at our final preview, mostly consisting of fellow actors and theatre people, was our most enthusiastic yet. It was after this show that the most surprising response came, from an actor friend who rushed up to me as I emerged from backstage and shouted, "Oh my god, you are all so fucking sexy! I wanted to fuck you all!!!" If that wasn't a positive endorsement, I didn't know what was.

Our opening night crowd was relatively dormant, as opening night crowds tend to be; everyone is nervous, waiting for the reviews, hoping that all goes well, so it's rare to find an exuberant, free, generous opening night crowd. We didn't give a shoddy performance that night, by any means, but we also didn't give our best show.

The party was held in the rehearsal room, but I didn't feel like I could let loose until after I saw the *Times*. Periodically, I tracked down Richard Kornberg, our press agent, and asked him, "Is it here yet?" He smiled knowingly and forgivingly at me and replied, "Don't worry, I will tell you when it is," and I aimlessly wandered around the party, picking at the food and sipping at my drink, unable to enjoy myself.

Finally Richard came up to me, grabbed my arm, and pulled me off to the side. "It's in," he whispered, "and it's great." Flooded with relief, I followed him into a downstairs room where the only copy sat—it was kept away from the party because some people wouldn't want to read it even if it was a rave—and devoured Ben Brantley's review, reading as quickly as my eyes would allow. My worst fear, that he and other critics wouldn't embrace the show's heart, was immediately laid to rest as line after line affirmed what I so strongly believed about the show, calling it "exhilarating" and "vigorous," and saying that it "rushes forward on an electric current of emotion." He also said flattering things about the entire cast, singling several of us out (always a good thing for our egos), but, disappointingly, he disparaged Michael's brilliant contributions. He did include a nice mention of Tim and the band, however, saying that they "lovingly and precisely interpreted" Jonathan's score. And then, as if he hadn't already made it clear how much he loved our show, he took his review over the top with its final sentences: "People who complain about the demise of the American musical have simply been looking in the wrong places. Well done, Larson."

I laid the paper down and looked right up at Richard. "That's what we needed," I said.

"Yes," Richard replied, "that's what we needed."

The next day, our entire run at the Workshop sold out within hours. Such was the power of a rave in the *Times*. We quickly extended our run for two more weeks, and promptly sold that out. Rumors began to fly around the cast and in the press about our moving to Broadway, and were confirmed a week after opening night by our commercial producers, who pledged to make inexpensive tickets available so young people would be able to afford the show. Soon, and with great rapidity, television crews descended on our theatre, and we all became adept at sitting in front of a camera for CNN or CBS or ABC or VH-1 and talking about our little show that had become such a huge, overnight smash. Print media joined in as well, with editors calling some or all of us in for lavish photo shoots. Within a matter of a few weeks, we'd traveled around town to various photographers' studios to pose for the *New York Times, Vanity Fair, Vogue, Rolling Stone, Time Out New York, Out,* and *Harper's Bazaar.* And night after night, we showed up at the theatre, where long lines for cancellations twisted down East Fourth Street, and performed the show to increasingly enthusiastic crowds. Celebrities began showing up, too, although we didn't get to meet many of them; the theatre had no easy access to the backstage area, so the celebrities tended to dash out after the curtain call to avoid being inundated by crowds of admirers. Danny DeVito and Rhea Perlman were the first ones to stay and say hello, and the cast surrounded them afterwards, giddily snapping pictures, shaking their hands, and drinking in their praise for our show. They had come to celebrate Rhea's birthday, so we spontaneously serenaded her with an R&B-influenced rendition of the birthday song, complete with intricate gospel harmonies, which seemed to thrill them.

All of this attention felt insane and yet deserved; we had all worked so hard to get the show where it was, and Jonathan had in some ways lost his life for it, pouring everything that he was into its creation. But the media machine had its own relentless, cyclonic energy, feeding off of itself, swallowing everything in its path, with the story about Jonathan's death sometimes overshadowing the story about his work. This seemed like a minor trade-off, however, if it resulted in more and more people finding out about Jonathan's words and music, thereby keeping his spirit alive that much longer.

My own personal publicity soon kicked in, with a request for an interview with the gay and lesbian newsmagazine *The Advocate*. I was pleased that they'd called; I had never been in their pages and wanted to do anything I could to raise my profile, both for the sake of my work and for the sake of gay and lesbian issues. I didn't believe that being an out actor was detrimental to my career. On the contrary, I had come out publicly three and a half years before in my bio for *The Destiny of Me* by thanking my then-boyfriend, David. (With the best of intentions, I'd naïvely called David my "partner for life" in my bio, only to break up with him a year and a half later, a fact that led to much subsequent teasing from friends and coworkers.) *Out* had run a feature story on me a year after my coming out to coincide with the release of the film version of *Six Degrees of Separation* (in which I'd recreated my stage role), but since then my profile had been too low to merit exposure in the press, gay or otherwise. So I jumped at the chance to sit down with a reporter from *The Advocate*.

Among the many subjects my interviewer and I discussed over our lunch at the Life Café was the state of my romantic life, which was currently a little confusing; I'd recently begun seeing a different ex-boyfriend, an actor named Marcus. We'd been involved with each other on and off for the past two years, although for the past year we'd been mostly off. However, as I told my interviewer, Marcus was not out publicly, nor did he ever intend to be. He so deeply, almost desperately, wanted to have a successful acting career that he refused to allow anything, including the hypothetical backlash that might result from being an out actor, to prevent it from happening. At times I'd felt as though I could never respect him for this decision, because, to me, the stakes for queer people in America, specifically young queer people, were too high for anyone with a conscience to justify remaining in the closet, especially if that someone was a public figure in a position to bring much-needed attention to queer issues. On the other hand, I recognized that each queer individual had a very personal choice to make: to reveal that aspect of his or her personal life or not to. Marcus was his own person, and I was my own person, and while I wished that he felt differently about being in the closet, I did love him, and I didn't want our differing politics, as personal as they were, to determine the outcome of our relationship.

A few nights after my interview, and with all of these issues swirling around in my mind, I went to dinner with Marcus at Angelica's Kitchen, one of our favorite restaurants. Inside, the dining room was quiet and mellow, and as we ate I enjoyed the glow of the restaurant's low, soft light as it flattered Marcus's pale, lovely features. I was feeling safe and in love and content.

And then I said, "I wanted to talk to you about opening night on Broadway."

I felt Marcus immediately tense up, his eyes clouding over. "What about it?"

"Well, I want you to be there with me."

He regarded me with suspicion. "Okay . . ."

"But you should know that there will probably be lots of press there. Lots of photographers."

"Well, then I can't go," Marcus replied, firmly sitting back and waving his arms in front of him, warding me off. And with those words, and that gesture, I knew in my gut, without even a coherent thought, that there was no future for us. Tears sprang to my eyes, surprising me with their force. As much as I'd wanted to believe that I could be okay with Marcus's choice to remain in the closet, the truth was that I wanted to share my life with him, and that meant all of my life. I wanted to hide nothing; I couldn't live my life any other way. And if he could not stand to be seen alongside me on one of the most important nights of my life, if he couldn't be there for me, then I couldn't be with him. I didn't feel any anger, though, in that moment, only sadness and a profound recognition in my heart of what was true. Suddenly, the abstract notions of personal politics had very real consequences indeed.

"I'm sorry," I said, crying, feeling no malice, just surrender. I truly was sorry. "I can't be with you. I'm sorry."

Marcus iced up, chewing his hurt into his lip. "Well, if that's the way you feel about it . . ." he said. We'd been down similar roads before, and he'd had similar reactions, but this time it was final.

"I really thought I could handle this, I really, really did. I thought a lot about it. But I can't." I tried to keep my throat from tightening up as I talked through my tears, still surprised by the intensity of my emotions. "I'm sorry. I'm sorry. I'm sorry."

Marcus shrugged, his mouth set tightly. "That's okay. I'm used to it with you."

He was right; I'd led him on, I'd opened the door to him after having closed it, only to close it again, and not for the first time. I looked away, stung.

We didn't talk much after that, and then paid the bill and went our separate ways.

Our commercial producers had announced our move to Broadway without knowing which theatre we would be inhabiting, but soon enough they settled on the Nederlander. I thought it would be the perfect house for our show: it was the only Broadway theatre situated below Times Square, on the slightly scuzzy West Forty-first Street, and it hadn't had a hit in many years. We'd swoop in there and clean the joint up, breathing new life into it, the same way we were breathing new life into the world of musical theatre.

Our rise to fame was happening rapidly. The *Times* devoted page after page of the March 17th edition of the Arts & Leisure section to our show, including a splashy, half-page, technicolor photo of the entire cast on its cover, miniprofiles of each one of us inside, and a thorough report on the genesis of the show and the aftereffects of Jonathan's death. When I read through my copy, gladdened by the balanced and compassionate writing I found there, I thought, *Yes. This is right. This is what happens when you are a part of something important.*

New rumors began to swirl that Jonathan would win the Pulitzer Prize for Drama for writing *Rent.* I thought that he should win—his work was having more of a cultural impact than any other piece of theatre that year—but I also thought that the Pulitzer committee would not award it to him. They had given the prize to only a handful of musicals in the past, and our show was youth-oriented and popular and probably not "literary" enough.

I'd been following the news of the impending Pulitzer announcement online, so I knew that on April 9th, we'd hear whether or not Jonathan had won. When that day came, we were all in the Nederlander, working through "Christmas Bells" on our new stage. It was snowing fairly heavily outside—a highly unusual occurrence in April—while we sang the recurring motif of the number over and over again: *"And it's beginning to snow."* The dual snowfalls, inside the theatre and outside, made me think that Jonathan was saying hello.

As I stood onstage on one of the tables, next to Daphne and Adam, I noticed a camera crew, a couple of reporters, and our producers enter at the back of the theatre. My heart started thudding, and I whispered to Daphne, "We're going to find out about the Pulitzer now."

"Don't think about it," she whispered back, and as she said it, Kevin McCollum, one of our producers, walked to the lip of the stage and asked Michael to stop the work so he could make an announcement.

"I just wanted to let you all know," he said, as coolly as possible, "that Jonathan Larson just received the Pulitzer Prize for *Rent.*"

I made an involuntarily crazy, relieved, inarticulate, joyful sound, a kind of a sigh and cheer, and raised my hands to the ceiling, feeling so many things all at once: foolish for caring so much about a damn award, so happy that Jonathan had been recognized, and so terribly sad that he wasn't there to receive his prize. Among the cast, there was a smattering of applause, and a few minor cheers, but overall the mood in the room was confused. Normally, in any other circumstance, we'd be able to go up to our friend who'd just won one of the most prestigious awards known to writers and give him a hearty slap on the back or a deep hug. But now we didn't know what to do.

• • •

A week later the mood was jubilant and nervous as we headed into our first performances in our new home. And from the moment we stepped onstage at our dress rehearsal, the twelve hundred friends and acquaintances and associates who'd packed themselves into the Nederlander erupted in a collective cheer. The sound of that many people clapping and whistling and hollering had a heady force that stopped us in our tracks. We had become something like rock stars.

In the long moments it took for the audience to quiet down, I locked eyes with my friends onstage, each one suppressing a huge grin, their eyes gleaming. I knew my eyes were also gleaming, and when at last the audience was silent, I took a deep breath and began.

The audience didn't stop screaming for the rest of the night, nor for any of our two weeks of previews. We all took well to our larger house, opening up our performances to fill it with our voices and passion and commitment to each other and to what we were singing. Any lingering doubts that anybody may have had about whether we were a bona fide Broadway show were eradicated.

I hadn't talked to Mom very much over the past two months because I'd been so busy with the show, but along the way I had kept her abreast of our developments. She had been dismayed by Jonathan's death, saying, "It seems like they should have known at the hospital that something was very wrong with him." She had often shared stories with me about using her nursing skills to correct doctors' misdiagnoses, saving several people's lives in the process, which always made me wish there were more nurses like her working in hospitals.

Mom hadn't been to New York for a visit since the Broadway opening night of *Six Degrees of Separation,* five and a half years before, so I was thrilled when she arranged a trip into town for *Rent's* Broadway opening night on April 29, 1996. Accompanying her were her brother Chris, his wife Bonnie, Mom's sister Roberta, and Mom's old friend Phyllis. Phyllis lived in Portland, Oregon; she and Mom had met in 1978 when they were nurses together at Island Lake Camp.

They had kept in touch ever since, talking on the phone or writing long letters stuffed with snapshots of their children. They had seldom seen each other over the years, but had managed to remain extremely close.

Because of my two shows on the day before opening night, I was only able to see Mom and everybody else on the day itself. We arranged to meet for breakfast, and Adam and I rendezvoused with them all at their hotel, eager to see how well—or how unwell—Mom looked. She had more energy than I'd seen in a while, although she did have a cane with her, just in case she needed it.

"I can't walk that far," she said.

"Well, we'll go just a couple blocks away to a diner," I said, eager to keep things light and easy and fun.

At the diner, Chris pulled out a copy of *The Advocate*. I glanced over to see Mom's reaction, but she remained pokerfaced. It had been so long since she and I had talked about my sexuality, and I wasn't sure what her current feelings on the subject were. I felt my cheeks redden.

"This was a very nice article," Chris said. "A great picture."

"Thank you," I said.

"Yes," Mom said, "it's a wonderful picture."

Bonnie chuckled. "Just don't let your Grandma see it." Everyone, including me, laughed, although I was eager to change the subject.

"Tonight," I said, "there are supposed to be a lot of stars coming."

Phyllis perked up. "Oh, really? Like who?"

"Well, the list they gave us had Michelle Pfeiffer on it, and Isabella Rossellini, and George Clooney, and Kevin Bacon, and some other people. We don't know if they'll all show up, though."

"Well," Phyllis said, "that's exciting."

"Maybe I'll just have to go up to George Clooney and ask him out on a date," Roberta said, and everybody laughed. I was glad we'd gotten onto another topic, but I was still afraid that Mom was tense over *The Advocate*. I let it go as best I could, and tried to give myself over to the generally lighthearted, easy mood. Mom was sitting among people she adored and enjoyed, and I loved watching her take us all in as we laughed at Roberta's joke. I was happy that she was still well enough to be there with us.

I left everybody at the diner so I could make my last-minute arrangements for the performance that night, which consisted mostly of writing cards to everyone in the cast, band, and creative staff. It was my ritual, and I made every effort to say everything I'd been storing up to tell my friends: about how much I loved them, and how much I loved their work in the show. By the time I was done it was already time to meet everybody again for dinner. We assembled at the theatre, where barricades were being set up to keep the paparazzi away from the stars, and I showed everyone the backstage area. Our attitudes were exceedingly midwestern; no one was overtly excited, including myself, but the sense of anticipation was palpable. Phyllis expressed the most excitement in her quiet way, her eyes glinting as she giggled and snapped lots of pictures.

Jonathan's friend Eddie was putting together a video documentary about *Rent,* and I asked him if he wanted to shoot us at dinner and if he would interview Mom for my purposes. He agreed, and I asked Mom if she would mind participating.

"Oh, no," she said. "That's fine with me."

As we all sat through our pasta dinners at the Italian restaurant down the street from the theatre, we chatted amiably enough, but didn't talk about the significance of Mom being there. I wanted to tell her and make her feel how absolutely excited and thrilled I was, but since our family had never been inclined to express ourselves so openly, I didn't bring it up.

As a result of the weight of all that was unsaid between us, I was relieved when it was time for me to head back over to the theatre. Mom was to return to the hotel now, change into her evening clothes, and then meet Eddie back at the theatre so he could interview her. I double- and triple-checked that she and Eddie were both still willing to do it, so desperately did I want a record of her on that night. I knew that it was probably going to be the last opening night of mine that she would ever witness.

She arrived at the theatre right on time for her interview, decked out in the same outfit (but not the same Elizabeth Taylor hairdo) she'd worn to Anne's wedding. I could tell right away that she had shrunk more than I'd realized; her clothes looked baggier on her now. She sat in the house with Eddie, and the cast gathered onstage with Michael. I tried not to cast my eye toward Mom, to see if I could tell what she was saying to Eddie, as all of us onstage joined hands in a circle.

"I just want to say how enormously proud I am of all of you," Michael said, radiant in his elegant dark suit, "and how proud of you and of his show I think Jonathan would be, and is, wherever he is." I nodded to myself, closing my eyes, freezing this moment, trying to feel Jonathan's presence, thinking that I could feel it, hoping that he knew what was happening.

By the time we were done with our onstage circle, Mom was done with her interview, and I brought Michael down off the stage to meet her. She looked tiny in her seat, her cane slung over the back of the chair in front of her. She didn't get up as she shook Michael's hand.

"It's a pleasure to meet you," Michael said. He and the rest of the cast and crew knew that Mom was ill, and he'd asked me to introduce him to her.

"Oh, nice to meet you, too," Mom said, her voice mild as ever.

"We're very glad you could be here," Michael said.

"Oh, I'm very glad, too. I wouldn't miss it for the world." She smiled, glancing up at me, and it was the first time all day that I'd really felt her pride and excitement.

"Well, I hope you enjoy it," Michael said.

"Oh, I'm sure I will. I've read such wonderful things about the show. And I always love watching Anthony onstage." Embarrassed and happy to be hearing this from Mom, I put my head down slightly and grabbed her hands in mine.

"It was great to meet you," Michael said.

"You too," Mom replied, and Michael shook her hand again and left.

I looked up at her, wanting to tell her how excited and sad and proud I was, but all I said was, "Well, I've got to get going backstage."

"Okay, Tonio," Mom said. "Break a leg."

"I will, Momma," I said. "I love you."

"I love you, too."

And I gave her a hug and a kiss and left her sitting there in the audience.

Pandemonium ruled backstage as everyone ran around to everyone else's dressing rooms with gifts and cards and flowers. We were already a hit, so all there was to do now was enjoy ourselves, and go out there and give a kick-ass performance.

Michael pulled me aside while I was getting ready and said, "I think tonight we have to start things off with a dedication to Jonathan." I nodded, glad that he'd brought it up. I'd been thinking the same thing.

When we all stepped out onstage, the entire audience leaped to their feet, cheering us for a long, long time. I drank it in, trying to calm the shaking in my knees. I scanned the crowd, finding Cy, who blew exuberant kisses to us (she'd already seen the show several times, becoming one of our first "Rentheads"); the Larsons, who clapped with their hands raised high, seeming so happy and sad; and my mom, up in the front mezzanine, looking small and lovely in her turquoise suit, slightly dwarfed by my brother Adam's hulking frame in the seat next to her. The vivacious, joyful, explosive cheering went on and on, and then finally, everyone took their seats.

I centered myself with a breath and said, "We dedicate this performance, and every performance of *Rent*, to our friend Jonathan Larson," and the audience immediately leaped to their feet once again, clapping long and hard, cheering, sending their love and respect up and out to us and him.

And then they sat once again, and we began.

I had never felt more focused and alive onstage, knowing that this would probably be the only time Mom would ever see this show that I loved so much. I sang to her as much as I could, wondering how she was feeling through it, wondering if the emotional intensity of some of the songs was too much for her to take. Some of them were almost too much for me to take—in Act Two, when we sang, *"How do you measure a last year on earth?"* and I looked right at her up in her seat, her glasses reflecting light back at me, I had to struggle through the knot in my throat. By that time, the show had zoomed by so quickly that I was wishing it would just continue on and on. I imprinted the night on my brain, telling myself, *Remember this. Remember this.*

In the reprise of "I'll Cover You" and then "Halloween" and "Goodbye Love," I battled with myself to keep it together, alternately stuffing down and channeling the swarm of grief and joy that had tangled itself up in my gut. Lines like *"Mimi's gotten thin / Mimi's running out of time"* kept doubling back on me, and it took everything I had to stay in the play.

I made it through all of it, though, as I had so many nights before, and, all too quickly, there I was at the end of the show, assembled onstage with my dear friends—my new family—holding on to them, singing *"No day but today"* with them, our hearts and voices unified, showering our friends and family with love and joy and grief. And as the lights faded on us on our final note, the audience exploded in a tidal wave of roaring, whistling, cheering applause.

During the curtain call, I finally started to let go, and tears streamed down my face, my chest heaving, as we bowed, and bowed again, and bowed again. I looked up and saw Mom joining the standing ovation and my heart burst open, and more tears sprang to my eyes. When we were finally done bowing I stepped back, sent my customary four strong claps up to Jonathan, blew kisses up to Mom, and walked off.

We all spent many, many minutes hugging each other tightly backstage, all of us spent and jubilant and alive, saying to each other, "I love you" over and over again. As I walked upstairs to my dressing room, a fresh blast of emotion hit me, and I braced myself on the banister, putting my head down, trying not to sob out loud as my cast mates passed by. Gilles stopped next to me, gently resting his hand on my shoulder.

"Are you okay?"

"Yeah," I said through my tears. "It's just . . . I don't know, I'm so happy. My mom was here tonight. I'm so happy she was here." My chin trembled as I spoke.

"Yeah," Gilles said. "I understand."

"Thanks," I said, and pulled myself together and went into my dressing room.

After I had glammed myself up for the party, I went back downstairs into the house so I could say good night to Mom; she'd already decided that she would skip the party and get some rest. When I found her she gave me a hug and said, "It was wonderful." Her face glowed.

"Did you really like it?"

"Oh, I loved it." She nodded emphatically, her eyes wide and bright. "It was very, very moving."

"I'm glad," I said. "I thought you would like it."

She grabbed my hands. "Tonio, you were great. I'm so proud of you."

I squeezed her hands, stuffing down my tears that were threatening to come at any moment. "Thank you."

"Now go have fun at your party."

"I will, Momma. I love you."

"I love you, too."

And I walked away from her again, feeling for a few moments like I was almost weightless, trying once again to imprint everything about this night onto my mind, my heart fuller than it had ever been. It was already the greatest night of my life.

falling and spinning

The next time I saw Mom was two months later, on July 1st. I only had one day off a week, but now that I could afford it with my Broadway salary, I planned to visit her as often as I could; I didn't know how much longer she would be around, so I wanted to make the most of the time she and I had left. I booked myself on an early-morning flight on Monday, with my return scheduled for Tuesday morning, getting me back into New York just in time for that evening's performance.

In the preceding two months, the show had continued its meteoric rise. We were nominated for ten Tony Awards and won four, including two for Jonathan. We won three OBIE Awards, including one for Michael Greif's direction and one that the entire cast shared for Outstanding Ensemble. Jonathan and the show won Best Musical from the New York Drama Critics Circle, the Outer Critics Circle, the Drama League, and the Drama Desk. We consistently sold out every seat and every standing room ticket at every performance. We sang "Seasons of Love" on *The Rosie O'Donnell Show, The Late Show with David Letterman,* and the *Today* show. Jonathan and our show were the subjects of segments on *Primetime Live, CBS News Sunday Morning,* and *48 Hours.* And in May we went into the Right Track Studios to record the cast album for DreamWorks Records, which had won the rights to our show after what was reportedly an intense bidding war among several labels. During the first month of our Broadway run, we didn't have one full day or night off, and yet no one in the cast had missed any performances.

And, as if that wasn't enough to keep my head from spinning off its axis, I had fallen in love. His name was Todd. When I met him, the day after opening night, he was just finishing up his senior year in NYU's Dramatic Writing Program where he was taking a playwrighting class with John Guare, the writer of *Six Degrees of Separation.* John had discussed *Rent* with his class (he was a big fan, having written about us in *Vogue*) and had encouraged Todd to get in touch with me, thinking we'd hit it off. I don't know if John was trying to set us up romantically, but midway through my first conversation with Todd, which began on AOL, moved to the phone, and lasted for hours, I was already smitten. His fierce intellect, his barbed sense of humor, his self-deprecating sweetness all came through loud and clear on the computer, and even more so on the phone. I just hoped he was cute. The next night I was going to find out; we'd arranged a date for after the show. Coincidentally, we lived a block and a half from each other in the East Village, so our rendezvous point was on the corner of Second Avenue and Tenth Street. He obviously knew what I looked like, but the only thing I had to go on for him was his description of himself in his Instant Message: "Some people say I look like Robert Downey Jr with short hair, others say a little George Clooney, but skinnier. I hate the latter. And the former is a bit too uppity for my tastes. He looks like a fop, too." Neither man particularly interested me, but I was charmed and intrigued enough to see how accurately he'd described himself.

Even before he came up to me and shook my hand, I knew it was him walking toward me as I leaned against the brick wall of the Second Avenue Deli. I was relieved to see that he was adorable, with big brown puppy dog eyes, a boyish face, short dark hair, and just the right amount of scruff on his cheeks. My crush was cemented.

We enjoyed a fast and furious courtship, even though I tried to make myself slow it down; with all that was going on in my life, with all of the pressures of the show and Mom's illness, I didn't think it was the best time to get involved. But we shared an unusually intense passion for music and film and theatre and books, and he was a night owl like I am, so our schedules were copacetic. And he loved lying in bed with me after I got back downtown after a performance, as we listened to the latest Superchunk CD or watched *Fearless* on laserdisc or as I read the most recent draft of his latest play or screenplay. And he made me laugh often, even when his humor was sliced through with meanness (his cynicism was a nice contrast to my generally genial outlook). And I soon found myself spending almost all of my time away from the theatre with him, hardly ever going home to my own apartment except to shower and change clothes. And I didn't care that Todd smoked, because he was conscientious about not smoking around me, and he did his best not to smell or taste like smoke when we got together. And even though the first time he took me home to his apartment, he wouldn't let me open the door to his bedroom (because, as I found out later, the floor was buried underneath an incomprehensibly chaotic pile of detritus—magazines and Starbucks cups and ashtrays and screenplays); even though I was wary of his intensity which bordered on mania (his thoughts seemed to charge forward ahead of him, like lightning, carrying his mouth along with them, but always full of keen observations and sharp witticisms); even though I wished that at times he wasn't so cagey about his family life or his romantic or sexual history (he alluded to making a habit of seducing straight boys in high school, but refused to go into detail as to how he went about doing so); even though there were times I felt pressured by him to come over when I was exhausted from the show and might have preferred a night off to myself; even though all of this was, on some level, perhaps a little too much too soon for me to take, the truth was: I loved sharing my success with someone who wasn't intimidated by it (he'd sweetly brought me consolation flowers when I didn't get nominated for a Tony), someone who appreciated the show and the impact it was having, someone who enjoyed my company for my sake and not because I was becoming a mini celebrity, someone who was genuinely attracted to me, whose body fit with mine, who enjoyed sex as much as I did, and, perhaps most important, someone who enjoyed long, meandering conversations in bed after sex as much as I did. And so I couldn't stop myself from saying to Todd one night as I lay next to him, "I think I'm falling." And even though he didn't say the same thing back to me, when he shyly gazed into my eyes and put my hand on his heart, I knew that he was falling, too.

So by July 1st, when I went home to see Mom, I wanted to tell her about him, but I didn't know how to bring up the subject; I didn't know how she'd feel about my having a new boyfriend. And as I was traveling home and thinking about what I wanted to tell her, dreading a probably uncomfortable, and possibly ugly, confrontation, I thought through all of our past conversations about my relationships with boys. I was reminded of the first time my queerness had come up between us: it had been in the fall of 1986, when I was fourteen, in the full, wild throes of puberty, and I was hanging out with an older kid from my high school named Ricky.

"Let's play Spin the Bottle," Ricky said.

Ricky was the ringleader of our group's little gatherings. He was dark-haired and olive-skinned, Italian (judging by his last name, D'Angelo), and older-looking than his eighteen years. Maybe it was his eyes: they were dark brown, and they seemed to hold some kind of secret. Whatever secret it was lit them up, giving him a sort of illicit authority when he talked, making me think of conspiracies or back rooms or money-laundering schemes, stuff that people got involved in when they were well out of high school. There was an energy about him that wasn't just gossipy or teenager-goofy; it was *naughty.* He was slim and quick and effeminate, which he made no effort to hide. In fact, he had, at one point the previous school year, dyed his hair a shocking pink, an unheard-of act for a guy to do in 1985, especially in Joliet.

I hadn't really known him for long, but he was the ringleader, and that night, as usual, we were at his house in Shorewood, the slightly more upscale community adjacent to Joliet. His loud, obese mother was also home, in the living room watching TV. She loved when Ricky brought his friends over. "Oh, HI, how are YOU?" she boomed in her nasal voice from her easy chair when I dropped in. "Nice to *SEE* you again!"

"Mom, we're going to be in my room," Ricky said.

"Okay, Ricky. See you all *LATER!*"

There wasn't any asking for permission in Ricky's house. He expected to get, and got, what he wanted. And what he wanted that night was all of us in his room drinking and playing Spin the Bottle. And that's what we did.

The players that night were Ricky; Bryan, an officer in Joliet West's ROTC who was Ricky's age, with that similar older-than-he-was quality, his New England accent an anomaly in our town; Doreen, whose dyed red hair was spectacularly sprayed and sculpted to swoop over her forehead, almost covering one eye, its side-part extremely low, near her ear, like a balding man's combover; Laura, compact and tough, sporting a New Wave pompadour, her hair poofed up on top and buzzed on the sides and in the back, but with a bonus tail stemming from the base of her skull; Frances, slim and pretty, with freckles, big blue eyes, and dark dark dark black hair, which fell around her face without quite as many products sprayed or gelled or moussed into it; me, at fourteen by far the youngest participant; and Andy Dick—yes, *that* Andy Dick, years before he was famous—also eighteen, my closest friend in the group and the real reason I was there. I had met Andy two and a half years prior, when I played the title role in *Oliver!* at Joliet West. He played Dr. Grimwig, a tiny role in Act Two, and in any other production undoubtedly completely forgettable, but not so in our production. Andy, gawky and skinny and unafraid to do anything for a laugh, sprayed his blond Afro—he looked like a tree, with his lanky frame and huge hair—completely gray (the shiny, silvery gray you only get out of those 'Streaks 'n' Tips' cans used for makeup effects in amateur theatre productions), and decided that his Dr. Grimwig was ninety years old and dying of emphysema. So his two-minute scene with me wherein he asked me how I was feeling, and then pronounced me well, stretched into four or five minutes, as he coughed and wheezed and sputtered and hacked up phlegm and ad libbed crazy exclamations. The audience loved it, laughing uproariously, and it took all of my concentration to keep from laughing. We became instant friends, and from that moment on Andy constantly made me laugh.

There we all were, in Ricky's room, ready to play our game. Violent Femmes' eponymous album blared from Ricky's stereo system, if you could call it blaring; his stereo was one of those Radio Shack cheapies with the tiny simulated-wood speakers, and everything that came out of it sounded pretty thin and sad, but we didn't care.

I hope you know this will go down on your permanent record, Gordon Gano, the Femmes' lead singer, sang.

Oh yeah? we all chimed in.

There wasn't much to Ricky's room: just a bed, his pathetic little stereo, and a couple of posters messily thumbtacked to the formica-paneled walls, posters of Duran Duran and Bauhaus and The Cure. We all sat on the floor at the foot of his bed, in a circle, clutching our wine coolers or beers or screwdrivers or plain old straight vodka. I was drinking wine coolers.

Gordon Gano sang, and we sang along:

> *Why can't I get just one fuck?*
> *Why can't I get just one fuck?*

I guess it's got something to do with luck
'Cause I've waited my whole life for just one . . .

Our Spin the Bottle rules went like this: the spinner got to tell the spinnee what to do, and everyone *had* to do whatever the spinner said. So it had elements of truth or dare, but without the truth, and with the essential Russian roulette factor of the spinning bottle.

"I'll start," Ricky said, and he spun. It landed on Doreen.

"Oh, shit," Doreen said.

"Doreen," Ricky said, "I want you to give Laura ear sex."

Doreen blushed and smiled, and Frances playfully hit her in the arm.

"Go Doreen," she said. Ear sex was a favorite activity in our Spin the Bottle games. I hadn't known it even existed until I started playing with this group.

Laura rolled her eyes and took a sip of her wine cooler, then went over to Doreen. Doreen kissed Laura's ear, really giving it a thorough licking. Laura squealed in delight. I still didn't quite get the appeal of ear sex; it seemed slobbery to me, messy, and not very tasty, but I was still intrigued. No one had ear-sexed me yet. In fact, I rarely got hit by the bottle. That had to change. I wanted some action. I swigged the last of my wine cooler and opened another one.

"Ooooooo, look at that," Bryan said. "Laura likes that."

Finally, Doreen and Laura broke apart, both of them grinning huge grins. Doreen tidied up her lip gloss and drank some of her beer, and Laura sat back down in her spot on the floor. She didn't wipe her ear. I resisted wiping it for her. Then Doreen picked up the bottle and spun it. It landed on Bryan.

"Okay, what is it this time?" Bryan said, rolling his eyes as if he had truly done *everything* there was to do.

"Hmmm," Doreen said.

Bryan's mouth gaped open in mock horror. "Uh-oh."

"French kiss Ricky."

"*Yeah!*" Andy growled.

Bryan smiled. "Okay." And he lunged at Ricky, and the two of them kissed, quite aggressively, Ricky holding on to Bryan's face, Bryan grabbing on to the back of Ricky's neck, both of their tongues working overtime. Ricky's eyes opened as he kissed Bryan, and with an eye facing me, he watched me watching them kiss. I could feel my cheeks burning, but I didn't look away.

The thing was, a couple of weeks prior to this get-together, during another hangout at Ricky's house (no Spin the Bottle that day), I wound up alone in Ricky's room, listening to The Smiths, when Ricky walked in and closed the door. I was lying on my back on his bed, propped up on my elbows, in red-and-white-striped shorts and a Meat Is Murder T-shirt. Everyone else was with Ricky's mom in the living room watching TV. The Smiths tape was almost over; I had been in there a while.

"Hey, what's going on?" Ricky said to me.

"Not much," I said. Suddenly the tape that was playing stopped with a click that felt more like a bang.

And without another word, Ricky sat down on the bed next to me and started to run his hand through my hair. I froze and felt my shorts tighten around my groin. Before this moment, I hadn't had any sexual thoughts about Ricky. I didn't find him attractive; he was too flamboyant and edgy for me, although most people would probably think he was handsome, with his mature, five-o'clock-shadowed square jaw and intense eyes and dark hair. But now there he was, with his hand resting tenderly on my head, and my heart started to race and my face started to heat up, and in that moment I definitely wanted him to do more to me than just run his fingers through my hair. But I said nothing.

He gently eased me down all the way onto my back, sitting next to me, and let his hand travel down from my head to my chest and then onto my stomach—I had never felt those spasms in my belly before, little jolts, when his fingers lightly brushed their way down—and finally his hand found its way into my shorts. *This* was what I wanted him to do, but at the same time I wasn't sure why he was doing it, I was so young, and small for my age, and I barely knew him. But then again it was just sex after all, it didn't mean anything anyway, and he obviously wanted to do it, so if he wanted to, that was all right. I stared at his fake-stucco ceiling, concentrating on my breath moving in and out. He pulled my shorts down and kissed my stomach, and there were much bigger jolts, *much* bigger, and then he put me in his mouth.

The lights in his room were on, and at any time, someone could have walked in. But I didn't stop him. I stopped staring at the ceiling and started to watch him as he went down on me. Without stopping, he looked up at me. I was motionless and didn't make a sound; neither did he. I started to feel raunchy, and for a brief second considered stopping him, but the silence in the room was so complete that I didn't want to break it by saying anything. I could imagine that this wasn't really happening. I could step outside myself and watch myself lying there like that, Ricky over me, his head moving rhythmically up and down, up and down, and from there I could still feel the incredible, delicious sensations of having his mouth on me, and it didn't mean anything, it really, really didn't—it didn't mean I was *gay* or anything like that, it was just a blow job, after all—and I didn't want to touch him, I just wanted him to touch me, the way that he was, that was all that we had to do, I hoped that was all he wanted to do, and it felt *so* good, it felt so *good,* and I felt and felt and felt and *felt* and I was going to come soon, I was going to come soon . . .

It didn't take long, and when I was done, he smiled at me, pulled my shorts back up, and left the room, just like that, closing the door behind him. I lay there on my back for a very long time. I felt myself sinking into the bed. It wasn't a pleasant sinking; it was more like the beginning of drowning. I didn't know why I hadn't stopped him. I started to think that I should have stopped him, I should have, but then I started to think no, it was harmless, what had just happened was harmless, it didn't mean anything, and no matter what, it had felt good, anyway. But it was so weird that neither of us had *said* anything. At least when I had fooled around with my friends Christopher and

Stephen, masturbating together and occasionally going down on each other, we had talked before and after, and sometimes during. Although I always felt silly talking during. Christopher, Stephen, and I had all been good friends first, and we all knew each other really well. We trusted one another. Our fooling around together didn't really mean anything anyway; at least I thought so. It was just the result of our desire to experiment, to get our rocks off. It was our little secret, and we told ourselves and each other that we only did it because we were horny teenagers who didn't have girlfriends.

But as I sat in Ricky's room staring at his ceiling, thinking about what had just happened, I couldn't remember why I had started hanging out with him; he and I had barely talked to each other in school. And now I didn't know what he was going to say about me to his friends, or when he might try something with me again. I didn't want anything more to happen. Already it was complicated. For all I knew, the entire school was going to hear tomorrow about the blow job Ricky D'Angelo gave me. I never should have let him do that to me. It was a mistake. Really, a *mistake*.

I sat up and shook my head vigorously to get my brain to stop spinning. I sat there, staring at my hands in my lap, and eventually, my brain spun down just enough, and I left the room and rejoined the group, tucking away the experience I'd just had, trying not to think any more about it.

Ricky hadn't spread the story around after all, as far as I could tell, and he and I had not spoken of it since, but now, two weeks later, there he was, pointedly eyeing me as he sloppily and hungrily kissed Bryan, and Bryan sloppily and hungrily kissed him back.

> *Mo my momma mama mo my mum*
> *Have you kept your eye, your eye on your son?*

I adjusted my position so no one would notice the stirring happening down in my crotch. A nice buzz was also starting to flit its way through my head, and I was determined to get it going stronger. I gulped down some more wine cooler.

> *Words all fail the magic prize*
> *Nothing I can say when I'm in your thighs*

At last, Bryan and Ricky broke apart. *"WHOOO!"* Andy yelped. "That was *EXCELLENT!"* Ricky kept watching me. He even gave me a silent-movie star one-eyebrow raise as he drank a little more beer. And, in spite of myself, I held his gaze.

> *Wait a minute honey, I'm gonna add it up*
> *I'm gonna add it up!*

We all joined in for the song's big finish, messily shout-singing over Gordon's screechy whine.

> *Add it up!*
> *Add it up!*
> *Add it up!*
> *When I take a bow and say good night*

There were more rounds of Spin the Bottle, and I got picked once, by Frances.

"Give Doreen ear sex," she said.

So there it was, this ear sex thing. Not the most appealing activity in the world, and with Doreen to boot, not the most appealing recipient imaginable. I was now drunker than I'd ever been, and the room itself, not just the bottle, spun a little, as I crawled on over to Doreen and brought my face up to her ear. The utterly unpleasant, synthetic odor of Aqua Net practically leaped off her hair into my nostrils and stayed there. A few prized blackheads poked out of the tight, shiny skin of her ear. I took a deep breath, and plunged in.

Well, the scent of Aqua Net was terrible enough, but it was nothing compared to the taste, a revolting combination of glue and metal. The spray had also left a sticky sheen all over her ear, stiffening even the tiny hairs that lined her ear's upper edges. There was nothing soft or inviting about licking her lobe or sending my tongue into her ear's recesses. I had to keep myself from gagging, but Doreen was giggling and squirming with what I assumed was pleasure. I was glad one of us was enjoying it.

I finished as quickly as I could, took a giant swig of my wine cooler, swishing it around in my mouth before swallowing, and tried to hide just how unpleasant that experience had been.

"Woo-hoo!" Doreen said. "That was gooooood!"

"Thanks," I muttered, embarrassed.

"Go Anthony!" Andy shouted. Ricky made eyes at me, a bemused smirk on his face. I rolled my eyes and spun the bottle. It hit Laura.

"Grab Ricky's crotch," I said, still trying to force the Aqua Net out of my taste buds forever. Ricky smiled at me and Laura laughed, and then she went right on over to him and grabbed. She even threw in a kiss for effect. Ricky kept his eyes on me the whole time.

Then Laura spun, and it hit Ricky.

"Okay, Ricky," Laura said. And she looked at me. Had he told her anything? "It's about time Anthony got some ear sex."

Ricky could not have looked more delighted. He grinned an enormous grin at me. My heart was now a thundering crazy creature trying to break free of my chest. If I had been blushing before, I must have looked like a giant blond-headed strawberry at this moment. The others' faces faded into the background; only Ricky filled my field of vision. And then there he was, next to me, and then there his tongue was, squirming around and around and in and over my ear, louder than I would have thought—but of course it was loud, it was in my *ear*—but it was warm, too, hot, actually, from his breath, and soft, and moist, and absolutely thrilling. So *this* was what people were talking about, ah, yes, this was nice, this was very very very nice, and what he was doing with his hand, rubbing my inner thigh (did anyone see that?), was also very nice, and before I knew it I was opening my neck up for him to kiss, and kiss it he did, and I was grabbing the back of his neck, and pushing his mouth into my neck, and into my ear, and he was grabbing my head and pushing my neck and ear into his mouth, and this was going on for what felt like an eternity, and soon I realized I was laughing uncontrollably, and kicking my legs out like a spastic puppy, and I saw and heard Andy whooping and clapping, and I saw Laura smugly taking a drag on her Marlboro Light, and Ricky's tongue was all over my ear, and he was kissing kissing kissing my neck, and then all of a sudden, he stopped and pulled away, giving my lobe one last quick lick.

"YEAAAAAAHHHHH!" Andy screamed. Since when had he become a crazed frat boy, anyway? "That was so *HOT!*" And he cackled, holding his hands to his mouth the way he did when he couldn't stop himself from laughing.

I was dizzy. I gulped more of my wine cooler, and suddenly felt bolder than I had ever felt. Like I could do anything with anybody, right then and there, never mind any consequences—nothing mattered, nothing at all. If Ricky wanted to have sex with me, I would have sex with him, so what if I barely knew him, so what if I didn't really want him, I wanted *somebody,* and he was there, and he seemed to want me, I didn't know why—I was so young and scrawny, no one ever seemed to want me—but he did, and that was way, way, *way* more than enough for me.

Sometime later, we all found ourselves in the driveway. It was dark and cool, and I was spectacularly drunk, feeling heated and slightly manic from the fuzz in my brain. I had already arranged with my mom that I was going to spend the night at Andy's house, and as I was getting ready to cram myself into his canary yellow Honda, Ricky came up to us.

"I'm coming over, too," he said. I felt my face flush and I looked away. I'd been hoping he'd say something like that.

"No problem with me," Andy replied, flashing me a goofy,

scheming smile, and we took off, Ricky in the back seat, me in the front, my stomach quietly but persistently flip-flopping at what I was about to do. Andy drove like a crazed monkey as usual, always the performer, screeching his tires and abruptly slamming on the brakes for no reason, then squealing away and swerving back and forth down the dark and silent suburban streets as if he were traversing the world's looniest obstacle course. I loved every second of taking these rides with Andy; I never felt unsafe, just absolutely entertained, and I guffawed the whole way.

In the short drive to Andy's house, Ricky's hand found its way onto my shoulder, giving it a squeeze and a rub, which I didn't acknowledge, but which I also didn't stop him from doing.

Later, Ricky and I were tangled in blankets on the floor of Andy's living room, moonlight spilling in through the glass patio doors. We were naked and fumbling (well, I was fumbling; Ricky was pretty adept) and Ricky was insistent and relentless. I followed his lead and went right along with him, dozing occasionally, to wake up who knew how much later to find his mouth on me somewhere. I'd start in with him again, touching him in ways I'd never touched anyone, with more abandon, ecstatic and spinning and drunk drunk drunk the whole time.

I had only kissed two boys before Ricky. It had always felt like a forbidden act with boys (never with girls), and even though my friend Stephen and I had touched each other and touched ourselves in each other's presence, we had only kissed once, when we were thirteen. Standing and facing each other in the dark of his bedroom, both of us naked, his soft, pale skin almost glowing, he reached out for me and brought his mouth to mine. We kissed for a minute or so, his tongue awkwardly probing its way into my mouth, both of his hands cradling my face, and then we stopped and pulled away, both of us flushed and breathing heavily and embarrassed. We jerked off and came on our own at a safe distance, and never kissed again and never spoke about it.

The other boy I had kissed was Josh, my friend at Interlochen National Music Camp. We had met the summer prior to my night with Ricky. Josh and I were cabin mates, but he was two years older than I, taller, dark haired, and handsome, and the large mole on his upper lip was a kind of beauty mark to me. He was also fiercely intelligent and intense and witty, and a really good actor (he had played Creon in Anouilh's *Antigone*), and I had a huge crush on him, my first real crush on another boy; in the couple of years I had spent fooling around with Christopher and Stephen, there had been no crushes anywhere to be seen, at least on my end.

One of the rituals among our group of friends at Interlochen was called starspinning, a name coined by Josh. We would gather outside on the soccer field beyond the boys' cabins, not long before the lights-out call, which didn't give us much time, and stand out in the middle of the field and lean our heads back, staring up at the spectacular splash of stars that only exists in the darkness of the middle of the countryside. We'd hold our arms out to our sides, like helicopter blades, and spin and spin and spin our bodies around, all the time still gazing at the sky, until we couldn't spin anymore. Then we would suddenly collapse to the cool, wet grass onto our backs, and as we lay still, the stars continued spinning and spinning and *spinning*, until at last they slowed and then stopped. Then, laughing and exclaiming "WOW!" and "Oh my GOD!" we would get up and start the whole process over again. Eventually, we would all just lie there and talk, or just lie there and say nothing.

One night, only Josh and I trekked out to the field. It was nearing the end of the summer. He lived in Los Angeles and I lived in Joliet, and I was very, very conscious of the implications of that enormous distance, of how little we would see each other, of the possibility that our friendship would probably fade with time. We starspun for a few minutes and then lay there on the grass in silence.

"Josh?" I said, after a while.

"Yeah?"

I didn't know how to say it. I propped myself up on my elbow and looked at him. He continued to lie on his back. I felt focused and calm and happy and scared, and I knew clearly and powerfully in that moment that there was nothing wrong with how I felt about him. I just didn't know how to say it.

"I really like you," I said at last.

He looked at me. "I know you do. I really like you too."

"I mean I love you." At Interlochen this wasn't such an unusual statement, and I had said it to Josh before, and he had said it to me, and I had said it to other friends, and they had said it to me. All of us at Interlochen unself-consciously loved our friends, and told them, and were told.

"Can I kiss you?" I asked.

A long silence passed. Josh regarded me, an unreadable expression on his face. I looked right back at him. My skin was tingling, and I was barely breathing, but I was calm. Finally, he leaned over to me, and we kissed.

The tiny needles of his stubble poked at my lips, which felt strange and surprising, but I was thrilled by our embrace and our kiss. It was more curious and tentative than passionate, but I was still ecstatic that it was happening. It felt absolutely right to be out under the stars kissing him.

When we finished kissing, we separated and lay back down.

"Thanks," I said.

"Thank *you,*" Josh said.

About six months later (three months after my night with Ricky), I was staying with Josh in his house in Los Angeles for a few days while I screen-tested for *Adventures in Babysitting.* One afternoon I found myself alone in the house, and I poked around in his room, looking through his books and tapes, when I found his journal. I held it in my hands, not sure what to do, and at last opened it. We hadn't talked about that night and that kiss, so I quickly flipped through the pages until I found this, scrawled in his tiny, almost illegible handwriting:

Tonight Anthony asked me to kiss him, and I did. I could feel his whiskers. EWWWWWWWWWWWW!!!

I didn't read any more, I just read those lines over and over and over and over again, my stomach plummeting and my cheeks on fire. How could he feel that way and not tell me? I had felt his whiskers too, and it was strange, it was, but I loved him, and he loved me too, and we had kissed, and it was so nice, and all this time I thought he thought so, too, but he didn't? He was *disgusted*? I stared at the page, at those two lines, and finally shut the book and put it back exactly as I'd found it, feeling terrible for having read it, for having snooped. I shouldn't have snooped, it was wrong, I deserved to see that, what did I expect to see? I'd asked for it.

I never talked to Josh about it.

But three months before that trip to Los Angeles, there I was on the floor of Andy's living room, drunk and naked with Ricky, kissing him, and enjoying kissing him, and enjoying him kissing me. And if there was stubble I didn't notice it or didn't care, and his skin was smooth—it was the first time that I'd really felt a boy's skin and noticed just how smooth it could be, almost like a girl's—and we were kissing and doing everything else, when I heard a voice. Ricky must have heard it too, because he stopped what he was doing and looked up at the voice with me.

"Um, excuse me," the voice said meekly.

Standing in the kitchen a couple of steps up from the living room was Andy's father. I didn't know him well—he was always so quiet when I was there, and Andy and I would usually hole up in his room and make silly audiotapes of commercial spoofs and radio skits when I came over—and at that moment when I looked up at him I wasn't filled with any kind of panic or embarrassment; I didn't feel caught or found out. I was just very very drunk, and I felt so good there on the floor with Ricky, and Andy's father was simply an interruption.

Ricky and I stared up at Andy's father for several moments, his body a silhouette, his hair a sloppy halo. He seemed to sway as he stood there. Finally, he said, "Sorry," and left.

Weird, I thought, and without a word, Ricky and I resumed our kissing, which continued on and off for the rest of the night.

"Guys? Guys? You gotta get up."

I cracked my eyes open, pushing Andy's irritating hand away from my shoulder, where he'd been shaking me awake.

"Stop," I said.

"Come *on,*" Andy said. "Get up. I gotta take you home."

I groaned. Ricky was a big lump beside me, still asleep. I looked over at him. I felt numb and stiff and slightly hungover. Looking at Ricky, his back to me, I remembered everything about the night before, but from a distance, as if looking at a blurry black-and-white photograph of myself performing in a play. I wondered what Andy thought, but I didn't ask him.

"Did you have fun?" Andy said.

"Huh?"

"Did you have fun?"

"I guess," I said. "Yeah."

I pulled on my clothes, and Andy took me home, leaving Ricky asleep on his living room floor.

Home at that time was an apartment complex called Cresthill Lake. Living in an apartment in Joliet had always filled me with shame; all of my friends lived in houses, as did almost everyone in our part of town, so I thought we should live in a house too. The complex looked like it had been shoddily assembled in another, grimmer town and plopped down in the middle of a field without any regard for the esthetics of its surroundings: traditional, suburban subdivisions complete with winding streets, sturdy oak trees, sculpted lawns, and modest single-family homes. Down the road was Cresthill Lake's slightly more affluent cousin, Colony West, a small development of identical two-family homes, which we called town houses for some reason, all painted a faded dijon yellow and adorned with dull brown trim. We lived in a town house in Colony West for the first few years of our time in Joliet, from when I was two until I was six, until we couldn't afford it anymore on Mom's nursing salary, at which point we moved down the street to an apartment in Cresthill Lake. Then even that apartment became too expensive, and a couple of years later we moved again to another, smaller apartment in Cresthill Lake.

The so-called lake was actually a large, oblong, scuzzy, sad pond, which more often than not featured a rusty dead bike stuck in the mud of its banks, and which gave off a disturbingly toxic odor on really hot days. Occasionally in the summer, potbellied tenants would sit on the edge of the pond adorned with Cubs hats and armed with fishing poles, lawn chairs, and tackle boxes. They would cast their lines into the pond's murky water and very seldom go home with a bluegill or two, flinging them into pickle tubs after the poor fish had flopped their way to oblivion on the drab grass. I guess the tenants ate the bluegills, although I would never have wanted to ingest anything that had come out of that pond.

The pond was ringed on three sides by the buildings of the complex, all exactly the same: three-storied with brown brick façades and tiny windows and cement steps leading to their entrances. In our building, on the east end of the complex, the apartments either faced the front, as ours did, or the back. Living in the front meant that out of our badly insulated, metal-framed windows we viewed a narrow strip of dark black parking lot, and beyond it a small cornfield; out the back window was the pond in the middle of a badly mown, perpetually yellowish-green lawn. A dilapidated, rusty jungle gym and swing set adorned the lawn, randomly situated at its edge in the farthest spot possible from the tenants.

I hated living there.

Nobody was home when Andy dropped me off—Mom was at work as a nurse in Joliet's maximum-security juvenile correctional facility, and Anne was probably out shopping, or at her boyfriend's house. I went straight to my room, climbed up my bunk bed (a leftover from when Adam lived at home), and snoozed for most of the rest of the day.

I woke up sometime in the late afternoon, groggy and disoriented, feeling more hungover than I had before my long nap, and stumbled out into the living room, an Isaac Asimov novel in my hand. Mom was home from work, puttering around in the kitchen.

"Hi, Tonio," she said. She looked harried and stressed, as she often did after a long day of passing out meds to horny, violent teenage boys.

"Hey," I replied, and plopped down on the couch. I tucked myself up in the nook of its armrest and opened my book. I didn't feel like talking. From the kitchen, pots and dishes clanged around and cupboards banged shut, as I sat and read about robots who helped solve crimes in the distant future.

Eventually, the noise from the kitchen subsided, and Mom stepped into the living room, in front of the TV, and stood there. I could feel her eyes on me. I kept reading, or trying to.

"Anthony," she said. I marked my place with my finger and looked up at her. She was very still, her arms folded across her chest, her eyes focused and sad. I waited for her to continue.

"I . . . got a call today," she began, and stopped.

"A call?" I asked. Alarm bells went off in my brain. I did my best to ignore them.

Mom took a deep breath. "Andy's mother called me today, while you were asleep." I could see her hands squeezing into the flesh of her arms. "She said . . . she said you were hanging out with Ricky D'Angelo last night."

I felt my palms start to sweat. I put my book down. "I *was* hanging out with Ricky D'Angelo last night."

She looked away from me for a moment, then into my eyes. She seemed angry now, and tired.

"Anthony, I don't want you around him anymore."

"What? Why?"

"Andy's mom told me—"

"Told you what?" I could now feel the old familiar hot righteous rush of an argument coursing through my body. I sat up very straight and put my book down.

"He's taking advantage of you, Anthony. He's older than you—"

"I knew what I was doing," I said, my voice rising.

"You're only fourteen, he's *much* older than you are!"

"I knew what I was *doing,* Mom. I wanted to do it. It was my choice. He didn't *make* me do anything."

Mom stopped for a second. She looked as if she was about to cry. "You're only fourteen," she said, again.

"I knew what I was doing," I said, again. "It was my choice."

Mom looked away again. A long silence passed. Her jaw was set. I stared at her from the couch.

"I don't want you around him anymore," she said, at last.

I didn't say anything.

"Please, Anthony."

"Mom . . ."

"Please."

I just sat there. I was not going to give her this. It *was* my choice, it *was,* and I could do whatever I wanted, with whoever I wanted, whenever and wherever I wanted to do it. We stared at each other, neither of us moving. I was not going to let her win.

After a long silence, Mom sighed heavily and went back into the kitchen, shaking her head. I opened up my book again but wasn't able to distinguish the words on the page anymore; they blurred and bled into one another. I was too keyed up. I could hear Mom sniffling from the kitchen. She always cried the way she laughed: silently. I felt weighted down on the couch. I knew I should do or say something, I knew she was waiting for me to do or say something, but I didn't want to make a move to comfort her or talk to her anymore. I didn't want to give in to her. So I stayed glued to the couch. Eventually, she went into her room and closed the door.

But I never did hang out with Ricky again.

In the first four years after the Ricky D'Angelo incident, I stayed away from messing around with other boys, only occasionally straying when I was feeling particularly lonely and horny. This self-imposed abstention from boys wasn't always terrible for me; I was also occasionally attracted to girls, just not as often, and not always as intensely. But I did have a couple of girlfriends during my senior year of high school, and when I was with them I didn't feel like I was sublimating some part of myself or hiding from my true nature. For the most part, I enjoyed the physical aspect of fooling around with girls as much as with boys.

But when I got to NYU in the fall of '89 to study film, I found a fast and emphatic friend in a fellow freshman named Keith. We spent almost all of our downtime together, bonding through long, rolling conversations about the movies and actors and plays and books we loved, talking intimately about our families and dreams and hopes and fears. It gradually dawned on me that we had been sort of falling in love with each other, as much as two eighteen-year-olds could, anyway. So we started to sleep together, and then we started to really go out with each other, even telling our friends about our burgeoning relationship. Keith became my first real boyfriend. And one night I decided I wanted to call Mom to tell her about him.

Mom and I chatted for a few minutes about our latest news, about the family goings-on, about school, all the while my chest feeling more constricted than usual, my voice feeling remote from my body, until I finally worked up the nerve to say, "Mom, there's something I want to tell you, and I don't want you to be upset."

Her voice got very quiet. "What is it?"

"I'm bisexual," I said. It seemed like the best way to say it, and it wasn't wholly inaccurate considering I'd had a sexual and romantic history with both boys and girls; I resisted limiting myself to one gender preference.

There was a long pause. I held my breath and listened to Mom's silence.

"How can you be sure?" she finally said.

"Well, I've been kind of going out with a guy. His name is Keith. We love each other." I held my breath again and listened for Mom's next words, whatever they would be. I pictured her moving around the kitchen, cleaning, as she always did while she talked on the phone.

"I can understand that two men can really think that they love each other," Mom said carefully. "But why can't you just be friends?"

"Because we don't want to just be friends," I said, my voice rising. I was trying to stay focused, trying to remain calm, but it was a struggle. "We love each other."

"Oh, Tonio," Mom said. "I don't understand."

"I don't know what there is to understand."

"Well . . ." Mom said, her voice trailing off. "I just worry about you."

"I'm not going to get AIDS, Mom," I said. I could feel my old, angry self-righteousness coming back to the foreground, in spite of my efforts to stuff it down and away.

"You'd better not," Mom said.

"I won't. I promise. I won't."

"You're so *young,*" Mom said, her voice resigned. "How can you know what you want to be?"

"I know I'm young, but I do know how I feel. And I'm careful. I don't want to get AIDS."

"Oh, Tonio, you'd better not get AIDS . . ." She trailed off again. I could hear water running. She was probably wiping down the kitchen counters now.

"Well, I just wanted to tell you about Keith," I said. "Because it's important to me to share my life with you."

"Okay," Mom said, sounding deeply tired.

"I'll talk to you later," I said then, stifling a sigh. "I love you." But I didn't feel it so much as say it.

"All right. I love you, too."

I hung up. The call hadn't been disastrous, but it had hardly been what I'd hoped for. I couldn't understand why she was so worried. She knew what good care I took of my body, how healthy I was. She knew I was smart and awake and alive. She had trusted me so much my whole life, giving me opportunities and freedoms other kids only dreamed about. I wanted her to trust me now.

The next family member to find out about Keith was Adam. When my brother flew to New York for a visit during his senior year in college, I hadn't yet told him about my relationship with Keith or anything about my sexuality. Adam stayed with Keith and me for a week in our one-bedroom apartment in the East Village, sleeping on the living room couch while Keith and I stayed in our bedroom.

One night, Keith and I were kissing under the covers, Keith on top of me, when the door opened.

"Anthony?" Adam said. Keith and I froze, and I looked up to see my brother's tall body in the door frame. He stood there for a moment, not saying anything more, and Keith and I didn't move, as alert and still as birds, until finally Adam said, "Sorry," and closed the door. Keith and I stayed still for another long moment, and then resumed our kissing.

The next day, Adam didn't say anything about what he'd seen. I didn't bring it up, until that night, when we were walking together on Avenue A.

"Keith and I are together," I said.

Adam didn't look at me. "Whatever," he said. We walked a few more feet in silence, my eyes cast down to the sidewalk, and then Adam said, "I don't get it, I don't get how you can do that, but whatever." And neither of us said any more after that.

For the rest of his stay, we didn't talk about the incident again. Adam, who'd become a prolific writer at college, started to spend most of his time in the apartment, furiously working on a new short story. It was about a senior in college from the Midwest who comes to New York to visit his younger brother, only to walk in on his younger brother having sex with a man. Adam showed me the beginnings of the story. I liked it, and asked him if I could write it with him. He said yes, and among the scenes I wrote was a dramatic, intense confrontation between the two brothers, in which the younger brother demands to be heard by his older brother, demands to be accepted. Adam and I went back and forth like this, writing our respective scenes, neither of us acknowledging that we were writing about ourselves. As had so often been the case in our family, we avoided directly confronting each other, but for the first time we had a new outlet through which we could express ourselves. But even as we wrote, we absurdly never admitted to each other that we were working out all of our issues through our story. Not that all of those issues actually got worked out, however; in both the story and in real life, the older brother left New York without coming to terms with what he'd learned about his younger brother's life.

Keith and I continued together for just over a year, although as time went on we began to fight, and I became less and less comfortable with the idea of having him as a boyfriend.

After my initial conversation about Keith with Mom, I didn't mention him again to her until several months later, when she came into town for the Broadway opening night of *Six Degrees of Separation*.

I called her at her hotel. "I want you to meet Keith," I said.

"Well, I want to meet him," Mom said, but I sensed the tightness in her voice as she spoke. She did meet him, spending a brief and tense visit with us in our apartment, sitting quietly on our desk chair, her arms loosely folded across her lap, her legs crossed, her meek voice barely reaching across the room. Keith's energy was generally high and nervous, and her presence that afternoon seemed to wind him even tighter than normal. His eyes darted around the room at twice their usual rate, and his hands fidgeted crazily with a pen, flipping it up and down, up and down, again and again, almost faster than the eye could follow. I found myself sinking down into the couch, feeling extremely monosyllabic, conscious of the slightest change of expression on Mom's clouded-over and mostly blank face. Later, when I asked her what she thought of Keith, she said, quietly, not looking at me, "Oh, he's very nice." And we didn't speak about him again for the rest of the trip.

A few months later, Keith and I broke up, and soon afterwards I began to see David. David was an actor who was taking time off from show business to work as the AIDS Walk New York team coordinator. I was the AIDS Walk team leader of the *Six Degrees of Separation* team, so David and I had to talk on the phone a lot, and I immediately warmed to his bright, charming sense of humor and his passion for his work. I asked him out, and he said yes, and we started spending a lot of time together.

In the meantime, Adam moved to New York and into my apartment, sleeping on the sofa in the living room. He and I hadn't spoken again about the whole sexuality issue, either negatively or positively, but I resisted sharing with Adam my relationship with David. Instead, I invited David over more and more often, and he would usually spend the night, which Adam didn't seem to mind, and after a couple of months Adam said to David, "Hey, I think you should move in."

I was shocked. "Really?" I said.

"Yeah," Adam said. "It would help out with the rent, and we all get along. It'd be nice."

"That sounds great," David said.

And even though Adam hadn't said so, I knew that he had accepted me after all, for which I was deeply grateful.

Even though Adam had accepted me, I still longed for a sense of peace with Mom. I would call her up and talk to her about my life, sneaking in a tidbit here and there about my relationship with David, and, when his name came up, she'd pretend it didn't bother her. But I'd always hear a rigidity, a resignation, in her voice.

Then, on Thanksgiving in 1992, a month after my twenty-first birthday, I wrote Mom a seven-page, urgent, handwritten letter:

Dear Momma—

This is the first letter I've written to you in I don't even know how long . . . and I'm as surprised as you that I'm writing it, but I thought it the best way to say everything I want to say to you, because it'll give you time to digest it and reread it if you want to, and then it'll be something you can ask me questions from or respond to. So, here goes . . .

Where to begin? Well, I guess first of all, I love you more than I can say. And, especially on this day of Thanksgiving, I am eternally grateful for the life you've given me. I know it was your support for me and my career and the choices I've made that have given me the confidence and responsibility and joy I have now. Thank you thank you thank you. (I can't say it enough.)

But there are some unresolved issues in our relationship, and I would love it if we could resolve them and move on and have a <u>totally</u> free, <u>totally</u> communicative relationship. I feel like we've been getting better and better, but I still see that we can be even more, and I think you agree. Do you?

A big thing is my relationship with David. I'm really torn up about how to go about saying everything I want to say, so what I'm going to do is tell the whole truth, and leave nothing out, and hope you understand. First of all, I've stopped pressing the issue of trying to get you to accept the fact that I'm bisexual, because I know it made you uncomfortable to talk about or even think about. And I understand that it's hard for you to accept. I really do. But Mom, is it worth it for you to be upset about something you can't change, especially if your being upset prevents you from being able to appreciate the extraordinary relationship I have with this amazing man? I'm genuinely asking. Because I've respected your wishes to not bring up the subject of my sexuality, and I've discovered I'd much rather be able to share with you the joy and fulfillment and issues and problems that are in my life because of David. I know you can talk to Anne about her and Ken, and Adam about his relationships, and I'd love it if you could do the same for me. Especially since I'm your son, and I'm in a relationship with David, and that's not going to change. And believe me, Mom, _please_ believe me that I'm not wanting to hurt you in any way by talking about it this honestly with you. I understand this might be uncomfortable for you (it is for me too), but I think, and I hope you agree, that a little discomfort in the moment is better in the long run, if it leads to more open communication. Do you agree?

I guess a reason I'm talking about my sexuality again after leaving it alone for a while is that I'm here at my friend Joan's house, and one of her sons is gay, and her other son is bisexual, and neither she, her husband, nor her daughter has the slightest problem with it. In fact, her son and his lover (who, unfortunately, has AIDS) are sleeping in the same bed in her house. I guess I'm telling you this to let you know that you're not alone (I know you know that), and also that it is possible for a family to acknowledge and accept other family members' ways of life without judgment. I would love it if I could bring David home, and have it be just as much a part of our family's life as if Anne brought Ken home, or Adam brought Christina (or whoever) home. I don't know if that will ever be the case, but I sure would love it, and I know David would, too.

The truth is, Mom, we could go on as we have been, not really discussing some of these issues, but don't you agree that we could have a much better relationship if we were able to talk openly about everything with each other? Even if that means we're temporarily uncomfortable? I hope you agree.

Above all, Mom, as I said before, I love you, I will always love you, and there's nothing you can do or say that will change that fact. Really. And it's only because I love you so much that I've been as straightforward as I have in this letter. Because it's so *much more worth it to me to have you fully be a part of my life (and vice versa) than to have all these things I feel I can't talk to you about. Do you feel the same way? I hope you do.*

Please give all of my love to Annie and Rachel. Please let me know what you thought (and think) about this letter. I love you, Momma. Take care of yourself, and I'll talk to you soon.

Love,

your son,

Anthony

I mailed off the letter but received no reply from Mom, in either a letter or a conversation. And as free and open as I'd felt while I was writing the letter, whenever I'd get on the phone with Mom my throat would close in on itself and I'd lose my nerve to ask her what she thought of what I'd written, and we'd go entire conversations without addressing a single point I'd brought up in the letter. Maybe it had been too much for her, I thought. Maybe I had been unfair. It was all well and good for me to sit by myself with my pen and paper at my desk, where I could safely pour out my thoughts, and then hide my head when I lobbed them over to Mom like a grenade. Mom hated confrontation, she'd had so much of it growing up, and I knew that, but it hadn't stopped me from trying to get through to her.

But finally, when we were talking about my plans for Christmas that year, I drew up my courage and said as nonchalantly as possible, "David would love to come home with me. He'd love to meet you and the rest of the family."

And without missing a beat, Mom said, "Well, that would be nice."

"Great," I said, careful not to display too much relief. New anxieties quickly followed, though: What if they didn't get along? What would Anne and Ken and Roberta and Rachel think? Would Mom let us sleep in the same bed in her house? Would the holiday be unbearably tense and difficult? But I didn't air any of those concerns, and Mom and I, as usual, didn't speak any more about it.

• • •

My anxiety proved to be groundless. Mom and David sparked to each other readily, although I imagined Mom had prepared herself to remain distant. But even if she had, her reserve melted in the face of David's rare and easy charm. He was exceedingly well-bred and had a kind of primal knowledge of how to socialize, how to chat and joke and compliment and listen attentively, all while eagerly sitting up straight, his face bursting into raucous smiles, his strong, clear voice resonating in all the right ways. He was a few years older than I and a real gentleman, and I watched Mom begin to take him into her heart, her eyes glinting during their conversations.

We had Christmas dinner at Roberta's house, feasting on a gorgeous meal she and her husband, Bob, both of them master chefs, had prepared for us. I felt almost giddy with relief as I wolfed down their food (they had been careful to provide vegetarian selections for me) and observed Roberta and Bob welcome David into their home and our family without a shred of reservation on their part. I should have known I'd have allies in Roberta and Bob; she'd always been a freethinking, self-made, slightly bohemian woman, and though I didn't know Bob well, I imagined she'd never allow herself to marry anyone who viewed life more narrowly than she. I also loved watching Mom quietly relax into a sweet, satisfied glow while she was in Roberta's presence. They were best friends, best sisters, soul mates, with what felt to me like a complete and utter understanding of each other's very being, even though they couldn't be more different at first glance. Mom was forever quiet and small, while Roberta was often boisterous and large. Mom had a cultivated sense of propriety, while Roberta had little, happily cursing her head off when she felt like it. Mom shrank from arguments, while Roberta seemed hungry for a good, chunky debate. Mom abstained from substances, including alcohol, while Roberta drank plenty of wine with dinner, even allowing herself to generate a healthy buzz, loosening her tongue and laughter even more than usual. And yet I never sensed any disapproval emanating from Mom toward her younger sister; I sensed only deep love, and an abiding connection and trust. I envied Roberta for that.

Little five-year-old Rachel glommed onto David with her usual zeal, begging him to repeat again and again their impromptu game in which he swung her around the room by her arms and legs, her chirpy squeals cascading out of her, her adorably chubby-cheeked face overwhelmed with joy. I watched Mom watching their game to see if she disapproved in any way of David's contact with Rachel, but Mom just beamed with pride at her child. After the fifth round, Mom said, "Oh, Rachel, you're going to make David fall over from exhaustion," to which Rachel replied, "No I'm not!" to which Mom said, without a tinge of reprimand, "Oh, Rachel, you're so silly," and then she settled into an easy laugh in response to Rachel's endless squeals.

I was proud of Mom and proud of David and proud of myself for the way the visit went between all of us. But as time went on I lost confidence in sharing our relationship with Mom, especially as it started to sour, and our fights grew more and more common (a pattern reminiscent of my relationship with Keith). A little over a year after bringing David home with me, I broke up with him to be with Marcus, whom I'd met while David was away on a German tour of *West Side Story*. I was fast becoming what one friend called a "serial monogamist," and I felt ashamed to tell Mom that David, this wonderfully engaging, sweet man, whom she'd perhaps begun to think of as a possible son-in-law, had not been enough to sustain me, for reasons that I couldn't articulate even to myself. (Was it that I was too proud to admit that I was young and immature and didn't really know the first thing about maintaining an adult relationship?) All I knew was that David and I had grown apart and that Marcus and I seemed to be more of a match. I halfheartedly told Mom about breaking up with David and about my new relationship with Marcus. She listened, but as our conversation went on to other topics, I could feel a shift in the landscape between us, I could feel old anxieties of hers resurfacing. And for the next three years my old, familiar constraint and fear ruled any talks I had with her about my romantic life.

Joliet seemed to be undergoing some sort of boom, I noticed as I drove into town from O'Hare airport on July 1, 1996: generic, identical new homes were sprouting up everywhere in newly minted subdivisions, and there were more five-store strip malls dotting the landscape than I'd ever seen. As always during my brief visits home, I was grateful that I had gotten out of Joliet's culturally anemic suburban sprawl.

I pulled into the tiny driveway of Mom's three-unit condominium and parked, pausing behind the steering wheel to take in a few steadying breaths. I had no idea what condition Mom would be in when I went inside, and I had no idea whether we would be able to have a conversation about my new boyfriend, Todd, on this trip. Staring out the windshield at the new row of houses where there once had been a cornfield, I resolved to talk to Mom about Todd no matter what. I grabbed my overnight bag, got out of my rental car, and opened the door to Mom's house.

The small house was full of people: Anne, five months pregnant, who stood in the kitchen chatting on the phone, wrapping its long cord around her fingers; eight-year-old Rachel, who sat in the living room on the lap of an older woman with long gray hair—a stranger to me, who I figured to be Mary, the woman sent from Joliet Hospice to help Mom take care of Rachel; and Mom, who lay in her usual spot on the couch, her thin legs bent in an upside-down *V* before her. No sooner had I closed the door behind me than Zelda, Mom's probably-half-beagle, maybe-half-Labrador, definitely-treasured mutt, let out her customary full-throated barks and leaped up onto me, attempting to lick my face off.

"Zelda Lou, no jumping," Mom said from the couch as sternly as possible, but having little effect.

"It's okay, Mom," I said, although a strong, heavy Zelda threatened to knock me over with the force of her affection. "Hi, Z," I said.

"Hi there." Mom had rescued Zelda from an abusive family soon after Zucchini's untimely death. She had lavished her with love and care, and Zelda had responded wonderfully.

"Zelda, get *down*," Rachel said, her little-girl voice doing its best imitation of Mom. Zelda didn't obey, of course, but I finally managed to shove her gently away so I could give proper hugs to my family. Rachel clutched me as tightly as always, Anne gave her usual half-second, lighter-than-air embrace, and Mom squeezed me into her with as much strength as she could muster, which wasn't a lot. She didn't look much worse than I'd seen her in April, though.

"Anthony, this is Mary," Mom said. Mary didn't get up out of the chair she was sitting in, but she smiled up at me.

"I've heard a lot about you," she said, her voice mild. I hoped she'd heard only good stuff. "Nice to meet you," I said.

Mom had made her little house into her cozy haven, surrounding herself with flourishing plants and shelves of books and her adored Charles Wysocki prints, and I perched myself on the sofa, taking it all in again. Sunlight streamed in through the windows. I was proud of her for creating such a comfortable environment for herself, even though I didn't share her taste for countrified furnishings.

I chatted with Mom for a little while, extremely conscious of the brevity of my visit, and hoping for an opportunity to be alone with her. Rachel and Anne didn't leave, though, and they began to talk intensely to each other, and soon Rachel whined, "No! I don't *want* to go!"

I glanced over at Mom and asked her softly, "What's going on?"

Mom worriedly watched Rachel talk to Anne as she answered. "Anne and Ken want to take Rachel up to the Smiths' cabin in Michigan for the Fourth of July."

"Why doesn't she want to go?"

"She's afraid of leaving me," Mom said, her brow furrowed. "She's afraid of being away in case anything happens to me."

"Well, that's understandable," I said.

"Yes, but it's important that she learns that she can go and that I'll be okay," Mom said.

"I guess that's true."

Rachel began to cry, her wails enormous and heartbreaking.

"Rachel, come here," Mom said, her voice a blend of authority and compassion. Rachel reluctantly headed over to Mom, her face twisted up from her crying.

"I don't want to *go,*" she said.

"Well, you have to go," Mom said. "You'll have fun."

"I don't *want* to have fun!"

"Oh, Rachel, yes you do."

"Rachel," Anne said, sounding like she was trying to control exasperation, "we'll have a good time."

"I don't *want* to have a good time!"

I decided to step in, putting my hand on Rachel's back, trying to soothe her. "Rachel, honey, you'll be okay. It's only for a couple of days."

"Noooooooooo," Rachel said.

"Well, Mom," Anne said, "I've got to get going. Ken's waiting for me."

"Okay, Annie," Mom said.

"Let me know if she changes her mind," Anne said as she left.

Rachel's crying had quieted down, and she stood staring mournfully at the floor. "Come here, honey," I said. I wrapped my arms around her and pulled her onto my lap, squeezing her tightly. She'd had so many difficult and transformative circumstances to get used to in her young life, and I figured Mom was often too weary to give Rachel the kind of attention that she craved. Rachel clutched me tightly and buried her face into my neck. I glanced over at Mom and saw how concerned and conflicted she was, but I didn't know what to say to her, and so in my usual fashion I said nothing.

"Rachel, honey," Mary said. "Why don't we go for a swim?"

I could feel her sigh in my arms. "Okay," she said. Part of me was sad to see her go, and part of me was relieved that I'd have time alone with Mom, and still another part was dreading that alone time.

"Have fun," Mom said.

"Oh, we will," Mary said, and then she and Rachel were gone.

For the first time since I'd arrived home, there was silence in the house. I glanced over at Mom, my head spinning around, trying to figure out where to begin our conversation.

"So how are you, Tonio?"

"I'm fine, Momma," I said. "How are you feeling?"

"Oh, pretty good. I'm just tired a lot. The radiation makes me tired. But I'm basically pretty good."

"That's good," I said, then sat in silence, waiting for the next move.

"How's the show going?"

"It's amazing," I said. "I'm having such a great time."

"That's wonderful."

"Yeah," I said. And finally I decided to say, "I got my third-ever HIV test. Negative."

"Well, you'd better stay negative, Anthony," she said, quickly.

"Oh, I will, Mom, I promise," I said, just as quickly.

"Don't ever take any chances."

"I won't. I haven't yet."

"Never, never, *never*, not even one."

I paused for a second, swallowed, not looking at her.

"But, um," I said, feeling the color rise in my cheeks. "The real reason I got tested now, too, is that—I was sort of waiting to tell you this until some more time had passed and so I could tell you in person—but I'm . . . seeing somebody."

My mother's hand started plucking at the stitching on the couch. She didn't say anything.

"He's really great," I said. "I assumed Adam had probably said something about him to you." Adam always told Mom everything about me.

"No, he didn't say much," she said.

I took a deep breath. "His name is Todd," I said.

"What does he do?" This was almost a mumble.

"He's a playwright and screenwriter." I could feel my cheeks really heating up now. "We've been going out for a little while. We've been taking it slow, but . . ." I sighed. "It's the best beginning I've ever had."

I looked over at Mom, who didn't look sad, at least, having this conversation. But she was very, very still, her only movement in her hand, as it plucked away at the couch. I sat and waited for her to say something, steeling myself. And after she remained silent for a long moment, I asked her, "How do you feel about that?"

She regarded me steadily, and then quietly said, "It was hard for me at first to grasp the whole thing about your sexuality, but now it's not, you know, it's not so hard. I know a lot of people are, and it's no different from having blue eyes or brown eyes, really."

And that was more than enough acceptance for now.

waiting

In August I got a call from Mom. "I'm going to have another surgery," she said. This one was to repair one of her vertebrae, which had been eaten up by a tumor; her cancer was now spreading into her bones. "If they don't repair it, and it collapses, I could be paralyzed," she said.

"I'll come home," I said.

"Good. I want you to be here."

So Adam and I flew home the day of the surgery, and headed right over to St. Joseph's Medical Center in Joliet. Mom was already in prep, and Anne, Grandma, Roberta, and Mom's friend—and our honorary aunt—Gloria were already in the waiting room. Gloria was one of Mom's oldest and closest friends, who, like Roberta, was almost the complete opposite of Mom, with her raspy, loud voice and vulgar, hilarious jokes. As with Roberta, I envied Gloria's ability to make Mom laugh so readily and fully. I was grateful she was there; she was a lively antidote to the silence my family tended to fall into.

As soon as I arrived, Gloria rushed up and gave me one of her tight, crushing hugs, kissing me on each cheek. "Anthony, how *are* you? How's *Rent* going?" Gloria had recently flown to New York to see the show several times over one weekend, reveling in the crowds at the theatre and the music pouring off the stage and the emotions washing over her as she watched the story unfold. She was now one of the show's biggest fans, although she had a lot of competition for that title.

"It's going very well," I said.

"Of *course* it is," she said. "How could it not be? It's *so* wonderful." And with that, she gripped my hand in both of hers and guided me over to everyone else in the waiting room. We all exchanged our hellos in our customary fashion—Anne and I shared a brief, insubstantial hug, Grandma and I barely made eye contact, and Roberta and I embraced.

"So can I see her?" I asked.

"They said she'll be out and on her way soon," Gloria said, her eyes wide and wild. "I can't stand this. I hate this waiting around, it drives me crazy." She clutched my hand even tighter. "I need a cigarette." And with that, she left.

In the wake of her departure, the waiting room felt more cramped than it already was with its low ceiling and too many chairs and tables for its small space. But there were windows all along one wall that let in the hazy, grayish, warm late-summer sun, a welcome addition to the usual fluorescent lights. Multicolored construction paper cutouts fashioned by children adorned the walls, and magazines—*People* and *Sports Illustrated* and *Highlights for Children*—littered the floor and tables.

Without Gloria's presence, the room grew silent, as I'd known it would. I contemplated heading outside so I could be with Gloria as she smoked, but I stayed put. I hated that I felt so stifled and still in my family's presence. Why couldn't I just be myself and open up? Why couldn't we all just turn to each other and say, "I'm scared for Mom, are you?" I knew Gloria had spoken for all of us when she said she couldn't stand all the waiting, but she was the only one who'd had the guts to actually admit it.

Gloria soon came back upstairs, and then an orderly in surgical scrubs poked his head into our waiting room.

"Mary's about to head into surgery. If you want to come out to say hello to her, now would be a good time."

We all jolted out of our chairs and filed out into the hallway. Mom looked tiny and frightened in her oversized hospital bed, with her thin, dark hair splayed out around her pillow, and her confused, milky eyes swimming and darting behind her glasses. We allowed one another to have a private moment with Mom, and as I waited for mine it occurred to me that this was the first of Mom's many surgeries for which I'd been present *before* she went under, not after.

When it was my turn I approached her bedside and held her slim, tender hand and said, "Hi, Momma." It was strange to be hovering over her, to see her so prone.

Her eyes were wet and her voice wavered as she said, "Hi, Tonio."

I felt calm and strong with her in that moment. "I'll be waiting for you when you get out," I said.

"I don't want to do this," Mom said quietly, almost in a whine. It was the first time I'd heard this kind of fear from her.

"You'll be okay," I said. And I believed it.

The orderly then said, "All right, we've got to keep moving, they're waiting for us in the OR."

We all trailed after Mom as they wheeled her to the elevator, her eyes locked on us the whole time. And as I stood there, watching the elevator doors slide shut, I refused to believe that this would be the final image I'd have of my mom: so small and frightened and alone, weakly waving to us from her hospital bed. It couldn't be. She'd survive the operation, I had no doubt. Or at least no doubt that I was going to allow myself to feel.

Hours and hours passed in the waiting room. Silence prevailed between us, as usual. Even Gloria was quiet. Anne broke out a Scrabble game, invoking an old family ritual, and Adam, Anne, and I huddled around the board for the next few hours, clicking our lettered tiles, building our makeshift crossword puzzles, giving us something, anything to do. Anne was usually the family champion, but on this day I won every game we played; it seemed the distraction of waiting for Mom was too much for Anne to handle, while it just helped me to focus even more on the game—something over which I could have some control.

The expected hour of the end of Mom's surgery came and went, with no word from any hospital staffer as to how she was doing. An uncomfortable anxiety crept around the outskirts of my mind, and I stuffed it away as best as I could. But when a garbled voice announced over the intercom, "Would someone from the Rapp party please contact the operator?" adrenaline flooded my system and I leaped out of my seat. *This is how it happens,* I thought. *This is how they tell you people have died.* I glanced over at my family and saw that they all were thinking the same thing. No one made a move, and then Roberta bravely headed over to the phone and dialed. I watched her face for some sign of dreadful news as she listened to the voice on the other end, but as usual she was simply stoic.

"What was it?" I asked when she hung up.

"They were just calling to say she's still under, it's taking longer than they thought it would, but it's going fine."

I realized I'd been holding my breath, and let it out. "That's good," I said.

"Oh, I can't *stand* this," Gloria said.

I was growing so tired of hospitals and waiting rooms and hospital food and hallways and hospital smells and waiting and waiting and waiting.

Finally, another orderly popped his head into our room. And we all once again leaped out of our seats. All those hours of dazedly sitting melted away in one moment.

"She's doing fine," he said. "The surgery was a success. She's in the ICU now, and in a little while you'll be able to go see her."

"She's okay?" Anne said.

"Yes, she's fine."

"Okay. Good."

And I thought to myself, *Well, I was right.*

After visiting her in the ICU—I was also growing weary of the all-too-familiar image of my mother surrounded by beeping, whirring machines, with tubes snaking out of her nose and arms—Adam and I headed back to the airport and back home to New York City.

A few days after my return, and for no concrete reason, I decided it was finally time for me to attend a group meeting at Friends In Deed.

On my night off, I headed down to the Friends In Deed offices, situated on Broadway just below Houston Street. Cy greeted me with a warm "Hello there!" and a hug; we had grown close over the past few months, since her visit to *Rent's* rehearsal room back in January. She had seen the show more than a dozen times since then, bringing practically every friend she had, and we had shared numerous dinners after those performances, talking about how much she loved the show and how the work at Friends was going and sharing stories about our lives in and out of theatre circles.

Thirty or so people shuffled quietly around the Friends In Deed offices, and then they all began heading into a serene, silent, cream-colored room lined with rows of chairs. The bulk of Friends' clients were there to deal with HIV or AIDS issues, and I immediately felt self-conscious, as if I were an impostor. Not only was I not affected directly by HIV or AIDS at the moment, I wasn't even ill, as I was sure many of these people were.

"I'm so glad you came," Cy said to me, as usual projecting grace and ease and a quiet joy.

"Well, I felt like it was time," I said.

"Well, good. Good, good, good." She grinned her gorgeous grin and grasped my hand in hers. "We'll talk afterwards."

"Okay," I said, and I found an unobtrusive, hidden seat in the middle of the third row.

Cy began the proceedings by welcoming everyone—giving special attention to any and all newcomers—and asking for everyone to agree to respect everyone else's confidentiality.

"Now I want everyone to close your eyes and breathe deeply and just get yourselves here," she said. Ah, this was a guided meditation. I could certainly handle that. "Notice any thoughts you're having," she said. "Just notice them. Picture yourself on the bank of a river, and the river is full of your thoughts, your feelings, your opinions. Now watch them as they float on by. Notice if there's anything lingering in your mind from outside of this room. From your day. See if you can let all of that be, if you can leave it outside this room. It will still be there when you leave here. Now notice the sounds of this room. Just listen to the sounds of the room, and notice them. There's nothing to do but be here."

As the meditation continued, I relaxed; my concerns over what the other people in the room might think of me began to evaporate.

"All there is to do in here is to tell the truth, to tell your truth, and to speak from your heart." She let this sink in. "Now open your eyes."

The room, which had already been tranquil, seemed even more so upon opening my eyes. I had never been particularly skeptical of meditation, but I had never really practiced it either, and right away I felt its power to alter my experience of reality, at least in this context.

I sat quietly and listened as, one by one, different people in the room raised their hands and Cy called on them. She conducted the group very much as she had led our meeting in rehearsal those several months ago—with confidence and intelligence and a keen and compassionate ear. Eventually I put my hand up, and Cy called on me.

"Well, I'm not sure where to begin," I heard myself say, my palms sweating already. It felt somewhat strange to be speaking so formally, in front of a group of strangers, to one of my friends. But I continued, not knowing what was going to come out of my mouth. "As you know," I said, "my mom has cancer, and I feel like I'm doing okay with it, but I don't know, I'm just trying to figure out how to deal with everything. Life's pretty intense right now, with the show and everything else." By "everything else," I was referring to my relationship with Todd, which had continued to intensify, but not always happily.

"You have a lot on your plate right now," Cy said. "A tremendous amount."

"Yeah," I said. And it was the first time that simple truth had been uttered, by me or anyone. I breathed in the relief I felt with its utterance. "And I'm going home to visit my mom as often as I can, and I don't always know what to say to her. I feel like we have a pretty good relationship, but there are things I'd like to talk to her about, and I'm afraid of upsetting her or saying the wrong thing."

"Okay, first of all, you need to give yourself a big break," Cy said. "You really do. You really need to let in the fact that you have a lot on your plate. An extraordinary amount. That's step one. You need to acknowledge the way things are."

This made a lot of sense. I breathed deeply. "Okay," I said.

"So you need to take extra care of yourself. You need to make sure you get enough rest, that you get massages, anything and everything to take care of yourself. This is a very, very stressful time. It's okay to have to take care of yourself."

"Right," I said, sighing again. I was much more likely in my life to keep going and going and going, rather than stop and slow down and tend to myself.

"And as for your mother," Cy said, "I don't know her, so I can't say what will or won't upset her. But what I can say is that I'm pretty sure that what any parent wants from their children is their love and support, and if you come from loving and supporting your mother when you're with her, if you speak to her from your heart, I can't imagine there's a whole lot you could say or do that would hurt her."

I nodded, taking all of this in, hoping she was right.

"If she's like most people, she doesn't want to leave things unfinished when she goes. She'd much rather talk about whatever there is to talk about. Now, again, I'm not guaranteeing that's the case for your mother, but after working with so many people who were dying, or were about to lose someone, I could pretty well bet on it."

I nodded again. And before I even knew I felt this way, I found myself saying, "I wish I knew how much time there was left."

"Of course you do," Cy said. "Of course you do. Unfortunately, there's no way to know. She'll go when it's her time, and that's all you can be sure of."

"I hope I can be there when it happens." Again, this was not something I'd thought about saying before it came out.

"And you may be, and you may not be. I've been with many people when they've died and I can tell you that it is truly one of the gifts of life, to witness someone crossing over into whatever's next for them. So in that sense, I hope it happens for you and your mother. But it may not, and that has to be okay, too."

"Yeah," I said. Over the course of our conversation, a field of energy, a tractor beam, had caught me, filling me with clarity and light and peace. And as I sat there, I felt an aching anxiety I hadn't even known to be there melt away, and then there was nothing left to say but, "Thank you."

"You're welcome," Cy said.

We soon got word at *Rent* that the entire cast had been invited to sing at the upcoming Democratic National Convention, to be held in Chicago. Since Mom was still at St. Joseph's, recovering from her surgery, I scheduled myself a later flight back to New York the day after the convention so I could head down to visit her.

On the flight over to Chicago, I thought of a story Mom had once told me from her days as a pediatric nurse.

"There was this little boy I was taking care of," she said, "and he was terminally ill, and we all knew it, but he kept hanging on and hanging on. He wouldn't die. It was so sad.

"And his parents were always there with him, giving him so much love and support, but he was in so much pain, and it really was time for him to go.

"So finally some of us nurses took his father aside and we told him, 'You have to tell your son it's okay for him to go. You have to give him permission.' And so the father took his son in his arms and he sat with him in a chair and held on to him and told him over and over that it was okay, that it was okay for him to go, and, well, after a few moments, his son died."

The convention was something of an anticlimax. On the one hand, it was exciting to feel like we were a small part of history in the making, and to sing our song in front of the thousands upon thousands of delegates gathered together there. On the other, it was disappointing to be relegated to a basement waiting room until it was our turn to perform and to miss the opportunity to meet any of the delegates. We also found out later that our performance hadn't even been televised except on C-Span, and that the real reason we were there in the first place was that David Geffen, who co-owned DreamWorks Records, was a big supporter of the Democratic Party and had pulled strings to get us this national exposure, which just so happened to be on the eve of our album's release.

I was still happy to be there, especially because it meant I'd have another opportunity to visit Mom.

When I walked into her hospital room, I was relieved to see that she wasn't hooked up to any machines, or even an IV drip, and that her room was airy and pleasant and bathed in sunlight. She was no longer in intensive care, with its mood of death and dread; she was now in a wing dedicated to physical rehabilitation, the hallways of which were full of patients practicing walking again or mastering their wheelchairs or visiting with their loved ones. There was life and hope here.

Mom was sitting up in her bed alertly—another relief to see—and she smiled when I came in. I gave her a hug and kiss, careful as always not to squeeze her thin frame too tightly.

"Hi, Tonio," she said.

"Hi, Momma. How are you feeling?" We both knew I didn't have long to visit her before I had to head back to the airport so I could perform in that evening's show.

"Oh, *pretty* good." Her customary response. But now that she wasn't smiling at my arrival anymore, I could see a new weariness in her eyes.

"How's your back doing?"

"Well, it's all right. I'm having a hard time walking. But it's okay."

I sat and held her hand and looked in her eyes, which were starting to well up a little.

"I'm getting very tired of all of this," she said, and slow, silent tears ran down her cheeks. "I really wish this wasn't happening."

"I hear you, Momma," I said.

"I don't understand how it all happened. I wish I could just be normal again."

"I know, Momma."

"I sometimes wish it was just all over, you know?"

I sighed. "Yeah, Momma, I do."

"I mean, I want to be here so I can see you kids and see Rachel grow up and see all of the wonderful things that are going to happen for all of you, but sometimes it's very hard to just feel so *awful* all the time."

I squeezed her hand. I thought about the story she'd told me, and I thought about Cy's words to me, and I said, "Momma, I just want you to know that if you need to go, you can go. I will miss you, and I'll be very very sad, but I'll be okay."

"Oh, Tonio . . ."

"It's okay, Momma, it's okay."

Suddenly, Mom's sister Amy walked into the room. My heart sank. Amy was mildly retarded, behaving in many ways like a six-year-old in a forty-something-year-old body, and I wasn't sure if she'd understand if Mom or I asked her to come back later so we could have privacy. Besides, it had taken a lot for Amy to come to the hospital; she lived in a special home, had to obtain permission to leave, and most likely faced a time constraint herself.

Mom wiped away her tears. "Hi, Amy," she said, her voice shaky.

"Hello, Mary Lee," Amy replied in her childish blurt, not really looking at Mom as she said it. Mary Lee was what all of Mom's family called her.

"Hi, Amy," I said.

"Hey." She didn't really look at me either, and took a seat, staring at the floor. I sometimes wondered if Amy wasn't so much retarded as she was severely emotionally traumatized; she struck me as someone who often had a lot to say, but who was deeply, terribly afraid to say it. We all sat there in silence, waiting for Amy to say something, and while we sat I longed for her to be gone so Mom and I could continue our conversation.

"So how are you, Mary Lee?" Amy said, at last. Again, she didn't really look at Mom as she asked this.

"I'm okay, Amy, how are you?"

"Fine," Amy said quickly, as if by rote. And then she sank into silence again. I glanced over to Mom, who looked at me impassively, resigned to the idea that our conversation was over.

"So are they taking care of you good here?" Amy asked.

"Yes, they are."

"That's good." I glanced at my watch; it was time for me to leave. I squeezed Mom's hand.

"I need to get going, Momma," I said.

"I know, Tonio," she said. "Have a good flight, okay? And have a good show tonight."

"I will." I leaned over and gave her a kiss, and then kissed her hand as I stood up. I turned to Amy. "Bye, Amy," I said.

"Oh, you're leaving?"

"Yeah, it was nice to see you."

"Okay," Amy said quickly, still not looking at me. "Bye-bye."

I turned to Mom and waved goodbye, hoping it wasn't going to be the last time I'd see her. She waved weakly from her bed, and I headed out.

births

The next time I saw Mom was about six weeks later, in October, the month of our birthdays. I flew home on my day off, trying to establish a new ritual of traveling home once or twice a month, a frequency that felt good, and yet seemed to be not often enough. I always remembered Grandma stopping me at Mom's front door once when I visited home back in '95.

"You need to be a better son to your mother," she'd said sternly, her intense blue eyes burrowing into me. I felt pinned, heat instantly rising up the back of my neck. I knew she was right. "She needs you."

"I will," I said, also wanting to say, *Easy for you to fucking say. You need to be a better* mother *to my mother.* But I didn't say that.

So in an effort to be that better son that I'd said I would be, I made my plane reservation, got myself to Newark airport on Monday morning, landed in Chicago at around noon, got in my little rental car, and tooled down I-55 to Joliet, blasting the radio the whole way. My old favorite radio station, WXRT, played Counting Crows, a band whose work I mostly tolerated and only occasionally liked, performing a song called "A Long December." It spoke to me of my journeys home, and I turned up the music and sang along over Adam Duritz's distinctively nasal croon:

> *And it's been a long December and there's reason to believe*
> *Maybe this year will be better than the last*
> *I can't remember all the times I tried to tell myself*
> *To hold on to these moments as they pass*

As I walked into Mom's little house, I felt the enormous contrast between the quiet of her world in Joliet and the noise of my life in New York, with its traffic and clamor, my late nights out with friends at bustling restaurants, my relationship with Todd, and performance after performance of *Rent* greeted with standing ovations and crowds of people waiting outside the stage door thrusting pens and programs and cameras into our faces to grab an autograph and a photo. These visits home, in fact, were pretty much the only chance I had to slow things down and be alone for a while, something Cy had encouraged me to do. Not that they were stress free, by any means. Just more quietly stressful.

I headed into Mom's serene, sunlit bedroom to find Anne gazing down at her week-old son Brendan, who was lying on the bed next to Mom. Brendan radiated pinkish redness, looking impossibly tiny and fragile and alien atop Mom's pristine white bed cover. Mom lay flat on her back next to him, her head turned so she could gaze lovingly at her first grandchild as he clenched one of her slender fingers in his tiny fist. She looked so at home there, as she always did around children, and at the same time she looked almost as tiny and fragile and alien as Brendan. I had to stop at the door and steady myself to keep from bawling at the sight.

"Hi, Tonio," Mom said quietly, smiling.

"Hi, Momma."

"Hey," Anne said. Her face glowed, her cheeks bursting in a grin.

"He's beautiful," I said, not because he was (how could newborns be called beautiful when they looked so strange?), but because I knew I was supposed to say so.

"Thanks," Anne said, now chuckling in the way that she did when she was excited and embarrassed. I sensed that she had become both more centered and more childlike in the wake of giving birth to her son.

I came into the bedroom and leaned over Mom to give her a kiss. Her lips felt papery and almost nonexistent. Brendan's head lolled around as he lay there, his big blue eyes roaming across the ceiling, the room, Mom, and me. He continued to clutch Mom's finger. I sat on the bed next to them and remembered the doubt I'd felt over a year ago, when Anne had reassured Mom that Mom would in fact live to see her grandchildren born.

"Can I hold him?" I asked.

"Yeah, but be careful," Anne said.

I hadn't been around many tiny babies before, and I was nervous about doing something wrong—holding him too tightly, supporting him in the wrong places, or worse, dropping him—but I cupped one hand behind his downy head and the other around his miniature back, and brought him to my chest. He looked at me hazily for a second, then continued his herky-jerky surveillance of his larger surroundings. I lightly bounced him up and down in my arms, only because I'd seen other people do that to little babies, and looked at the two of us in the mirror across the room. We looked strange together; I was pale and large and he was red and tiny. I knew I wanted children at some point, but at this moment the responsibility of protecting and providing for such a vulnerable being seemed much more than I'd ever be able to handle.

"If he's too heavy, I can take him," Anne said, although there was no way that he could ever be too heavy for anyone except Mom. But I was relieved to hand Brendan over to Anne; nothing bad could happen to him now that he was in his mother's arms.

Brendan had been born on the 14th, five days before Mom's birthday—a nice coincidence at a time like this. Her birthday had been two days prior to my visit, and I had agonized over what to get her. She didn't need anything material these days, and this birthday was probably going to be her last, so what on earth could I have gotten her that would be fitting? I finally decided to buy her a dozen white roses, and had them sent to her at home. Better than nothing, I thought. Besides, she loved plants and flowers.

When I called her on her birthday, her hello sounded especially weak and sad.

"What's wrong, Momma?" I asked.

"Oh, Tonio," she said. "It's so sad. It's so sad."

"What is? What happened?"

"Sarah got hit by a car. She's dead. She died."

"Oh my god." I had to think for a second about whom she meant. And then it hit me: she was talking about one of Rachel's friends, an adorable and insatiably energetic little blond girl who lived a couple of doors away. She was forever poking her face up to Mom's glass patio door, screeching for Rachel to come out and play with her. It seemed impossible that this was the Sarah Mom was referring to.

"How did that happen?" I asked.

"Oh, I don't know, she just ran out into the street and some idiot was barreling down Gael Drive and he ran over her." She sniffled. "It's so sad, she was such a wonderful little girl."

"That's terrible," I said. "How's Rachel?"

"She's devastated. Oh, Tonio, it's so sad."

I could hear Mom crying in her nearly silent way on the other end of the phone. I wished so much that I didn't have to just listen to her, that I could see her, that I could be there to hold her hand. "I'm sorry, Momma," I said.

"Yeah," she said. "Me too."

After hearing this news, I didn't know how to tell her that I'd called to wish her a happy birthday. But then she said, "Oh, and thank you for the beautiful flowers. I love them."

"You're welcome," I said. "I'm glad you like them."

"They're wonderful. Thank you."

"Well, I was going to say happy birthday, but it doesn't seem like it's too happy."

"No, it's not, but thank you for thinking of me. Thank you for calling."

"Of course, Momma. Of course."

"This is a hard time," she said. "Very hard."

I breathed in deeply. "I know, Momma."

"I love you, Tonio."

"I love you, too. I hope Rachel's okay."

"She'll be all right. She's such a strong little girl."

"I know." I sighed. I wished I could be there rather than on the distant, cold phone. "Okay, well, I'll see you Monday. Have a good weekend, if you can."

"Okay, Tonio. Goodbye."

"Bye, Momma."

I hung up and sat staring at the floor for a long time. Calling Mom was hard enough without her having such sad news. At least when I was with her in person I knew I could be a little helpful; on the phone, quite the opposite was true.

And two days later I was with her, and even though she looked no better than the last time I'd seen her, even though I knew that this really was the beginning of the end, I felt more settled, more connected to her, as I sat in the recliner next to her bed watching her watch her grandson. My nephew. The roses that I'd sent her sat in a vase on her dresser; they had opened up spectacularly, their perfect white blooms enormous and beautiful. I had neglected to send Mom anything on so many previous birthdays and Mother's Days that I was proud to have finally come through with a gift that pleased her and gave her room a touch of light and life.

Soon Anne gathered up Brendan in his baby blanket, gave me a perfunctory hug goodbye, and kissed Mom on the cheek, something I'd never seen her do. And then there Mom and I were, alone together for the first time in almost two months. I moved from the chair to the edge of her bed so I could be closer to her. It was then that I noticed the IV in her hand connected to a gray plastic box.

"What's that?" I asked.

"Oh, it's how I get my pain medication now," she said. "I self-administer it with this button. It regulates the dosage."

"That's cool," I said. *Cool?* What could possibly be considered cool about pain medication? I tried to remember all the things that Cy had told me to think about these visits: be with her, don't judge myself, just talk and listen from my heart. I took her hand in mine. "How are you feeling?"

"I'm okay," she said.

"That's good." She really was okay in a certain sense of that word, in that she was still alive, and still able to talk and think, but there were so very many ways in which she was not okay.

As I sat there with her, I tried to fight the need to fit in everything I ever wanted to talk to Mom about. I kept my voice measured and calm. I kept a steady, easy grip of her hand in mine. I watched myself from outside of myself as I talked to her about how well *Rent* was going.

"I'm so happy to hear it," she said. "It's such a great show."

"What were your favorite parts?" I asked. I realized I'd never talked to her at length about what she actually thought of it.

"I love that song that goes, *'Will I lose my dignity?'* It's so beautiful."

"Yeah," I said. Given her condition and her steady decline, it made sense that she'd connected to that song in particular.

"Jonathan was so talented," she said. "Those stupid emergency rooms. What a waste." Mom had watched the *Dateline NBC* episode detailing the two hospitals' misdiagnoses of Jonathan's aneurysm, telling me at the time, "Anybody with any sense looking carefully at his chest X-ray should have seen the swelling. It was there plain as day." She had often shared stories with me of saving patients' lives when she worked in hospitals, mostly from rectifying mistakes that doctors made. She prided herself on her diagnostic skills, deservedly so.

"I almost wish his death couldn't have been prevented," I said. "It's easier to think that than to think it might have been avoided."

"It's very sad," she said. "He seemed like such a nice man."

"He was," I said.

"What a shame."

"Yeah." Death was now more present in the room than it needed to be, so I decided to broach a different but still potentially difficult subject instead. "I wanted to share a letter I got with you," I said, my throat tightening ever so slightly.

"What is it?"

"It's kind of a fan letter, but what's different is that it's from a kid who's having trouble coming out. It means a lot to me." I carefully monitored her face for any possible glimmer of resistance but didn't see any, so I pulled out the letter and handed it to her. It was typewritten by a seventeen-year-old kid named Shale who lived in Highland Park, an affluent Chicago suburb. He wrote some flattering things about my work in *Rent* and then went on to say:

I have been struggling with something for a while now, and I thought maybe you would be the person to talk to about it. I realized this year that I'm different, that I like boys, but I'm not entirely comfortable with it. People say it's a choice, but why on earth would I ever choose to be some way that society doesn't accept? I don't know anybody I can talk to about it. I hope maybe you can offer me some advice.

I watched Mom read the letter, her brow slightly furrowed but her face expressionless. When she was done, I said, "This is why I'm publicly out, so kids like Shale have someone to look up to."

"That's nice," she said, quietly.

Emboldened by her willingness to talk, I continued, "I really feel like this is part of my life's work, Mom." I'd never said anything like that, but in the instant that I said it, I knew it was true. "It's part of what I want to do with the time that I'm here. You know there are kids who are in much worse situations than Shale, whose parents kick them out of the house for being gay."

"I know, that's terrible. I'll never understand that."

"So if I can make a difference at all by talking openly about myself, I'm glad." As I said this, I kept waiting for Mom to object, or to shut down, but she didn't. She just regarded me, her eyes warm and a little sad.

"I think it's a good thing, Tonio," she said, still quietly, but sincerely. I squeezed her hand. I had been so prepared for this conversation to be difficult, for it to turn dark and fraught with tension, that I had to let down my guard and allow in the fact that it was going well. "People can be so cruel," she said. "A parent doing something like that to their own child."

"Yeah," I said. Relief was spreading through my body. "So anyway, I just wanted to share that with you. I wanted you to know about all of that."

"Well, thank you. It's very nice, Tonio."

On something of a roll, I decided to open up another potentially tricky subject, my relationship with Todd. I pulled out of my backpack a little folder I'd brought with me. "I wanted to show you these," I said and handed her the folder. Inside were two black and white portraits of Todd that I'd taken. "That's Todd."

She regarded them for a moment and then said, "He's so *dark*. He's like the opposite of you."

I smiled. "Yeah."

"He hasn't shaven," she said.

"He doesn't shave very much, no."

"He's cute," she said.

"Yeah," I said. "I wish you could meet him."

"I wish I could meet him too."

"He'd come for a visit, but I know that's not really possible."

Mom sighed a little. "No, I don't think so."

I sighed as well. "He told me to say hello to you and that he's thinking of you."

"That's nice."

I was happy that she was so willing to talk about Todd (and now that he and I had been solidly seeing each other for five and a half months it really was a bona fide relationship), but the reminder that she was in no condition to meet him encroached on my sweet mood. So I introduced another new subject, this one happier than the last.

"Can you tell me about my birth again?" I asked. It was almost my birthday, and I wanted to hear all of Mom's stories about my childhood again before she was gone.

"Sure, what do you want to know?"

"I don't know, the whole thing. Weren't you going to have me at home?"

"I almost did. But not because we'd planned it that way. Your labor was so short. You were an easy baby to have. You were ready to come out and you just came right out."

"And was my umbilical cord really that long?" I knew that it was, but I wanted to hear her say it again.

"It went all the way from me and down to the floor and up to you in the doctor's arms."

"Why was it so long?"

"They don't know. I think it's part of the reason why you're smart."

I smiled. "I don't know, why would that be?"

"Well, who knows?" She smiled. "And then the doctor put you in my arms and when I held you, you looked right at me, you looked right into my eyes. And I knew then and there that you were special."

It was nice to see her smile. I knew I was being self-indulgent, asking her to tell me all over again such lovely stories that I already knew, but she was enjoying herself as well. I had heard this story of my birth so many times that I felt I'd seen it played out in a movie. I even had an image of the obstetrician in my mind: a red-faced, middle-aged, chubby man with glasses, marveling at my impossibly long umbilical cord. I then saw the gauzy close-up of my radiant mother, sweaty but aglow from just having given birth, cradling the tiny pink version of myself, the two of us gazing lovingly into each other's eyes, as sweet music played in the background. And all was well with the world.

temper

.Back home in New York, the warm glow I'd felt from being in my mother's presence quickly faded, and into its place crept a nagging, raw, harsh edge. I was starting to fray, to grow tired of holding myself together night after night onstage, of staving off the low hum of dread and anticipation that I would soon get news that Mom had died. I was physically spent from the rigors of eight shows a week (with an almost impossible five of them in just three days on the weekends). I loved doing the show, and was grateful for having a job, which was already affording me a more comfortable life for myself than I'd ever known, filled with good food, good friends, and lots and lots of enthusiastic fans. But with all of the attendant stresses, I would grow impatient and irritable at the slightest provocation—in one instance, I had to restrain myself from nastily chewing out a deli counter clerk for being slightly less than attentive to the person in front of me.

Todd bore the brunt of my new bite.

"I need to talk to you about something," he said one afternoon before I had to leave for the theatre. "About what you said yesterday."

It didn't matter what it was that I'd said—I was now off and running. "I can't *do* this right now," I snapped.

And then he was off and running: "You never can. I can never talk to you about this stuff."

"My mother's *dying*, Todd." And as I said those words I knew I was playing a terrible, patently unfair trump card.

"I know she's dying, you think I don't know that?"

"Of course I think you know that."

"So I can't talk? So I have to be silent?" he said.

"Yes," I said, my eyes burning. "Yes. Just for right now. Just *right now*. This will be over but *right now* I can't handle it." My forceful voice and lashing hands scared me but I couldn't stop myself.

"You're asking me not to be *myself*," Todd said. "You're asking me to stifle myself."

"No I'm not, I'm asking you not to *come at me* with stuff. Not *now*."

"I have to be able to express myself, though," he said. "Or this isn't a relationship."

I knew in many ways he was right, but I couldn't say that. Instead I said, "Todd, I need you to just *be there* for me."

"But what about me?"

Fury leaped out of me. "This is *NOT ABOUT YOU RIGHT NOW!!!* This is about my mother who's dying—my *mother* who's *dying*—and I can't take it from you right now!"

"Then I can't be in this anymore," he said, his face darkening, his eyes hooded. "I can't give up myself like that."

"Fine, then go!"

"You'd really like that, wouldn't you."

"We have to stop this conversation, I can't have this conversation anymore, we have to *stop*, just *stop*."

And then I slammed the door and went off to the theatre and poured all of that rage and drama into the show; I sang my heart out and felt purged of the morass by the end of the night. And as much as I didn't want to fight with Todd, I couldn't bear the thought of being alone at this time with everything going on, I couldn't fathom facing it by myself. When I went home and saw Todd, he seemed to have forgotten whatever it was that he had wanted to talk about in the first place, and we were calm again. Later, as I lay with him, I knew that I couldn't keep hiding behind Mom's illness, I couldn't keep using that to prevent necessary conversations from taking place, but I didn't say that. He deserved more than I was able to give him, didn't he? But I also deserved a little more patience and understanding from him, didn't I? At the very least we could try to find a compromise. But these thoughts chased themselves around each other, not finding their way out, and I just lay there with my head on his chest, which had become my favorite position, and began to drift off to sleep.

During my next visit home, I tried to talk to Mom about my temper, which was beginning to frighten me.

"I get so angry sometimes, Mom," I said. As usual, my new openness with her caused my words to threaten to lodge themselves in my throat. I wondered if she could hear how small my voice sounded.

"Well, that's natural," she said.

"I have such a temper," I said.

"Well, it's okay. Just don't hurt anybody."

I was surprised to hear her talk about anger this way; she'd always had such a hard time allowing herself to get angry, and she'd come from a household in which her own mother's anger was often swift and toxic and violent and destructive. Mom had only really lost her temper with me on a couple of occasions, both of them during my adolescence. The first occurred when I was thirteen and gave her a brattily hard time about going to bed on time the night before a big speech tournament.

"You have to go to bed *now*," she'd said. She had cornered me right outside my room, her hands on her hips, her mouth set tightly, and her voice a little bit louder than normal, its pitch lower, its sound amorphous, like a muffled French horn.

"I can go to bed whenever I feel like it," I'd retorted. "You can't *make me* do anything I don't want to do." I knew how ridiculous I was being. But I hated—*hated*—Mom telling me how to live my life.

"Anthony, if you don't go to bed *right now* you're going to be in big trouble."

She had never really punished me, so I couldn't imagine what sort of big trouble I could be getting myself into. I couldn't resist smirking, nor could I resist saying, "I don't give a shit."

And with that, faster than I could see or move to stop her, Mom's left hand leaped from the side of her hip to connect with a stinging, shocking slap to my right cheek. She had never, *never*, laid a finger on me, aside from a couple of long-forgotten spankings I'd received as a toddler. I couldn't believe it, and as I stared her down, shaking my head, I heard myself say without thought, "If you *ever* do that again, I swear to god I'll slap you back." And I turned around into my room, slamming the door.

In our usual fashion, neither of us spoke of this fight, and I let it go. But a few months later, when we were living in New York during rehearsals for the play *Precious Sons*, I had grown restless with Mom's constant presence; I wanted to be an adult *now*, I didn't want to have to answer to her or have her follow me around the city—and I do mean follow. I took to walking very quickly down the street, leaving Mom huffing and puffing behind me as she implored me to slow down and walk with her. But I just ignored her and kept up my pace, not even looking at her when she occasionally caught up with me at a crosswalk.

In the text of *Precious Sons*, the mother and father, Bea and Art, constantly bicker, playfully putting each other down, until the playfulness turns sour and escalates to an all-out war. One of their more common exchanges in the play is:

> Bea: *Shut up, Art.*
> Art: *Oh, Bea, shut up yourself.*

Pretty basic and silly, but the rhythms of the play had seeped their way into my subconscious after I'd spent hours every day listening to the same bits of dialogue. During rehearsals for a play, the text often takes on the life of a song that I can't get out of my head, and I find myself parroting back phrases wherever they fit in conversations. One afternoon in the middle of the rehearsal period, I was reading a book in my bedroom while Mom was on the other side of the wall, in the living room, reading a book of her own. There were often long stretches of silence between us these days, but this stretch was broken with her voice wafting through my open door.

"Anthony, are you studying your lines?"

I put my book down and glared at the ceiling. I didn't *need* to be studying my lines; memorizing lines was always easy for me, and I was already mostly off book.

"No, I'm reading," I called out.

"Well, don't you think you should be studying your lines?"

"No, I don't, Mom." It was unusual for her to get all stage-motherish on me, but here she was doing it, and it pissed me off.

"I really wish you would do some work today."

"God, Mom, can't you just leave me alone?"

"Oh, shut up, Anthony," she said.

And I said automatically, with no thought, "Shut up yourself." And suddenly there she was, having stormed out of her seat into my room, and for the second time in my life she reached back and planted a giant slap on my face, on my left cheek this time. Before I knew what I was doing I reached out and slapped her back, hard, only I missed her face, hitting her glasses instead, sending them flying into the wall.

"I *told* you if you ever slapped me again I'd slap you back," I roared. Tears leaped to Mom's eyes, her chin crumpling, as she blindly groped for her glasses.

"I *told* you," I said again. And wordlessly, she fumbled her glasses back onto her tear-streaked face and left my room.

She never did slap me again, and, as usual, we didn't talk about the fight afterwards.

Eleven years later, in her bedroom in Joliet, sitting on her bed while holding her hand, as gentle classical music wafted through the room, I asked her if she remembered these fights.

"Well, yes, of course I do," she said. "They were very sad."

"I'm really sorry, Mom," I said.

"Oh, Tonio, it's okay. It was a long time ago."

"I'm sorry I was so mean to you during that time. I'm sorry I left you in the dust on the street."

"Oh, you were just going through a phase, I knew that."

"But still, it wasn't very nice of me."

"Well, it was hard, but I knew you were growing up and you needed your space and on some level I understood that. I didn't always like it. You were always such a sweet boy, so it was hard to see you lose some of that sweetness."

I sighed. "I'm sorry, Momma."

"But you're still a sweet boy."

"Lately I don't feel too sweet. I'm so on edge."

"Well, but that's natural. You're going through a lot right now."

I gulped slightly before I said, "And things have been hard with Todd."

I still didn't know how she'd respond to the subject of my relationship with Todd, but without missing a beat, she said, "Well, it sounds like Todd is very needy."

I was surprised that she was engaging so fully in the conversation. "I guess he is, but I've been hard to deal with lately, so it's not all him."

"Well, as I've tried to tell Annie over the years, the most important thing in a relationship is communication. Your dad and I needed a lot of help with that. And we didn't get the help we needed."

This was also new, to hear her talk openly about her relationship with Dad. And the serenity with which she was discussing all of this with me was also new; I didn't sense any of her usual discomfort. She continued to look at me steadily and hold my hand, exuding peace and patience and more than a little love.

"Do you think you guys might have stayed together if you'd had that help?" I asked.

"Oh, I don't know. We were both pretty young, and there's a lot of things we both could have done to try to make it work."

Another new piece of information. I'd never heard her take even partial responsibility for the divorce.

"Did you really love each other?" I asked, settling into the conversation more readily. It was much easier for me to ask questions of Mom than to reveal more of my own issues with Todd. And I knew that there wasn't going to be a lot more time to discuss all of these things with her.

Mom nodded slowly. "Yes, I think we did. He was very good to me, and I was very happy to be married, and I loved you kids so much, and he was always a nice man. But then we just started having problems."

"Have you talked to him lately?" I asked.

"Oh, he calls every once in a while to see how I'm doing. He never changes. Good old Doogles." Her teasing mangling of Douglas into Doogles had existed since I was a child. "He always says he's still learning."

I smiled. "Well, he is, though. What's wrong with that?"

Mom laughed. "He's been learning the same things over and over and over again. You'd think sooner or later he'd get it right." She sighed.

"Well, it's nice that he calls you," I said. I always felt the need to defend Dad to the other members of our family who were often hard on him, even though he sometimes drove me crazy as well.

"Yes, it's nice. He still doesn't know how to talk to me, though. He just rambles on and on."

Now it was my turn to laugh. "Yeah, but he's getting better at stopping the rambling if you tell him that he's doing it too much. You just have to get him back on track."

"Oh, I don't know, Tonio," Mom said. "I don't think he'll ever really change. He's not a bad guy, he's just sort of clueless sometimes."

"I guess."

I was happy that Mom had opened up to me. And as usual with these visits, lurking around the edges of the warmth I felt in her presence was the now-familiar dread that soon these moments would be gone.

Back in New York, back in the grind of eight shows a week, I rarely spent time in my apartment; I enjoyed running around like crazy, and I had little reason to be in my home except to get clean clothes, since I was still spending most nights at Todd's place, even though time with him was becoming increasingly difficult. But I still didn't like the idea of spending nights alone, with all that was going on, so I weathered our storms, and took solace in our occasional peaceful nights.

I still shared an apartment with my brother, but since we had upgraded to a slightly bigger place we now had two other roommates, and the four of us pretty much pulled our own weight, taking care of our personal space and whatever messes we might make in the common areas. For the most part, everyone was tidy and mellow, although my small room was becoming overrun by my ever-growing CD and book collections, and I longed for an apartment with more space and privacy.

Even though the mood was generally easygoing, Adam and I had had our share of roommate-style arguments over the years. But since I rarely saw him anymore we hadn't had a good fight in a while. One night when I got home from the show—a rare occasion when I was going to sleep in my own bed, since Todd and I were in the middle of a major tiff (there was that pattern again, of escalating fights with my boyfriends)—Adam came out of his room, his arms folded across his chest. An imposing figure at six-foot-three, he looked even scarier at the moment, with his large brow knitted and his imposingly chiseled jaw tightly set.

"We need to talk," he said. My pulse immediately quickened, and I faced him down in our narrow hallway.

"About what?"

"Where the hell have you been? You're never here."

"What do you mean?" His steady gaze felt like a blazing hot searchlight.

"It's like you're a fucking ghost, you're never here."

My voice started to rise in volume. "So *what*?"

"So it'd be nice if you pulled your own weight for once."

My fists clenched tightly. I was already set off and began to yell. "What the fuck are you talking about?!? I'm not even here, I'm not even doing anything to the apartment in the first place, so what's the fucking problem?!"

"That's exactly my fucking point. It'd be nice if you were here, if you took a little initiative, or something. If you made a little effort. You know, did a little something extra. It'd be a little bit of common courtesy. It wouldn't kill you."

I couldn't believe he was laying this on me. I started pacing, my voice getting more and more shrill, my chest tightening, my head pounding. "Where the fuck do you get off being the fucking head of household?!?"

"It's not just me, Anthony, Walt was bitching about it the other day, too."

This was something I *really* couldn't stand, to hear a complaint from someone other than the person complaining. "Well why the fuck doesn't he tell me himself?!?"

"Because you're never *here.*" Throughout the conversation, Adam's voice had not altered in volume, and he stood in the hallway impassively, his arms still folded, like a statue guarding a palace or temple. Losing control of myself, I kept pacing furiously, feeling the weight of this moment crushing down on top of all the other pressures and struggles of the last few months.

"Do you have any *idea* what my life is like right now?!?"

"How could I? I never see you."

In spite of myself, tears welled in my eyes. I fought off hyperventilation. Somewhere in the back of my mind was a rational, calm eye watching my hysteria, but I couldn't get a grip on myself. "I'm working my *ass* off, I'm working so *hard,*" I sobbed.

"Get off it, we're all working hard. You're nothing special."

And before I knew what I was doing, I charged at my brother and spastically whipped my fist into his shoulder as hard as I could, matching every word with a blow. *"Leave—me—the—fuck—alone."* He didn't move at all as I hit him, didn't try to stop me.

"You'd better calm down," he said.

My chest heaved. "Fuck you, leave me *alone,*" I said again. I charged away from him, my head spinning, and headed into my room for a second, then wandered down the hallway like a drunken moth.

"Why are you freaking out so much?" Adam said impassively.

"You have no *idea* what it's been like for me. I have no help anywhere, I'm doing it all *myself,* I'm exhausted—"

"What about Todd?"

"Todd is no fucking help, either, he just comes at me and *at me* all the *time* with all the things I'm not doing, and then I come home for once and *you* come at me—"

"I'm just trying to tell you what's going on here."

And there I was, leaping at him again, my fist pathetically plowing into his shoulder. Once again, he did nothing to stop me. "I can't *take* it right now, leave me alone, leave me alone, leave me *alone.*"

"Why are you freaking out so much? Calm down."

I flew away from him again, my mind racing, and I tried to find that quiet part of myself, but it was locked away and I was drowning drowning drowning. "I feel like I'm going to explode," I wailed. "I can't take anything more right now. Mom's dying, Mom's *dying,* and I can't do all of this, I'm sorry, but I can't, I can't."

"I know Mom's dying," Adam said. It was the first time such words had come out of him.

"I just have too much, I have too much to deal with right now," I said, my voice sounding and feeling foreign to me. "Please leave me alone. Please leave me alone. Please leave me alone."

Adam remained inert, his voice calm and clear. "Well maybe we should talk about all this so you don't keep freaking out," he said.

"I'm talked *out,*" I said. "I talk about it so much with so many people, I'm exhausted." That wasn't true; I didn't know why I was saying it.

"But you never talk to me about it."

And somewhere through my craziness it dawned on me that Adam was being as gracious to me as he'd ever been—he hadn't hit me back, he had offered to help, he had said he wanted to hear from me how I was feeling—and my pulse slowed.

"I mean," Adam said, "I'm going through the same things too, you know."

I stopped and leaned against the wall, gradually coming back down to earth. Tears still flowed, but they were slower and somehow truer now, no longer hysterical. "I'm sorry," I said. "I'm sorry."

"Maybe you needed to let off some of that steam."

"I just . . ." I began, and couldn't finish.

"It's okay, everybody freaks out sometimes."

"Yeah . . ." I said.

"Hopefully Todd can be more supportive."

"I don't know. I don't know sometimes," I said.

Adam looked at me steadily. "I just want to be able to talk to you, too," Adam said.

I could barely bring myself to look back at him, I felt so ashamed and sickened by the inanity and volume and violence of my outburst. "I'm sorry," I said again.

"I've never seen you like this before," Adam said.

"I'm sorry I hit you."

"Believe me, if it had hurt I would have stopped you. I would have clocked you."

I couldn't help but laugh a little.

"Sometimes people need to let off steam," Adam said. "You shouldn't keep it all bottled up."

I sighed. "You're right. I'm doing my best." But letting off steam was still a somewhat terrifying prospect; it could lead to disaster if left unchecked.

"Life sucks right now in a lot of ways," Adam said.

"Yeah."

"It sucks, what's happening with Mom. It sucks."

"Yeah," I said.

"I mean, we have no way of knowing what's going to happen, you know?"

"Yeah," I said.

"But you have to find ways to get this off your chest."

"Yeah," I said.

We stood there in silence for a long moment. My shame melted away and in its place emerged more love for my brother than I'd ever felt. We'd crossed over into a new world with each other. In spite of, or maybe in some ways because of, my brush with temporary insanity.

"Just talk to me when you want, okay?" Adam said. "There's no reason you have to let yourself get so burnt out."

I looked at him and nodded. "Thanks," I said.

"No problem."

holding fast

On my next visit home, I walked into the house and realized there was no eager Zelda panting and pawing at me as I opened the door. Of course—she was too much for the hospice workers to handle, so she'd had to go. I was sure that Mom missed her. And then I realized that there was no gleeful little Rachel running to give me a hug, either. Mom had mentioned during my last visit that Anne would take Rachel when the time came. Well, I guess the time had come. In their absence, the stillness of the house took on an almost holy quality, bathed in the sunlight streaming in through the glass patio door and the windows. I stood there and breathed in the quiet.

Tom, one of the hospice workers—a small, gentle, mild man with a dark mustache and slightly rumpled clothes—emerged out of the hallway and walked right up to me.

"Nice to see you, Anthony," he said. We'd met briefly, once before.

"Nice to see you, too."

"I knew you were coming home today. Mary didn't even have to tell me, and I knew. She was so up and happy when I got here." He smiled as he said it, but his words didn't sound right, at first. Mom was excited I was coming home? I thought my visits with her were always so serious, why would they be exciting to her? If I had still been the angelic boy she talked so fondly about, who wowed the crowds singing "Where Is Love?" at eight years old, I might have understood. But now? As an adult I'd brought her so much concern and worry and more than a little heartache that, without realizing it, I'd come to think she half-dreaded my visits.

"That's nice," I said.

"She's sleeping now—she just fell asleep—but I'm sure she'll wake right up when you go in."

"Thanks," I said.

Now Tom became slightly—only slightly—more serious. "I want you to know, if you need to talk about any of this, you are more than welcome to talk to me."

I nodded, not intending to open myself up to yet another person, but not wanting to blow him off, either. "Thanks, I will," I said.

"I know this must be very hard for you. So I just wanted to let you know I'm here."

I nodded again, feeling cornered by his kindness. "Thanks, I appreciate that."

"Well, I'll see you soon. Have a nice visit."

"I will." And I shook his hand and headed down the narrow hallway, the cheap floor creaking under the dingy carpet in the same spot it always had, and walked into Mom's room.

She lay on her back, her lips chapped and parted, her bony, nearly translucent hands splayed out at her sides. I realized that, in all these months of visiting her, this was the first time that I had been in her room while she slept. It was the first time I could just stand there and take in the ravaged shell that her body had become. I quietly seated myself in the recliner next to her bed and stared at her, listening to her shallow breath, watching her tiny chest rise and fall, rise and fall, and for the first time in all of these months, I saw, really *saw*, that all of her was no longer there. For the first time, I imagined what horror she must be experiencing every day, how impossibly hopeless she must feel as she lay day after day fixed to her bed, waiting for the phone to ring or some friend or loved one to drop by or for the nurse to take her vitals or change her dressings or empty her colostomy bag or refill her Demerol cartridge or feed her. How was she abiding this? And for the first time in all of these months, I sat next to my mother as she slept and I lowered my head into my hands and I wept, as quietly as I could, my face hot and slick with tears. This was not right, not at all, not any of it, not for her, not for anybody, but especially not for her.

As silently as I was attempting to weep, I couldn't stop myself from sniffling, which must have woken her up, because her meek voice called out, "Who's there?" And as soon as I heard her voice I clamped down on my tears, quickly wiped my face, and steadied my voice as much as I could—I didn't want Mom to know I had been crying. I didn't want her to feel she had to comfort me, since I was there to comfort her. Wasn't I?

"It's me," I said.

"Oh, hi, Tonio," she said. I stood up and clasped her hand, which had already reached toward mine. "I didn't know who it was at first."

"It's me, Momma," I said. She smiled, and I knew then that Tom had told me the truth: she was happy that I was there. I smiled back. "I didn't want to bother you while you were sleeping," I said. "I know you need to rest."

"Oh, I get plenty of rest," she said. "That's all I do, is get rest." She smiled ruefully. "I'm all rested up. This medication makes me so sleepy. That's why I try to keep it to a minimum." That's when I noticed a handwritten note on her Demerol cartridge: "Do NOT touch this without permission."

"Yeah, but if you need it," I said.

"I take as much as I need," she said. "But I hate to feel all sleepy and loopy. I don't like that."

"I understand." I sat then on the bed in what had sort of become my customary spot, careful not to jar the mattress too much or knock into her weak and sore legs. As I held her hand and she looked up at me, I hoped there wasn't any evidence remaining of my recent tears. We looked at each other in silence for a moment, not sure where to begin our conversation. I was curious how long Rachel and Zelda had been out of the house, but I feared that asking Mom about it would depress her, so I said nothing.

Breaking the silence, Mom asked, "So how are you? How's the show?"

"I'm fine," I said, relieved. "The show's going great still. Daphne's leaving, which is really sad."

"She is?"

"Yeah, she got a movie. I wish she wasn't going, but I know she has to do what she has to do."

"Well, she's very talented. All you guys are talented."

"Yeah . . ." I said. "Oh, the Clintons are going to come to the show."

"Really? That's exciting."

"Yeah. There's going to be all this security, and Secret Service sharpshooters on the roof. It's going to be pretty wild."

"I bet. That's wonderful."

"Yeah."

"So you get to meet the president," she said.

"Yeah. Apparently they're going to come up onstage after the show and we're supposed to line up and they're going to shake all of our hands and take pictures with us."

"You'll have to show me the pictures when you get them."

"Of course."

"This is all so exciting, Tonio," she said. "What a wonderful show, it's so nice that it's such a success."

"Yeah . . ." I was filled with a genuine happiness to be able to sit with Mom like this and give her updates on *Rent*'s success, but I also felt the pressure of the inexorable forward movement of time. How many topics, how many questions, could I cram into this moment? What could I think of now to ask, to say, since who knew how many more opportunities I'd have to do that?

She saved me from having to choose the topic, though. "So Joe wrote me a very crazy letter," she said. Joe was her brother, a manager of a Sizzler franchise who lived in southern Illinois with his wife and kids. Apparently in recent years he'd become something of a religious zealot, taking to wearing an oversized plain wooden cross fastened around his neck by thin twine. "He kept telling me to let go, that Jesus would come and take care of me." She did her best parody of his thick, slow, flat voice. " 'Let go, Mary Lee, let go!'" She rolled her eyes. "The card's right there, you should take a look at it."

I picked up the card and regarded the childish scrawl with which Joe had fashioned his message. There it was, with exclamation points and everything: LET GO!!! "That's crazy," I said.

"I don't hear from him or see him in months and months, and then suddenly out of nowhere, there he is, telling me to let go. It's almost like he wants to get rid of me." She smiled as she said that last bit, surprising me with her gallows humor. I found myself giggling with her.

Shaking my head, I put the card down. But even as Mom and I chuckled at Joe's over-the-top message, I wondered if there was any part of her that was thinking about taking his advice and letting go.

Later, I rifled through her closet—with her approval—looking through mementos of my career, which she'd kept in various cardboard boxes. She had always been better at such things than I, for which I was grateful. Embarrassing headshots of an eight-year-old bespectacled me gave way to old Playbills from the short-lived Broadway flop of *The Little Prince and the Aviator* (we previewed for two weeks and then closed, without ever performing an opening night). Underneath those were other clippings, including copies of the issue of *Seventeen* that featured me—along with my cast mates from *Adventures in Babysitting*—and an interview from when I was twelve, appearing in a

Milwaukee summer stock theatre production of *Oliver!* I recognized in the grainy picture accompanying that article a badly mauled haircut I'd given myself a few days before, which Mom had tried to fix to no avail. "Oh, *Tonio,*" she'd said as she amateurishly snipped away. "Look what you did to your beautiful *hair.*" I didn't know why I'd done it—it was one of my rare childhood moments of blatant rebelliousness.

As I flipped through more papers, I came across an audiocassette. I picked it up, surprised to see the call letters of our local radio station—WJOL—typed on the tape's label.

"What is this?" I asked.

"Oh, that? Don't you remember? We did an interview together when *Adventures in Babysitting* came out."

"Oh yeah . . ." Mom's memory had always been sharper than mine about most things, as this once again proved. But now it was coming back to me—the two of us sitting in a cramped and decidedly unglamorous studio in mostly deserted downtown Joliet on a hot summer day. My little claim to local glory, if it could be called glory—even when I went to see *Adventures in Babysitting* at the Louis Joliet Mall, I had to pay for my ticket, and the ticket taker and rest of the staff had no idea I was in it. This being my first movie, I didn't know that such experiences would continue to be the case in years to come.

"Can we listen to it?" I said. It was one other thing I wouldn't be able to share with her when she was gone, and I wanted to seize the moment while I could.

"Sure."

I popped it into her boom box and turned it up. As we listened I was struck by how much firmer and stronger and deeper and more substantial her voice sounded on the tape than it did now. I sounded young, but I also seemed to be trying to talk with as low a register as possible, to sound like a serious actor.

"Oh, I've always been very proud of him," Mom said on the tape. I watched her listening to herself and wondered how she felt being confronted with a time and place before this illness had begun to stalk her.

I sounded cocky. "I really want to move to New York and just keep working as an actor," I said. "I'm really primarily a theatre actor, and that's where I have to be." I laughed now. Yes, those things were true, but did I have to be so *serious* about it then? Couldn't I have lightened up a little? I remembered the huge chip on my shoulder I'd had about Joliet, which had only somewhat faded.

"Well, we'll see about when he's moving to New York," Mom said on the tape, trying to sound lighthearted. It had been a point of conflict between us—I had been all ready to just pack up and go, and she had wanted me to finish my high school career in Joliet. At the time of the interview, I had only my senior year left, but I was so ready to get the hell out.

The interviewer asked a few more innocuous questions and thanked us, and that was that. I stopped the tape and realized I'd been holding Mom's hand. Her expression seemed more melancholy than it had before the tape began. I wondered if it had been a mistake to bring it out, to remind her of everything.

"That was interesting," I said.

"Yeah," she said. "I was never comfortable being in the spotlight."

"But you handled yourself well," I said. "You sounded comfortable."

"Well, I don't know. I'm just a normal person. I'm just your mom."

Back in the closet I came across my baby book. It was white with "Baby's Milestones" written in sparkly silver letters on the front, underneath a simple line drawing of a bouquet of roses. I flipped through it briefly. It was packed with pictures and cards and page after page of Mom's impeccable handwriting, recording every detail of my early years.

At 8 ½ months Anthony is very bright and sociable. He can pat-a-cake, wave bye-bye, do so big, and shake his head 'no-no' appropriately.

At 9 mos. winks and blows kisses.

At 15 mos. is a real climber—so fearless and so brave. He fell twice and cut his tongue one day and his lip the next.

At 19 mos. 2 days Anthony climbed out of his crib for the first time (darn!) He was very proud.

"You can keep it if you want," Mom said.

"I'd love to."

"I want you to have all of that stuff in there," she said. I looked at her from my spot on the floor of her closet. Her eyes were clear and solemn and peaceful. Her voice gave no trace of sentimentality. This was just part of what she had to do now; relinquish her hold on her things, give them up to whom she chose. "And if there's anything else of mine that you want, you have to let me know, okay, Tonio?".

I sat silently for a moment. I was glad she was brave enough to say this, that she was dealing with everything head-on, but I didn't want to make this decision. I looked around the room.

"I want to give Adam first choice on the books," she said. "That's something he told me he'd like."

"That makes sense," I said. "He's reading so much now."

"But let me know if you want anything."

"Well, I said," my eyes falling on her Bose radio, "I think I might like to have your radio."

"That's fine," she said.

"I know how much you love it," I said. "And I love music so much."

"I know you'll appreciate it."

"Yeah." I then got up, still holding the baby book, and sat next to her once more on the bed, holding her hand. Her eyes held mine. We hadn't looked at each other this much since I was a little child.

On the flight back to New York, amid the antiseptic gray and blue interior of the plane, I pulled out my baby book and started reading it, and before I knew what was happening, hot tears poured out of my eyes and my breath started coming in gasps. Out of the corner of my eye, I half saw a flight attendant walking toward me, and I quickly averted my face, staring out the window at the pure blue sky and the rolling white clouds below. The baby book held so much love, so much care and concern and effort and work and hope. The enormity of Mom's love and the gift it had bestowed on me and the terrible truth that for so long I had in many ways squandered that love, all of these things collided and spread over and through me, pressing into my chest, flooding my eyes with tears. As I choked back great, gulping sobs among strangers on an airplane, I felt horribly exposed but also surprisingly safe. I was in a different dimension, thirty-five thousand feet above the earth, where it seemed for a moment that anything was allowed.

When the tears subsided, I continued staring out the window, my breath settling, my throat releasing its gigantic lump. I watched the clouds drifting by, calm now, cleansed, marveling at the power of these moments, their sudden, almost violent ability to overcome me, and their subsequent evaporation, as if they never had happened at all but for the peace and clarity that they left in their wake.

taking leave

The day the Clintons came to the show in April 1997, we all had to march through metal detectors and pass by numerous Secret Service agents stationed throughout the building, including the backstage and dressing room areas. Apparently there were snipers on nearby rooftops in case anyone tried anything foolish.

Almost a year into our Broadway run, it had become commonplace for cast members to take time off, but not on this day. No one wanted to miss being a part of this command performance.

We were in our offstage positions, ready to go on, when the Clintons arrived. The entire audience gave them a rousing standing ovation, complete with whoops and cheers and whistles. When everyone finally settled down, I marched out onstage with the rest of my fellow cast members and took my customary spot front and center.

The show began as usual with the house lights fully illuminated, so we had a clear view of the audience, and I quickly scanned the seats until I found the president and his family. There he was, right on the aisle of the sixth row, his chin resting in his hand, his eyes alert. An electric surge coursed through my spine and lingered in my fingers—after hundreds of performances, I was once again more than a little nervous.

And I began.

Throughout the show, periodically, I glanced over to see if I could tell how the Clintons were responding. And I can't say that I could—Bill sat in the same position the entire time, his chin in his hand, Hillary was straight-backed and alert, and Chelsea was the same. Earlier in the run, when Tom Cruise and Nicole Kidman had come, we had all remarked backstage that Tom was beaming from his seat, glowing like the superstar that he was. Bill, on the other hand, didn't seem unhappy, but didn't seem to be aglow either.

We'd been told before the show began that we were to line up at the end of the performance, that the Clintons would walk onstage and do a quick meet-and-greet, and then be whisked away. The whole event was to take about five minutes.

So after the last chords of the finale rang out, after we sang our last *"No day but today,"* after the curtain call and the screaming of the audience, we dutifully created our receiving line. One by one, the Clintons made their way to each of us. Bill was taller than I'd imagined and incredibly charismatic, with a palpable gravitational pull that drew me to bask in his presence. He shook my hand warmly and said, "Thank you for your performance," smiling and looking me right in the eye. When Hillary shook my hand, I said, despite my embarrassment at being cheesy, "We share a birthday." She smiled and responded, "Well, I'm honored." Chelsea was poised and even glamorous, unlike her reputation. A couple of her friends had tagged along, each of them well-coiffed, well-dressed, and articulate.

Surprisingly, the Clintons lingered. Either we had been misinformed as to what we should expect, or they had liked the show so much that they wanted to hang out with us all the more (an explanation I liked to believe). They spent a good half hour onstage, mingling, chatting, and posing for pictures. I decided that I wanted to say something of substance to the Leader of the Free World, so I made my way over to Bill when he was between conversations and said, "I just want to thank you for the work you've done on behalf of the gay and lesbian community." He'd received some criticism for not doing enough, and while I agreed with that criticism to a point, I still felt quite sincerely that he had done so much more than any previous president had, and I wanted him to know that I appreciated it. He replied in his soft drawl, "Well, thank you, but there's so much more to do." I said, "Yes, but you've done a lot." And I believe that he appreciated my saying so.

I spent my next three weeks at the theatre in anticipation of Daphne's imminent departure. She was the first of the original cast to be leaving, which didn't seem fair or right, since she was one of the three of us who had been with the show from the beginning. But I refrained from trying to convince her to stay, from telling her how part of me was angry that she was leaving so soon. It was her choice, after all, and her prerogative, and who was I to argue?

I tried to drink in and remember every moment of her performance night after night. We didn't share that many scenes, but I had the privilege of sitting onstage and watching her heartbreaking rendition of "Without You" every night, with her wonderfully raspy voice sailing through the theatre, her arms reaching out, groping for some kind of solace. I listened to her attack "Out Tonight" with increasing fire and abandon, seeing in my mind's eye her daredevil assault on the bars and staircase of the fire escape that led from Mimi's loft to Mark and Roger's. I stood helplessly by as she broke down and cracked her heart wide open in "Goodbye Love." And I held her ever more tightly as I carried her into our apartment in the finale, laying her down gently, and standing off to the side as Adam's Roger sang of his love for her.

As the days wore on, I became all the more grateful that the line *"Thank God this moment's not the last"* was true, for the moment, anyway.

On Daphne's last night, Jesse was fighting a flu, so he wasn't in the show with us, a cruel twist of fate that prevented all of us from sharing in her final moments together. The cast and crew and producers and Michael and Tim and everyone else in the building who could fit crammed into our tiny, unglamorous basement greenroom before the show for a champagne toast. Daphne was alert, tightly wound, like a tiger, staving off the brewing emotions that were no doubt lurking just below her surface. She and Mimi had always shared a fierce resolve, a pitched effort to be strong at all costs, which made her vulnerability, when it did show through, all the more poignant. But she didn't seem ready to show that vulnerability here and now. If she had, I don't think any one of us would have been able to stem the tide of sadness that would have overwhelmed us. Instead, we all solemnly held aloft our plastic cups of weak champagne and toasted our friend and colleague, who said, "To Jonathan," before she downed her glass in one quick gulp.

As had happened on so many nights, the show took off like a rocket, riding stratospheric currents of unstoppable energy and heart and commitment. Familiar faces filled the audience. Todd was right in the front row, flashing his smile and sign-language "I love you" to me (we were in the midst of a pretty good spell without a lot of fights lately, and he had become an extended member of the *Rent* family, so it was vital that he be there to witness what was really the passing of an era). Cy was in the middle of the orchestra, her proud beaming face a beacon of love and support reflecting back at us. Jonathan's parents were right next to her, a complex blend of stoicism and fulfillment. And there were lots of regular Rentheads scattered through the front two rows, some gripping each other's hands in anticipation of what they knew would be a heady and heartbreaking evening.

We powered through "Rent" with more than our usual explosiveness, making every note, every gesture, every moment matter. The audience's outlandishly enthusiastic screams at the end of the song matched our efforts.

Habitually, I would head down to the greenroom during "One Song Glory" and "Light My Candle," but not on this night. The entire cast and crew hovered in the wings to witness the last time Adam and Daphne enacted their sweet and funny and sexy introduction to each other, and we cheered with the audience when it was over.

On and on through the night, I stole every chance I could to watch and witness this closing of a chapter in my long association with this show that I loved so much. Daphne's performance that night was a pitch-perfect mixture of willpower and sexuality and desperation, peppered by that steely exterior of hers. But by the time "Without You" came around, her veneer of strength was beginning to crack along with her voice, and it took every ounce of resolve I had not to crumple.

Daphne had lost her mother to illness years ago, and often during the run of the show she would turn to me offstage and just check in with me. "How are you doing, Papi?" she would say, and I knew she was asking specifically about how I was doing with regard to my mom, without actually saying those words. "I'm okay," I would reply, and that was usually the extent of our conversations about the subject. But just the knowledge that she knew something of what it was like, that she was aware enough to reach out to me in that way, had provided such comfort. And I couldn't bear to see that go.

Nor could I bear to witness Adam losing her. Their bond was so strong, so full of deep and abiding love and respect for each other. They had carried each other through this incredible journey, on and offstage. On this last night of Daphne's run, when she as Mimi lay dying in front of him and he reached for his guitar to begin playing and singing his farewell song "Your Eyes" to her, I held my breath—everyone onstage and in the theatre seemed to as well—when he couldn't bring himself to begin the song, but instead bowed his head for endless and tormented seconds, unable to begin saying his last goodbye to his beloved. The entire theatre was absolutely silent in that impossibly full and painfully arrested moment, watching him breathe and gather his strength, until at last, at last, he lifted his head, plucked out his tentative notes, and somehow through his tears sang his lament.

shifting
ground

On May 5, 1997, my next visit home, I lingered longer than usual at the health food store on my way to Mom's house; I didn't want to see how much worse she had gotten in the weeks since my last visit. I needlessly wandered the small store's aisles, knowing that there was nothing for me to get that I hadn't already gotten, knowing that the clock was ticking on the time I'd be allotted to spend with Mom before her final moments, which seemed to be arriving soon. And yet I couldn't bring myself to walk out of the shop and get in my rental car and drive the last couple of miles to her door.

Finally, I paid for my nondairy vegetarian frozen dinner and my chips and my juice, and I headed home, numbly staring at Essington Road as it spread out ahead of me. At the corner of Essington and Black Road I noticed for the first time a large new prefab building made of blond brick, the sign for which told me it was a funeral home. I wondered whether that would be Mom's funeral home.

Spring had arrived in Joliet with full force, bringing balmy

235

breezes and clear blue skies and myriad buzzing insects and singing birds. Gael Drive looked almost picturesque on days like this, were it not for the drab uniformity of its houses' architecture, and the too-wide, unseemly expanse of its cracked and faded pavement. I pulled into our driveway and cut the engine, pausing in the car before I got out, steeling myself as much as I could without creating too hard a shell.

"Hello," I called out as I opened the door. I put away my groceries and headed to Mom's room. There I found Terry, one of Mom's hospice workers, beginning to shampoo Mom's hair. She smiled as I walked in.

"Hi there," she said. A small plastic bin filled with water rested on the bed next to Mom's pillow, and her head was gently propped up by another bin, there to catch the sudsy rinse. Mom regarded me as steadily as always, her large brown eyes looking even larger without her glasses on, the effect of which was augmented by the tightness of her skin over her skull. She weakly said, "Hi, Tonio," as Terry softly massaged shampoo into Mom's hair. I sat at the edge of her bed and watched, holding Mom's hand. Terry went about her task with care, tenderness, and love, and Mom simply gave herself over to the comfort. I looked up at Terry's face and noticed that she was crying softly as she finished rinsing the last of the suds out of Mom's sparse, thin hair. I wondered whether she felt such sadness for all of her patients, or whether Mom was special.

When Terry was finished she kissed Mom delicately on the top of her head, wiped her eyes, and said to me, "Have a nice visit," before she left the two of us alone.

"Hi, Momma," I said.

"Hi, Tonio." I wondered whether there was any part of her that was ashamed that she couldn't perform the simple task of washing her own hair. "How was your flight?"

"Fine," I said. "How are you feeling?"

"Oh, I'm tired," she said.

"I can imagine."

"I'm glad you're here, though."

"Me too, Momma," I said. "Me too." She seemed to be farther away than before, less tethered to her body. I gripped her hand tightly, but not so tightly, I hoped, that I caused her pain. "Momma," I said, "I wanted to ask you something."

"What is it?"

"Remember how I told you about the wall at the Nederlander?"

"Yes."

"I was wondering if you could write something for it, so I could put what you wrote there."

"Of course," she said.

The wall had begun early in our previews on Broadway, when celebrities had started to attend our show. Our doorman had decided to ask them to sign the alley wall that led to the stage door. They obliged, and right away, the cast extended the invitation to friends and family as well. Now, over a year after opening, barely any empty space remained. Since Mom had only come to the show on opening night, in the flurry of activity before and after the performance, I had forgotten to bring her backstage to sign the wall. Now I could laminate whatever she wrote and affix it to the concrete.

I noticed a small stationery box on her bedside table. "Maybe you could write on the inside of this," I said. "It's sturdy."

"Sure," she said.

I carefully cut open the flaps of the box and handed it to her.

"I have to write with this pen," she said, pointing to an oversized, extremely light pen resting on her bed tray. I handed it to her.

"Thanks, Momma," I said, and I rose off the bed so I wouldn't be hovering over her. I sat on the floor in front of her large bookcase, busying myself by looking through her collection: Anne Tyler, Raymond Carver, Barbara Kingsolver, and shelves full of others. I wondered how many of them she had read. One of her favorite T-shirts had the words SO MANY BOOKS, SO LITTLE TIME emblazoned on it.

For many minutes I sat there, occasionally glancing back at Mom to see how she was doing. She was lost in concentration, focused entirely on her note. I envisioned taking it to a laminator and proudly sealing it to the wall, sharing what she'd written with my cast mates and friends who would stop by the theatre. It seemed to be taking her an especially long time; she must have had a lot to say. Finally, as I was flipping through her copy of *Ellen Foster,* I heard her quietly say, "Okay, Tonio, I'm done."

I eagerly got up and headed over to her bedside and took the piece of cardboard out of her hand. And as soon as I looked down at what I held, I saw that she hadn't taken so long to write it because she'd had a lot to say; she had taken so long because it had been a physically draining and difficult task. Her normally pristine handwriting had been reduced to almost illegible, wavering scribbles. I gasped, the heat rising in my face; I had not thought that what I was asking her to do would be this difficult. I felt selfish and inconsiderate, stupid and ignorant. And then I read what she had written.

Dear Anthony,

My heart is filled with so much joy, pride and happiness in this wonderful production that you truly deserve to be an important part. I can't express the joy in my heart I felt when you stepped onstage on opening night and let us have what you have to give to the audience. I've dreamed of this for you and knew you would achieve it. I'm also happy you were a part of the show from the onset to opening night.

All our trips to Chicago in our "beaters" were fun because you are fun, full of interesting info.

As your Mom, I felt like my heart could go up to the ceiling giving off spangles of light and gold stars. I know good things will come to you and that you'll honor them with your talent. AND I'LL ALWAYS BE WITH YOU! I LOVE YOU FOREVER.

MOM

By the time I got to the end, tears had sprung to my eyes, my breath had tightened, and before I knew it, I was gripping my mother's hand tightly, while turning my face away. "Thank you," I said through my sobs. "Thank you so much."

She just gazed at me with peace and love and stillness. "You're welcome, Tonio," she said. I looked at her, unable to stop my tears, and as she held her gaze, she gently raised her free hand and ever so lightly rested it on my forehead, softly stroking my hair. She didn't say anything more. She just watched me as I wept, holding my hand and soothing my brow. I had been so afraid of letting go in front of her, of burdening her with my sorrow, but of course my weeping wasn't a burden to her. She was my mother, and this was one of the things mothers were supposed to do: provide comfort and love to their children when they were in pain.

"Thank you," I said again.

Later, Roberta stopped by. She enveloped me in a bear hug in the kitchen. I hadn't seen her since *Rent*'s opening night on Broadway, although we'd spoken a couple of times since then when I'd wanted to know how Mom was doing without asking Mom herself. Roberta and her husband, Bob, had moved from Southern California to a Chicago suburb a couple of years ago to be closer to Mom after she got sick, and Roberta had become Mom's primary caretaker, as well as assuming the role of executrix of Mom's small estate.

"How are you holding up?" I asked her.

"Okay." Her big eyes were wider than normal and a little hollow, but strength was, as always, emanating from them. "I'm going to see how our Mary Lee is doing."

When she left the kitchen I stood there, not sure what to do in this house that had been mine but no longer felt like mine. Especially with its pervasive, stifled air of illness. Restless, I grabbed the phone and checked my messages, discovered there were none, and then found myself staring at the wall. I thought about calling Todd, but, even though we were in a relatively calm moment together, I never knew how he would be on the other end of a phone, so I decided against it.

Mom slept the rest of the day, and I spent some time just sitting with her, watching her shrunken chest softly rise and fall with her shallow breath. I gazed at the bone tumor that had emerged on her forehead, just below her hairline, her pale skin taut and shiny over the bump. I considered her Demerol pump for long moments, and contemplated disobeying her handwritten sign and pushing the button. I rose and looked at the plastic bag that was collecting her urine, lashed to the end of her bed. The urine looked dark and murky. What did that mean? I wondered whether she was dreaming, and whether her dreams were drug-addled fantasies or calm visions of what might be waiting for her in the next life, if there was a next life. Or was her body so wrapped up in its battle against her disease that it could spare no energy for dreaming or anything else, leaving her in a state of total blankness?

I wanted desperately, selfishly, to be there by her side for her final moments. To live that dramatic deathbed scene from so many movies with her, where I would tell her I loved her one last time before she closed her eyes forever, and I would watch her breathing slow and slow and slow and then stop, and I would witness that beautiful transcendent moment when a soul leaves its body. I could practically hear the orchestral accompaniment. I wanted to have that experience with my mother, with all of its melodrama and beauty.

And I wanted this to happen sooner rather than later. How much longer could she possibly hold on? She had already confounded everyone's expectations by living for over four years after her initial diagnosis. Her mind even seemed to be starting to slow down. All signs were pointing to the end. So what was she waiting for?

The next morning after I awoke, I went to her room and sat next to her for a long while. She barely stirred, even when I said hello and squeezed her hand. She seemed to be smaller and smaller every time I looked at her.

"Momma?" I said, louder than before. "Momma?"

Her eyes finally opened, taking a long time to focus. "Hi, Tonio." Her voice was faint.

"I want to stay," I said, not knowing before I said it that it would come out of my mouth. She looked at me and considered this. What I didn't say, but what I think she knew I meant, was *I want to stay because I think you are about to die, and I want to be here when you do.*

"Are you sure you can?" she said.

"Yeah," I said. "My understudy can go on for me. I want to stay, Momma."

She blinked slowly several times.

"All right," she said.

I took a deep breath. "Do you want me to call Adam and have him come home now?" What I didn't say was *Maybe if Adam comes home, and he and Anne and Rachel and I are all here with you, maybe then you will finally be able to say goodbye and let go.*

She looked away, her brow furrowed, and said, "I don't know."

"Don't you want to see him again?"

"Yes . . ."

I tried to swallow down the guilt that was now crowding its way into me as I pressed forward; I was uneasy with the idea of forcing my mother's hand in her own death. But I kept on with it anyway, trying to engineer as much of an opportunity as possible for the end to arrive. "He can come as soon as you want him to, Momma."

She looked at me again, and I felt keenly that she knew what I was saying. She blinked slowly, holding me in her gaze, then blinked again, the vein in her forehead pulsing, her eyes so sad. And then finally, she said quietly and clearly, "Okay."

When I left her to sleep some more, I braced myself against the wall of the hallway as a fresh wave of tears flowed out of my eyes. I had bawled so much already—wouldn't all these fucking endless tears eventually get used up? Wiping my face, trying to control my breathing, and without thinking, I stumbled to the phone in the kitchen and dialed Friends In Deed, asking for Cy.

"This is Cy."

"Cy, it's Anthony," I said, managing to speak around my sobs.

Her voice became low and intense. "How are you?"

"I don't know," I said, my words tumbling out. "I'm home and my mom seems like she's going, it seems like it might be the end, maybe, and I thought I was ready, but I don't know . . ."

"Is she conscious?"

"Yeah, she's conscious, but I don't know, she seems like she's fading, and I can't stop crying, you know? I just can't stop crying. I feel like my heart is breaking, like it's breaking out of my chest." I sighed deeply. "It's so *hard*."

"Yes," Cy said. "It is hard. But that's what hearts do," she said. "They break. But if you let them, they break open."

I caught my breath, trying to let in what she was saying, concentrating on her soft, soothing voice. "Yeah," I said.

"That's what's happening to you. Your heart is breaking open. You have to let that happen. Don't stand in its way."

"I don't know," I said. "I don't know if I can do that."

"Of course you can," she said. "It's already happening. There's nothing more you have to do except let it continue. The only way out is through."

"What do you mean?"

"There will be another side to this, I promise you, but you can only get there by going through what you're going through. It might not seem like that's possible right now, but trust me, it is. The only way out is through."

I rested my head against the wall as I listened to her lovely, calm voice, and twisted the phone cord in my hand. I breathed in, swallowed, and managed to say, "Okay."

"Just take good care of yourself, and be there for your mother. That's all you have to do. That's all you can do."

"Okay," I said again.

"Your heart is just pouring out some of the love that's in there. That's all that's happening. You have a lot of love in there. You will come through to the other side of this."

"Okay," I said again. "Thank you, Cy."

"Anytime, honey. I hope you know that. Anything you need, you let me know."

We said goodbye, and then it was a matter of calling Adam and arranging his travel. I was relieved to have a task to focus on.

"I think she's going," I said to Adam, trying to maintain my composure.

"Are you sure?" His voice was steady.

"Well, I don't know, but I asked her if she wanted you to come home, and she said yes."

He sighed. "Okay," he said.

Fifteen minutes later, I sat across from a travel agent, my eyes raw, my nerve endings ablaze, watching as she clicked away at her keyboard looking for a reasonable last-minute fare for Adam. A bereavement fare, it was called. I might need to supply some sort of a note from a doctor, she told me; she'd have to check into that. She was chipper and efficient, and her chipperness, which would usually be a comfort, set me on edge. Didn't she realize the magnitude of the reason she was booking this travel? Couldn't she tell I was sitting across from her in extreme pain?

As she was typing, I heard the opening chords of R.E.M.'s "Everybody Hurts" piped in over the office radio, and it took everything I had not to break down right there at the travel agent's desk. I was turning into a sentimental fool, unable to function normally. I had to get ahold of myself. But Michael Stipe's reedy, expressive voice had never felt more resonant, his words more true.

I picked Adam up from O'Hare, relieved to be out of the oppressively silent house, grateful to have another task to accomplish. Adam's huge six-foot-three frame looked absurdly comic emerging from the jetway. We gave each other a brief hug and said our hellos, saying little else on the trip home.

Late that night, when Mom and Adam were asleep—my brother slept so much when he came home, as if the atmosphere in the house was infused with opium that affected only him—I finally decided to call Todd and tell him what was happening. While I dialed his number, my stomach locked up in dread. I listened to the rings and hoped for a helpful response.

"Hi, honey," he said. He seemed to be in a good mood. That was a relief.

"I just wanted to tell you I'm going to stay longer," I said. I braced myself to hear how disappointed he was; he often resented my being away from home, away from him, even for important reasons. "I think it's near the end," I said.

But he wasn't disappointed. Or if he was, he didn't say so. "I'm sorry, sweetie," he said. "I'll take care of the cats, you don't have to worry."

I'd been steeled for a bad reaction, so I had to adjust to what I was hearing. "Um, great," I said. "Thanks."

"Just be there for her," he said.

"I will." Disarmed by and grateful for this lovely moment of kindness from him, I stuffed down tears. It was these moments, and my hope that they would become more common, that sustained me through our rockier times. I said, "I love you, honey."

"I love you, too," he replied.

Later that night I still couldn't sleep, so I busied myself with responding to e-mails. As I sat at the kitchen table in the middle-of-the-night silence of Mom's house, listening to the low hum of the refrigerator, basking in the glow of my laptop's screen, I felt the return of my old sense of productivity and comfort. Night had always been my favorite time when I lived at home; there was no one to bother me, nothing to heed but my own will.

I became centered and clearheaded as I typed, glad to get caught up, glad to keep the connection to my life in New York alive. But in a pause in my finger's rhythm, I heard a tiny sound from very far away. I froze. It was muffled and high-pitched, a plaintive cry that I realized was coming from Mom's room. I leaped out of my chair, my heart thudding, and her words reached me as I headed to her room.

"Somebody? Somebody? Help? Somebody?"

I made it to her doorway, where in the moonlight I could make out her darting eyes, and her bony hands clutching at her bedspread. I rushed to her side.

"Momma, I'm here," I said. "I'm here. What's the matter?"

"I'm . . . thirsty . . ." she gasped.

"Here," I said, grabbing her sippy cup, a curly straw poking out of its spout. "Here you go, Momma." I gently lifted up her head and brought the straw to her lips, which clamped down desperately on the straw. Her eyes were huge as she gulped the water down. She barely registered my presence. She swallowed, breathed, then slurped some more.

"You okay?" I asked.

She nodded, her eyes still wide, looking more at the ceiling than at me. I eased her head back down to her pillow, tucked her quilt up to her chin, and smoothed her brow.

"Thank you," she whispered.

"Whatever you need, Momma, I'm here." My adrenaline was still firing through my veins, my heart only now slowing its crazy pace. "Go to sleep, Momma," I said.

I stayed with her for a while, until I was sure she was asleep, my fingers lightly stroking the tightened and shiny skin of her forehead.

Word spread throughout Mom's massive family that she seemed to be on her way out, and over the next few days more and more relatives descended on the house. It was a pilgrimage to a deathwatch. Grandma, whom I hadn't seen since Anne's wedding, was the first, accompanied by Diana, her shadow-daughter. Both of them were stoic and firm, their features pointy and formidable. Joe was next, his comically large wooden cross flopping against his chest, his tinted glasses above his sad mustache giving him the air of a guest star on an episode of *CHiPs*. One day Grandma brought Amy, whose sad-sack face was even sadder, and they lumbered into Mom's room to sit silently and watch Mom's labored breathing. Chris made it down from Wisconsin, his kindly, bearded face struggling to contain his fear and grief as he walked through the door.

I felt as though I had to defend against an invasion. Even though this wasn't my home anymore, even though I had hardly been here at all, especially compared to Roberta and Anne, I was strangely territorial. I didn't want Grandma and Diana and Joe to take up any of the time Mom had left. Grandma especially; she had caused Mom such heartache over the years. I avoided her presence, afraid of what I might say, what might spill out of my mouth. My edges were so raw, I knew I would have very little self-control.

And then one afternoon we were all in the living room, a group of silent zombies, not talking about why we were all there, none of us having the guts to bring up the words "Mom" or "death," let alone both in one sentence. The television was on, and Grandma, Diana, Mom's hospice worker, Terry, Joe, and I were dumbly staring at it. I was sitting as far away from Grandma as possible, crammed on the floor between the window and an easy chair, huddled down like a fugitive.

Oprah was on, and her guest was Ellen DeGeneres. Ellen had recently come out publicly, which had made huge headlines and garnered huge ratings for her sitcom, and Oprah was talking to her about all of this and about her relationship with her girlfriend, Anne Heche.

From across the room, I heard my grandmother say, "What are they talking about?" She had trouble hearing.

Terry said, very matter-of-factly, "Ellen DeGeneres is talking to Oprah about coming out as a lesbian."

Grandma screwed her face up. "Well, she's a person, but—"

And before I could stop myself, I shouted across the room, "But what? She's a person but *what*?"

Grandma looked stunned for a second, then said, "But why does she have to talk about it? It's private."

I wasn't going to stop now that I had gone toe to toe with her. "People talk about their husbands and wives all the *time,*" I said.

Grandma glanced around the room, looking for support, but everybody else remained silent. Then she sort of shook her head and muttered, "Well, that's why I don't watch talk shows. Private things should be kept *private.*"

Restraining myself, I got up and went into my room, my blood pumping, proud of myself for speaking up, although embarrassed to have done it in such a forum, and disappointed that I hadn't taken it further, that I hadn't annihilated the enormous elephant in the room: my failure to openly acknowledge my own sexuality to Mom's extended family. If they were going to make a scene at Mom's funeral about Todd being there, I knew I would not be able to restrain myself then.

Later that day, after Grandma and the others had left, I sat with Mom. Her room was so quiet, her chest's movements so tiny.

I said to her, "Momma, I think I know what song I want to sing at your memorial." I didn't know whether she could hear me. She seemed almost comatose. Lightly and tenderly, I began to sing:

> *I am waiting for the light to shine*
> *I am waiting for the light to shine*
> *I have lived in the darkness for so long*
> *I am waiting for the light to shine*

It was a song from *Big River,* a show we had enjoyed together over the years. I held her hand as I sang, knowing she probably had no idea what was happening, knowing this would probably be the last time she'd hear me sing, if she could hear me at all. And when I was done, she squeezed my hand ever so slightly, and then she faintly smiled and said, with her eyes closed, "That's nice."

I kissed her forehead. "I'm glad you like it, Momma," I said.

The next night, Roberta stayed behind when the others left, and she, Adam, and I opened a bottle of wine and went through some of Mom's personal effects. Mom was a great keeper of mementos, so there were many boxes in the basement crammed with letters, cards, and assorted knickknacks. We huddled on the floor together, sipping our wine, the musty cardboard boxes strewn around us.

"Look at all this *crap,*" Roberta said, laughing.

"I know," I said, also laughing. I felt giddy, on my way to a slight buzz. We passed around items of particular interest, such as home-made Mother's Day cards a preadolescent Anne had given to Mom and drawing after drawing Adam had made as a kid.

"God," Adam said, "I don't remember doing *half* of this shit."

I found an old leather-bound journal and opened it. It was writ-ten by Grandma, the pages filled with her angular, careful script. Faded black-and-white photographs were taped to some of the pages, the first such photographs I had seen of Grandma as a young woman. She had actually been pretty. Striking even, with her strong jaw and sharp eyes. I flipped through the journal and came across a note she'd written to Mom, when Mom was a baby asleep in her crib. Mom had been born in 1941, right before Pearl Harbor was bombed, and Grandma wrote that she sometimes wondered if she should have brought Mom into such a horrible world, full of violent, evil, terrible people. She wrote that life was hard and there is precious little joy in it. She wrote that she wished Mom would never have to know some of the pain she had experienced. I read the letter aloud to Adam and Roberta. "Wow," I said. "That's a lot to lay on a baby."

"Jesus," Roberta said. "Well, that's Dolores."

We sat quietly for a moment, regarding the heaps of stuff around us. I sipped my wine and said, "How much longer do you think she'll last?"

Roberta chuckled ruefully. "God, I don't know. She's certainly hanging in there, isn't she?"

I chuckled, too, in spite of myself. "What the hell is she waiting for?"

"She's so damn stubborn," Roberta said. "She's always been stubborn, our mother got that right."

Adam said, "You'd think she'd be sick of Joe just standing over her, breathing heavily and shit, and want to get the hell out of here."

We all laughed. Roberta wiped her eyes and said, "I should just go in there with a damn pillow and get it over with. It's the only way she'll leave, that's for damn sure."

I chuckled again, shaking my head. And part of me wanted Roberta to do just that. The ugly truth was that this waiting around was getting tiresome.

The next day, I stood in Mom's room with Tom, the hospice worker. We were looking at the color of her urine, collected in a clear plastic bag at the foot of her bed. Earlier in the week, it had progressively darkened, growing murky and thick, like caramel, a sign of renal failure, one of the surest indications of impending death. But now it was clearing up again, becoming the color of weak tea.

"What does that mean?" I asked him.

"Well, it seems to me that she's bouncing back a little," Tom said.

I chewed my lip. "So how much longer do you think she has?"

He looked right at me. "There's no way to know, really," he said. "Maybe a few days, maybe a few weeks. With your mother, she's so strong, we've been amazed she's made it as far as she has."

I watched her sleeping there, wondering if she was aware of our conversation. I wanted so badly, almost obsessively, to be there when she died, to have that dramatic moment of closure. Why wouldn't she give me that?

Tom put his hand on my shoulder. "Maybe you should think about going back to New York. I think your mother would want you to be there, rather than waiting around here."

I regarded him for a moment, and then nodded. "Yeah," I said. "I think you're right."

I made my arrangements to leave the next day—Mother's Day—and when the time came, I packed up my belongings and loaded up my rental car. I went to Mom's room to say goodbye, surprised to see that when I kissed her forehead, her eyes opened gently.

"Hi, Tonio," she said, her voice feeble.

"Hi, Momma. I'm going back to New York, okay?"

She blinked several times. "Okay," she said.

"I love you, Momma."

"I love you, too."

"I'll see you soon, okay?"

"Okay."

I kissed her again and walked to her doorway, pausing there for one last look. I signed "I love you" with my right hand. And ever so slowly, she raised her left hand and, trembling slightly, signed "I love you" back.

floating

On the morning of May 22nd, a week and a half after I left Joliet, the phone rang. It was Anne.

"Anthony?" she said, her voice tight and clipped. "We think you should come home today."

"Are you sure?" I asked.

"Well, the hospice people seem to think this is it," Anne said.

"Okay," I said.

I had last spoken to Mom a few days earlier. After several attempts to reach her, only to be told by Diana or Terry or Roberta that she was sleeping, I got her on the phone in a rare lucid moment.

"Hi, Tonio," she'd said, her words slurred, her voice weak.

"Hi, Momma." I couldn't bear to hear her like this, to be so far away and not be able to see her, to be unable to hold her hand.

"How are you?" she asked.

"I'm okay, Momma. I miss you," I said.

"I miss you, too."

I didn't know what else to say. To ask her how she was doing seemed absurd. So I didn't say anything for a moment.

"How's the show going?" she asked.

"It's fine," I said. I didn't tell her that earlier in the week I had stayed home because I could barely bring myself to get out of bed, let alone perform in front of twelve hundred people. I didn't tell her that I didn't know what to do in those moments of grief except stare at nothing. I didn't tell her that on those days I felt like I was moving underwater, that all things seemed dim and untouchable.

"That's good," she said.

I sighed and said, "Well, I should let you rest, Momma." As if she could do anything else.

"Okay," she said.

"I love you, Momma," I said.

"I love you, too."

But now, after the phone call with Anne, it was time to call the airline yet again and book a flight and get Adam's travel sorted out and call my stage manager to tell him that I was going home and then pack— for how many days was never clear—and get a car to the airport and go home and see her for what might be the last time, although that was never clear either. Task after task after task. One foot in front of the other.

At Newark airport, Adam and I made it to our gate with time to spare before boarding. We had hardly spoken during the day's activity, except to cover the logistical details. We sat in the waiting area, grimly watching the CNN feed on the airport monitors. Or at least looking in their direction—I was processing none of what was being reported, thinking instead only of going home. Would this really be the time?

Right before the gate personnel started calling us to board, I had the impulse to check in to see how Mom was doing. I hadn't called home all day, knowing that Anne or Roberta would have called us if anything had changed. "I'm going to call home," I said to Adam. He barely looked at me when he quietly replied, "Okay."

I dialed my calling card information into the phone and then dialed Mom's familiar ten-digit number. Two rings, three rings, four rings, and then Roberta's voice said, "Hello?"

I could tell she was crying.

"Roberta?" I said, gripping the cold metal pay-phone cord. "It's Anthony."

"Oh, Anthony," she said. "It's over. She's gone."

The ground tilted. I rested my head against the phone, staring at the floor, watching my tears splash down at my feet.

"When?" I managed.

"She just went a couple of minutes ago," Roberta said, "right before you called."

I swallowed. "Okay," I said.

"Oh, I miss her so much already," Roberta said, her voice keening.

"I know," I said.

"It was peaceful," she said. "She just went to sleep."

I fought off a sob. "Really?"

"I was right there with her," she said. "I was holding her hand. She just went to sleep."

"That's good," I said.

"I love her so much," she said.

"I know," I said. And then I asked, "Will you leave her there until we get home?"

"Yes," she said.

"Okay. I just want to say goodbye, you know?"

"Okay."

I was gripping the phone so tightly. "We have to get on our flight now," I said.

"Have a safe trip."

"Okay. See you soon."

I hung up and held on to the phone, trying to stop my tears.

Only another couple of hours and I would have been there. The timing seemed horribly unfair.

I breathed deeply and slowly walked over to where Adam sat. He looked up as I approached.

"She's gone," I said. More tears sprang out of my eyes. Adam just stared at me for a moment, nodding ever so slightly, and then he gently stood up and put his hand on my shoulder, his eyes wide, his face almost expressionless. I moved in to give him a brief hug, which he stiffly reciprocated, and then we wordlessly gathered our belongings and boarded the plane.

We sat silently in our cramped airplane seats, next to a fidgety, anxious man, waiting for the plane to taxi and take off. The fidgety man seemed terrified of flying; he kept staring out the window, rubbing his hands on his lap, clearing his throat incessantly. I knew Adam also didn't love flying, and I hoped this man's fear wouldn't bleed over into him.

I couldn't bring myself to ask what Adam was thinking or feeling or wanting. I felt incredibly alert, even as my chest caved in on itself. I focused on my plastic tray table as it faced me in its upright and locked position. I made sure my seat back was also in its upright and locked position. I checked to see that my carry-on was safely stowed beneath the seat in front of me or in an overhead bin. I even watched the flight attendants as they did their safety demo. I tried to hold back my tears, afraid of freaking Adam out, afraid of making a scene, but there they were anyway.

And then we took off, and as the plane made its lazy turns toward Chicago, my breathing gradually became steady and a kind of spaciousness and peace followed. Here I was floating above everything that had happened today and this year, away from it, able to see just the purest facts of it. My mother was dead, and I was flying with my brother to see her one more time before they took her body away, and then we would hold a funeral and memorial service and that would be that. It was simple, really. There would be people to call and inform, there would be arrangements to be made, there would be family to see, and there would be no more waiting for the end, no more hoping she would at last have some respite from her daily grinding discomfort and pain, no more wondering how much worse it could get before it was all over.

In the air, flying incredibly high across the landscape of the eastern United States, I automatically set about a task that reminded me of my actions in the wake of Jonathan's death: I looked through my laptop's address book to figure out who I would need to inform that Mom had died. Who most urgently needed to know? I hadn't called Todd yet—after getting off the phone with Roberta, I had just boarded the plane. Todd was in Los Angeles, having all kinds of work meetings, but I was sure he'd be able to come to Joliet for the memorial service and funeral. At least, he'd better. Of course he would, why would I even question that? Mom had made it clear he was welcome. (When I had told Mom that I hoped Grandma wouldn't object to or make a stink about his presence there, Mom had said, quietly, sternly, "She'd better not.") But who else needed to be told? I wasn't relishing the thought of breaking the news to people, but I knew that I could and should do it. Not for the first time, I imagined myself playing a scene in a movie in which I informed someone of my mother's death. It was the sort of event that took place in the movies and on television hospital dramas.

So I checked off the names of those I would inform, sitting next to a silently slumbering Adam. (He had always had the knack for falling into a deep sleep the instant a plane began speeding down the runway for takeoff. He thought it was his way of dealing with his anxiety about flying.) One name jumped out at me: Phyllis Wagner. She was Mom's old friend from Portland, Oregon, who had come to *Rent*'s opening night. Mom had always had an enviable knack for keeping in touch with her friends—this in the days before e-mail and mobile phones—but none were as close to her as Phyllis. Phyllis and Mom shared a propensity for taking in what Mom called "human strays," although Phyllis did it officially, as a state-recognized foster mother, specializing in kids with severe medical problems. She often sent long, handwritten letters to Mom, their accompanying envelopes spilling snapshots of her latest children. Many of her kids didn't make it past their childhoods, and some were just passing through Phyllis's home on their way to somewhere else, but some she wound up raising as her own. Somehow she and Mom found time to spend hours on the phone laughing and laughing, even when telling stories of the suffering they witnessed all day long.

When Mom had gotten sick, Phyllis hadn't been able to come to visit her except when they had rendezvoused in New York for *Rent.* I wasn't sure that Roberta would be calling her, so I thought I should be the bearer of the news.

When we landed and emerged into O'Hare's harsh fluorescence, I headed to the pay phone and first left a message on Todd's voice mail that I had to talk to him as soon as possible, and then dialed Phyllis's number.

"Hello?" she answered after one ring.

"Hi, Phyllis?" I said. "It's Anthony. Anthony Rapp."

She must have known why I was calling, because I could hear a hesitancy in her voice. "Oh, hi."

"I'm sorry to be the one to tell you, but I just wanted to let you know that my mom died tonight."

She sighed. "Oh," she said. "Okay." She caught her breath. "Thanks for telling me."

I tried to concentrate on my own breathing. "Yeah, well, I wasn't sure if anyone else would have called you yet, and I wanted you to know."

She sniffled. "Yeah, well, I do appreciate it."

And before I knew that I was going to say it, and feeling my face moisten with fresh tears, I said, "I just wanted to thank you for being such a wonderful friend to my mom for all of these years. I know she loved you so much and you were always such a good friend to her."

"Well," Phyllis said, "she was always such a great friend to me, too." I could hear her crying on the other end, but her voice remained as steady as she could manage. "She really was one of my very best friends."

"Yeah," I said.

"I'm going to miss her so much," Phyllis said.

"Yeah," I said again.

Then Phyllis heaved another big sigh and said, "Well, I really do appreciate you telling me."

"You're welcome."

"Take care of yourself."

"You too, Phyllis."

I hung up and realized that Adam was probably wondering what the hell I was doing. I found him sitting dazedly in one of the waiting area seats, his long legs splayed out in front of him, staring into nothing.

"I called Phyllis," I said, wiping my face. "I wanted to let her know."

He nodded. "That's good," he said, quietly monotone. Was his head swimming as much as mine was? Was he taking each moment as it came, or was he shutting it all away? I didn't want him to explain himself if he didn't want to, so I didn't ask.

More silence followed on the ride home, with me driving, since Adam had long ago lost his license due to a speeding ticket he'd never paid. Even though I was the younger of the two of us, I often felt like the adult, the responsible one. Not that I minded; it was familiar, as familiar as the flat streams of headlights zooming by across the median on I-55.

More silence, as we traveled past the good old Louis Joliet Mall, which was a couple of miles before Mom's house. The town seemed the same as always, just more developed, with even more monotonous strip malls and model homes lining the road.

More silence, as we turned through the six-way intersection onto Gaylord Road, nearer still to Mom's house. I kept my eyes trained on the pools of light out in front of our car, my hands gripping the steering wheel.

More silence as Gaylord turned into Cedarwood Drive, and we passed our old apartment complex, the one that was partially destroyed by that tornado a few years prior, and we then passed the subdivision where our townhome, which was destroyed by the same tornado, used to be. We finally turned onto Gael Drive, and into our driveway, and I shut off the motor.

How many times had I traveled that same trajectory in my car over the years? Never feeling like this, though. Not like this.

The silence finally broke when we opened the door to Mom's house and stepped inside. The lights were dim, and already the house seemed empty. Roberta and Anne got up and gave us hugs and kisses and then we sat for a second.

"So she's in her room?" I said. My face was heating up, but my voice was clear, for the moment, at least.

"Yeah," Roberta said. "She's there."

"I'll go first," Adam said.

"Okay," I said. I gripped the side of the chair. Then I said, "Where's Rachel?"

"At home," Anne said. "She said goodbye before."

"Okay," I said. I couldn't look Anne or Roberta in the eye. I clenched and unclenched my jaw.

A couple of moments after going into Mom's room, Adam returned to the living room, his large eyes wide, his face a little paler than usual.

I stood up and made my way to her door. I paused before looking in her room. And then I looked in, and saw her lying there on her bed.

My hand gripped the doorknob and quickly closed the door behind me. A sound began to emerge from my throat, from my gut, from my chest, a moan I had never heard myself make, a low sound, a horrible, frightening sound, and though I had already shed so many tears, there were fresh ones, streaming down my face, uncontrolled, unbidden, wet and wet and wet, and there was Mom, or rather there was her body, her shell, beautifully laid there on her bed, in a simple white nightgown, under her simple white quilt, a simple white rose resting on her chest. It was clear that she had been tenderly settled there by Roberta or Terry, and I was so grateful that they had taken such care, and I was grateful to get the chance to see her one more time, and at the same time, I was more certain than I had ever been that we are not contained in our bodies; there was nothing left of my mother in that shell on that bed, that impossibly pale body that only slightly resembled Mom. It was far, far too pale and still and, well—dead, yes dead, she was dead, dead dead dead—and I would have given anything at all to have one more chance, one more moment to tell her I loved her—even though I knew she knew it—and to hold her hand, and then I reached over and touched her hand, and my fingers felt her cold and rubbery dead dead dead skin, and there was no life in that skin, no sense of her, no possible way that all of who she was—all of the love she had, all of the life she lived, all of her mistakes and all of her energy and all of her friends' and family's love for her—there was no way that all of that was contained in that body, that empty dead body.

And there I was moaning and keening and wailing like some kind of primal animal let loose and roaming around this house that had this death in it, and I looked up and saw my reflection in the large mirror that Mom had always had in her room, and I didn't recognize my own face twisted up in agony. I looked again at my mom's body, which was not my mom but only her body, and saw the eerie and horrible way her lips had begun to pull away from her teeth in a death grimace—what a terrible and frightening phrase that was—and my chest was cracking open, and I pressed my palm into my chest to stop my heart from bursting through, heaving in huge gulping sobs. Then the door opened and Adam poked his head in. "Are you okay?" he said.

I wanted to say *of course I'm not okay I'm not at all okay I'm in agony I hate this more than anything I've ever hated before in my life, and all of that time I was waiting for her to die, all of that time we spent laughing about it and hoping for this moment, all of that time, I would give it all back ten thousand times over to not have to go through this right now, what I'm going through right now, I hate myself for ever having said or thought those things, no I'm not okay.* But instead I caught my breath and said, "Yeah."

"'Cause you were making some crazy sounds."

And I said, swallowing, "I'm sorry."

And he said, "Well, okay," and then he closed the door and left me alone with Mom. With her body. I looked in the mirror again and saw an insane person staring back at me, a wild-eyed, red-faced, horror-stricken insane person. More wails came, bigger than before, unstoppable, and I told myself that the only way out is through, the only way out is through, the only way out is through, but there didn't seem to be any way out, any end to this drowning. Then slowly but surely my breathing became regular, and those horrible sounds stopped coursing through me and out of my throat. Eventually I was able to look at my mother's body and just see her there, or at least an aspect of her, and I leaned down and kissed her cold forehead, which felt not like her forehead at all. Then, with some semblance of myself restored, I looked at her one last time and left her in her room, closing the door behind me.

Unsure if my eyes were still wild or if my smeared face was still flushed, I headed out to the living room and sat down again, not looking at anyone. The undertakers, two silent men in cheap polyester suits and soft voices, had arrived and quietly announced that they would be taking Mom away now. I sat and watched with Adam and Anne and Roberta as they lumbered back to her bedroom. They came out several minutes later wheeling my enshrouded mother, their heads bowed as they passed by, and all my tears were gone for now, as I witnessed my mother leave her home, carted away by these two strangers.

through

I was finally able to speak with Todd when he called the house later that night.

"I'm sorry I couldn't call sooner," he said. "I was watching a movie with my friends."

"It's okay," I said. And I supposed it was.

"So what's happening?"

"Well," I said, not sure of how I was going to say it. Then I decided. "It's over. She's gone."

"Oh, honey . . ."

"Yeah," I said in the silence that followed. "When can you get here?"

"Do you want me to come?"

Did I want him to come? What kind of question was that? "Of course I want you to come. When can you get here?"

"Well, I have some meetings tomorrow, so I guess I can fly there like the day after tomorrow, is that okay?"

I guessed it would have to be. "Okay, as soon as you can."

"I will, I will," he said. I couldn't tell if he wanted to come, or if he was only coming because I wanted him to. But did that even matter?

"Good," I said.

"How are you doing?"

How *was* I doing? I wasn't even sure. I was exhausted and spent and yet very alive and present and sort of wide open. "I'm okay." I sighed. "I'm okay."

"I love you."

"I love you, too."

The next day was filled with delegating the various arrangements—securing the location of the funeral and memorial; renting a piano so I could sing at the memorial, as I'd promised Mom I'd do; telling more people of her death; getting food sorted out; meeting with the priest to select the readings and songs; creating and printing up the program for the memorial. Roberta took the lion's share of the work, as she had done for the past couple of years. (She'd come to only half-jokingly nicknaming herself "The Boss.") It felt strangely similar to putting together a theatrical production.

I stayed fairly steady throughout the day, relieved after the long, long wait for Mom's death. Her house was sun dappled and filled with talk and activity, but a new emptiness lingered. And when I took a shower that day I had to hold myself up against the slippery tiles while a fresh wave of sobs overcame me. I stood in the steam and let out the grief. And then, as had happened the night before, it gradually lifted, and my breathing returned to normal, my head cleared, and I finished my shower and got back to helping create a fitting tribute to the life Mom had lived.

When Todd arrived the following night it was already late, and by the time we got home, the house was still and dark. Adam and his girlfriend, Devin, who had arrived earlier in the day, were the only other people sleeping at the house; Anne and Rachel were at their home, and Roberta was at hers. Todd hated flying and had to medicate himself before every takeoff, so he was loopy when he got off the plane. But already the effects were wearing off, and his familiar neurotic energy was showing through.

"So this is Mom's house," I said in a stage whisper, wanting to mark the occasion somehow.

"It's nice," he said. "Lots of plants."

"Yeah, she was a big plant lover."

Todd paced around, taking in everything with his lightning quick eyes. He was always proud that he could register many details of a place within mere seconds.

"Lots of books, too," he said.

"Yeah, she loved to read." I was nervous having him home with me. And I could tell he was nervous. He hadn't been able to look at me.

"Are you sure it's okay that I'm here?" he said.

"Of course I'm sure," I said.

"'Cause I don't feel very comfortable."

"What do you mean?"

"I don't feel comfortable," he said, agitated. "This isn't my house, you know I don't feel comfortable in other people's houses, I need my things, I need my chaos and environment and all that, you know that."

I couldn't believe he was already complaining, that he was making this moment about him. "Well, what do you want to do about it?"

"Oh, that's helpful," he said. "You should be trying to make me feel comfortable, not mocking me."

"Mocking you? How was I mocking you? I was asking you a question."

"Look, I'm your *guest*, I shouldn't have to figure it out, *you* figure it out."

"Figure *what* out?" I struggled not to raise my voice and wake up Adam and his girlfriend.

"How to make me feel more comfortable!" Todd was also trying not to raise his voice, balling up his fists, his eyes wide. I felt too raw for this conversation, but I tried to breathe and stay in it, to contain it.

"Todd," I said, "try to calm down."

"I am calm!" he said.

"Todd, can you just try for a second to sit and talk quietly about this?"

"Stop fucking condescending to me!"

I reached for his hand. "Come here, please," I said. "Sit with me. Please."

And reluctantly, he sat on the couch, under Mom's old hand-painted HOME SWEET HOME sign.

Todd clutched my hand tightly and said, "You're not being very helpful."

As much as I wanted to scream at him for being such an asshole, I stopped myself. I breathed in and out. "What do you mean?" I said.

"This is a very awkward situation for me," he said. "I don't know how your family will be, I don't know them, I don't know this house, I don't feel comfortable."

"Okay," I said.

"And you're not being very helpful."

"Todd, I need you to be a little helpful too right now."

"Of course, it's always about you! When I ask for something I need, you never can give it!"

Where was this going? "Todd, my mother just died. My mother just died and I can't really get too much more into this right now, let's just go to bed and we'll see how you feel tomorrow, okay?"

"I'm not going to be able to sleep, I slept on the plane."

"Well then just lie down with me, okay? Please?"

"Why does it always have to be what *you* need?"

I stuffed down another outburst. "Okay, Todd, whatever you want to do, that's fine."

"Stop fucking condescending to me!"

And we went around and around like that for what felt like hours, and may very well have been at least an hour or more, until he tired finally of running in the same loop over and over and followed me into Rachel's old room.

We lay down in the dark on our backs, holding hands. I stared up at the ceiling in a long silence, swallowing all of my impulses to rage at Todd. Why was I still with him when he was so fucking exhausting? Sometimes it seemed the only reason I stayed was that he was the only person in my life who had closely witnessed what I'd gone through in the past year, and if I lost him I would lose that connection to my own history. Yet here we were at another dead end, spent, unable to muster any words that might make a difference.

"I'm sorry," he said after a long silence. He didn't usually apologize, so that was something.

"It's okay," I said. Not that it was, not really.

"I just got freaked out."

"It's okay," I said again.

"I just didn't know what to expect."

"It's okay," I said once more.

And we lay there together, and I listened to our breathing, as confused as ever but grateful for his apology and starting to feel some comfort from his presence at this most difficult time. Suddenly, before I knew it, I was overwhelmed with the desire to make love to him, to connect with him, to be with him and love him and have him love me. And I rolled over and kissed him with more passion than perhaps I ever had, not knowing where it was coming from, not really caring, momentarily wondering if it was somehow disrespectful of us to be having sex in a house in which someone—and not just any someone, but my mother—had just died. But none of that mattered now. Even though I didn't always know why we should still be together, I still loved him. I needed him to know how much I did, and I needed him to make me know that he felt the same way. And above all else, I needed not to be alone.

On the following day, the funeral was first, to be followed by a luncheon at the park where the memorial would then take place. I hadn't been in a church since Anne's wedding and felt the familiar tightening in my chest as I passed the basin filled with holy water, almost reflexively reaching in to make the sign of the cross, but stopping short of getting my fingers wet; I was too much of a heathen to desecrate the holy water. I purposely didn't hold Todd's hand; I wasn't ready to put our relationship in Grandma's face. She stood near the door, receiving people, and I walked right up to her.

"Grandma, this is Todd," I said, trying to make my voice sound assured.

She immediately took his hand and shook it. "Nice to meet you, Todd," she said, looking him in the eye.

"Thanks for including me," he said.

And without missing a beat, she replied, "Well, of course, you're part of the family." I couldn't believe those words had come out of her mouth, but there they were. Todd and I shared relieved glances as we made our way to our pew and sat down.

The coffin was closed, and on its lid rested a color portrait of Mom, set in a tasteful frame. It was the portrait that had been taken on Anne's wedding day—the one featuring her coiffed hair and too-red lipstick. Mom had never had any sense of glamour, or even style, beyond sweatshirts and jeans, so it struck me as odd to see her publicly represented in this way. But I imagined that Roberta must have thought it was the most flattering picture of Mom, even if it didn't really look like her.

I wondered if Anne and Adam and Rachel felt as calm as I did, sitting in the church, listening to the priest intone his prayers and recite his homily.

After the Mass, my uncle Chris read a prepared eulogy, and I gripped Todd's hand, simple tears leaking from my eyes—the first of the day—as I listened to Chris's calm, quiet voice fill the church. He had been such a loyal and good brother to my mom, and I knew how much she had valued his friendship and counsel, and how much she had supported him through his life's vicissitudes.

But mostly as I sat there, I was looking ahead to the secular comfort of the memorial service, which Mom had wanted more than a funeral. It was like a show, with a program that Roberta had designed rather beautifully. It featured my favorite portrait of Mom: a black-and-white photograph from her student nursing days, complete with an old-fashioned white cap perched atop her head. She looked young and open and calm and much more herself than in the color portrait on her coffin, even though the shot was in black and white and she was sitting in a formal pose. And the memorial would feature entrances and exits and music and the whole works.

So after the last hymn was sung, and accompanied by the clatter of the church bells' peals in the bright spring air, we all piled into our caravan and rambled over to the park.

There was only one substantial park in Joliet, Pilcher Park, and I wasn't sure that Mom had spent any time there, but it turned out to be a lovely setting for her memorial. The previous days had been filled with intermittent showers and blustery winds, but on this day the sky was blue and clear.

I made my way to a small clearing ringed by old oak trees with Grandma and all of Mom's brothers and sisters (save Katrina, who was in some sort of feud with Joe and refused to come), Rachel and Adam and myself, Devin and Todd and Dad, Tom and Terry and the other hospice workers, Gloria, and other friends and coworkers of Mom's. I wondered how Rachel was feeling being around Lucie, her birth mother, and her two brothers, Nathaniel and Matthew, on a day like this. She was only nine years old, and I wondered how she was processing what was happening—I was having a hard enough time myself, at almost three times her age. But I had to help set up the service, so I didn't have an opportunity to check in with her.

After we all munched on the comfort food that was awaiting us in the park, we made our way to the folding chairs that had been set up for us, and found our seats. I was glad to see that the piano delivery I had arranged came through, and I conferred with my accompanist, Beverly, whom I knew from my days at Joliet West High School and who had graciously agreed to donate her services today.

"How you doing, honey?" she asked.

"Okay," I said. And it seemed to be true. If anything, I felt a little numb around the edges, and even a little remote, but basically I was clear and present and, for the moment at least, at peace. "Thanks again for doing this."

"Oh, honey, I'm honored, truly."

I had become the de facto emcee, so when everyone was seated I took to the microphone and began.

"Um, thank you everyone for coming to this," I said, feeling less self-conscious than I thought I might in front of Mom's family, who looked up at me with a strange mixture of passivity and expectancy. I took a deep breath. "We want this to be kind of informal and everything. Some of us have prepared some things to say, but when we're done with our part, please feel free to share whatever you'd like." After witnessing the reluctance of everyone in Mom's family to say anything at Grandpa's funeral, I wasn't sure how well they would do at this today, but I retained some hope that they would rise to the occasion. I continued, "Mom asked me to sing, so I'd like to do that first."

I had originally planned to sing only "Waiting for the Light to Shine," as I'd discussed with Mom, but I'd also decided recently to sing "Without You," and I'd worked up a version of it with Beverly. I looked to her at the piano, and she began the introduction's lovely and mournful arpeggios, and I sang. As I stood there in the sunlight, singing for my mother and the people who loved her who had gathered here, I felt like a conduit for the clarity and simplicity and beauty of Jonathan's words and music. I had anticipated having to contend with a closing up of my throat as I sang, but it didn't come; instead, I continued to sing freely and strongly.

After the piano's last note gently subsided, Adam read a poem he'd written years before, which Mom had requested he recite today, and Rachel and Anne read prepared speeches. Anne's voice rang out strongly, and she impressed me with her uninhibited, fearless presence, her eyes meeting ours as she spoke in a direct address to Mom.

"I guess I'm a lot like you," was her touching refrain. She and Mom had often been at odds, and Mom had worked hard to bridge the gaps that existed between them, so to hear Anne likening herself to Mom now struck me as a generous acceptance on her part, a final peace offering.

When Anne was done I opened up the floor to anyone else who wanted to contribute, and Grandma was the first to take the microphone. I wondered what she would manage to say on this day that her eldest child was being remembered. I was happy that she was taking the opportunity to say something, but I hoped it wasn't going to include a lot of talk about sin and hell and heaven and her Catholic God. This was, after all, the secular part of the day's events.

"I was always very proud of Mary Lee," she began, her voice more subdued than normal, her eyes downcast, but her proud face tilted up into the sunlight. "She was my firstborn and always managed to live her life with a very strong will and a lot of determination. I saw her raise her three children by herself, never complaining about the hardships she faced, and then I saw her face this illness with courage and grace. She never failed to make me proud of her."

As she continued, I kept waiting for her to say she loved her daughter, but that one word, "love," remained unspoken. It seemed unbelievable that she didn't—or couldn't—say it, but I was glad that she had at least spoken.

Dad made his way to the microphone then. I was proud of him for braving the potentially hostile eyes and ears of some of the members of the Baird clan, not to mention those of Anne and Adam, but if they were unhappy that he was there they didn't show it overtly. He deserved the opportunity to pay his respects just as much as anyone else.

"Thanks for the chance to say something," he began, shifting from one foot to the other, one hand in his pocket. "I met Mary quite a few years ago now, as many of you know, and then of course we were married and had our three wonderful children together . . ." He searched for words. "I learned a lot from Mary," he said. I hadn't heard him say anything like that before. "I learned about love and commitment, and even though we weren't able to make our relationship work, I always admired her so much and knew what a remarkable woman she was . . ." His face clouded over, and tears sprang to his eyes, which he quickly covered with his free hand. "Uh . . ." he said. "She was a gentle and kind woman and a wonderful mother to our children, and, uh, thank you for letting me speak."

I was touched by his sentiments and his courage. I wondered if Anne and Adam were merely tolerating his presence, or grateful for what he said.

A couple of other friends and family members spoke, and then I closed the proceedings by singing "Waiting for the Light to Shine." Again, my throat remained clear and open. As I sang, I hoped that today had been a suitable memorial for Mom. So much of her spirit had departed, bit by bit, well before her body had ceased functioning, and her death had been so long in coming, that we were ready to lay her to rest now. We were all ready to begin, at last, the long process of moving on.

tyson

For myself, moving on began with going back home to New York, which I did the next day, but not until after Adam, Anne, and I shared a ceremonial Scrabble mini-tournament. As we sat around Anne's kitchen table shuffling through our tiles, searching for our best moves and most impressive words, I wanted to ask my siblings how they were feeling, whether they were experiencing the disorienting mixture of relief and exhaustion and peace and guilt and love and sadness and freedom that I was experiencing. But the words caught in my throat. It was precisely the kind of question we had never asked each other, not ever, for any reason. Why? And why was I still abiding by our unspoken rule not to go there? After all, it wasn't that long ago, on the night I had flailed and ranted at Adam, that he and I had communicated openly. But the door seemed to have closed.

During our game, Todd, who had accompanied us to Anne's house at my request, but who had opted out of the game, sat sullenly in the next room, reading. Or trying to read. I could feel his impatience and anxiety building, even without seeing him—his sighs and groans had become audible—but I ignored him, resenting him for not being able to just be there and hang out while we played our game, which he knew was an important ritual. At one point, he got up and leaned in the doorway and whined, "How much longer are you guys going to play?"

I clamped down on my rising irritation and said as calmly as I could, "I'm not sure, we're going to play a couple of games. They take a while." I glanced at my brother and sister to see if they were picking up on our tension; I didn't want to argue with him in front of them.

"I should have just stayed at your house," he said. "Why can't you take me back there?"

The house was a twenty-minute drive in each direction. There was no *way* I was about to leave for all that time, in the middle of our game. "I'll take you home when we're done," I said, still trying to maintain my calm. Todd sighed and rubbed his eyes and skulked back into the other room. I resisted my urge to follow him and grab him and shake him and scream at him until he just got off my *back* and let me spend some time with my brother and sister whose *mother* had just died, and this was the time we had to spend with each other and this was how we dealt with that time, this was what we did in our *family,* and maybe it was ridiculous that our family couldn't do anything at moments like this but play a fucking board game, but it was *my family* and if he wanted to be with me then he had to accept us and how we managed our lives and why couldn't he just grow the fuck *up* and leave me the fuck *alone*???

My cheeks reddened as I reached in the Scrabble bag and pulled out fresh tiles. Anne and Adam and I finished our games quietly, except when Anne and I had to challenge Adam's usual attempts at playing invented words, at which point we all laughed at how silly he thought we were that we would accept "tumiscal" or "jumbation" or some other concoction, without a fight.

"Adam, you're nuts," Anne would say every time.

"You're just jealous," he'd reply, his eyes glinting. And Anne and I would share a knowing chuckle as we removed his errant letters from the board.

And just as quietly—with a hasty hug and a muted goodbye—Adam and I left Anne's house (with a sullen Todd in tow) and flew back home.

Back in New York, Todd and I continued our circular fights, which included a rehashing of why the hell I had stranded him at my sister's house so I could play a fucking game. I had hoped that Mom's passing would alleviate our stress, but it didn't. Maybe he had hoped the same thing, too. I was in constant turmoil to decide whether to break up with him, but I always panicked at the thought of being alone now, and I told myself that his capacity for sweetness, which had shown itself periodically throughout our time together, would carry the day in the end, and all of our struggles would be worth it.

I also couldn't bear to end yet another relationship, leading to yet another person out in the world resenting me, after having split up with Keith and David and Marcus. I needed to prove to myself that I could make a relationship work, that I didn't have to run away when things got difficult, as my father had.

As relieved as I was at having to endure no more uncertainty over Mom's condition, I was also spent, and a couple of weeks after my return, I asked for a week's vacation from the show, which the producers kindly granted. Todd had to be in LA for writing meetings, where he was getting put up in a free hotel room, so I figured I should just head out there with him. I had friends in LA, and it was an escape from my daily grind. Not that I liked LA much; I found its clichés—shallow, pretty people driving expensive cars; too much traffic; never-ending rays of impossibly bright sunshine—to be entirely accurate and distasteful. But LA was near the water, and the thought of spending at least a little bit of time by the ocean appealed to me.

On one of our first nights there, I drove to Santa Monica by myself and took a nice long walk on the beach. Mom had come to LA with me a couple of times when I was a kid, for screen tests and auditions, but we'd never made it to the beach together. The one time that I was aware of her being at the Pacific Ocean was in San Francisco when I was eleven, while we were traveling with the national tour of *The King and I.* That ruggedly beautiful beach was rocky and windy and the water was freezing, but she had enjoyed it, and I thought she would also have enjoyed the sandy beaches of Southern California. Maybe I was wrong, though, because I didn't recall Mom ever going on about wanting or needing to return to the ocean on either coast. But something about taking a walk in her honor made sense.

As I strolled along in the lovely, gentle breeze, basking in the orange and peach and violet sunset, listening to the mild and steady rhythm of the surf, I thought Mom would have loved it as much as I did. I didn't care if I was blithely reaching for a meaningful moment that didn't exist; during the hour or so that I spent out there, I felt very close to my mother indeed.

Michael Greif was currently in La Jolla, a couple of hours' drive south of LA, rehearsing the California company of *Rent,* so I decided to drop in on him. Todd was busy with his work, which was fine with me; we needed some time away from each other. Though our fights had lessened a little bit since the trip had begun, I could never trust which Todd I'd be dealing with—the patient, kind, open, easygoing Todd, or the distrustful, jealous, nagging, needy, neurotic Todd. His jealousy had been driving me mad for a while now. While I had been faced with many opportunities to be unfaithful, with so many people paying me so much attention in the spotlight of *Rent's* success, the truth was that I hadn't even tried to kiss anyone, as tempted as I had sometimes been. It was a heady experience to come out of the stage door at the Nederlander and face any number of adorable and sexy young men (and the occasional adorable and sexy young woman), some of whom openly flirted with me. But I had made a commitment to Todd to be monogamous—at his request—and I had been proud to honor that commitment.

Not that Todd ever really trusted me. Word would get back to him that I had looked someone in the eye as I talked to them outside the Nederlander (and, truthfully, I may or may not have been flirting by doing so; it depended on the person), and he would grill me.

"Who was it? Did you give him your phone number? Am I going to have to worry about you two?" he'd say.

"I don't even know which person it might have been, Todd," I'd reply, avoiding the phone number question, because there had been times in which numbers had been exchanged. "And just because I looked someone in the eye doesn't mean I wanted to fuck them." (Which was only sometimes true.) "And no, I didn't give him my phone number," (again, only sometimes true) "and no, you have nothing to worry about. People are going to think that I want to fuck them just because I talked to them, Todd, that comes with the territory, you have to know that."

"But why do you have to talk to everybody all the time?"

"Because it's important to me," I said. "I never wanted to feel like I couldn't connect with the people who appreciated my work. I never wanted to feel untouchable or something." Which was true, but it was also true that I enjoyed the attention and occasional flirtation.

"Well, you sure have a knack for making me feel special," he said.

"Oh, give me a fucking break. How many more ways do I have to show you how much I love you? I can't ever prove I'm not doing anything, I can only tell you that I'm not."

"Oh, that's reassuring as hell."

"God, Todd, it's like I'm on trial or something. Seriously, what the fuck can I do? I can only tell you, I can only swear on my mother's grave, that I'm not doing anything. With *anybody.*"

But these conversations never seemed to alleviate his anxiety or dampen his jealousy, and I came to feel as though I had to police my every thought while I talked to any fan or glanced at some hot guy on the street or even dreamed about someone else, for fear that somehow I was being unfaithful.

●   ●   ●

So it was a relief to have some time alone on the long car ride to La Jolla. I was looking forward to reconnecting with Michael, and I was curious about how this new cast was shaping up.

I made my way onto the campus of the University of California in San Diego, where the La Jolla Playhouse produced their shows, and wandered into the rehearsal room. The cast was in the midst of a run-through of Act Two, just beginning to line the edge of the stage for the reprise of "I'll Cover You." How apropos, I thought. Another funeral. Michael quietly waved me over and gave me a hug. I sat and took in this cast, all of them attractive and with huge voices and a lot of energy. It was surreal, however, to see a whole new group of people singing these songs and embodying these characters. But they approached the work with heart and commitment.

When they were done with the run-through, Michael announced my presence. I reddened as I waved hello, and one by one they came up to shake my hand and chat. It was strange, as though I were an elder statesman, but I enjoyed the opportunity to impart some wisdom here and there and to have a glimpse of their process.

After rehearsal, some of the members of the cast joined Michael and me for a bite to eat at a local Italian restaurant. I sat next to a cast member named Andy, whom I found to be adorable, but I couldn't tell if he felt the same way, so I kept my flirting to a minimum. As we were leaving, I offered a ride home to anyone who needed one, and he was the only person who took me up on it, so I thought the feeling might be mutual.

Even though I had never cheated on Todd, I longed to know if my attraction to certain people was returned. Knowing whether the feeling was mutual might satisfy some of my urge to go further. But I didn't ever ask anyone for fear that it would get back to Todd, or that I might tempt fate.

So during the brief drive from the restaurant to Andy's apartment complex, I fought back the desire to ask him head-on how he felt about me. Instead, I made idle chat.

"So, are you having a good time in the show?" I asked him.

"Yeah, it's really wonderful."

"Are you getting to be friends with the other cast members?"

"Yeah, some of them, especially. We're becoming like a family, you know?"

"I do."

I glanced over at him as I drove, wondering if he was doing the same while I wasn't looking. But soon enough we reached his destination, and he gave me a brief hug good night and went upstairs, and I drove off to my hotel room alone.

I had become an e-mail junkie over the past year, answering as much of my fan mail as I could, and striking up a few lovely friendships with some of the early enthusiasts of the show via AOL. E-mail had also served as an easy distraction from the reality of my mom's illness. And now that she was gone and the waiting was over, the last thing I wanted to do was sit in a strange hotel room in silence, alone with my thoughts; I had to keep finding ways to occupy myself. So as soon as I sat on my hotel room bed, I popped open my laptop and signed on to the annoyingly familiar generic male voice proclaiming, "Welcome! You've got mail!" and I opened up my inbox to discover an e-mail from Andy.

It was really nice meeting you tonight, I read. *I hope we can keep in touch.* On a whim, feeling impulsive as hell, I typed in his screen name to see if he was online, and lo and behold, he was, so I sent him an instant message.

"Hi."

"HI!" he typed back.

"Thanks for your e-mail," I said. I felt my cheeks flush, and my heart rate picked up steam.

"No problem."

"It was really nice to meet you, too," I said.

"Thanks."

And before I stopped myself, I typed, "I think you're really cute."

I hit the "send" button and waited for his reply. It was a smiley face. Followed by, "Thanks, I think you are, too."

I had crossed a big line, but invigorated by his response, I wasn't going to turn back now. "Really? I wasn't sure. I never know for sure, you know?"

"No, I really do. I really do."

Beaming, I shoved to the corner of my mind the nagging feeling that I was treading on dangerous territory. I resented Todd for all of the times I hadn't said to others what I was now saying to Andy. I became incredibly aroused.

"If I didn't have a boyfriend . . ." I said.

"I know," Andy replied.

"Oh well," I said.

"Yeah."

And we continued to type at length, sharing more stories about what it was like to work on this amazing show we were both in. I told him about my mom, and he listened and offered heartfelt condolences and told me about his family back in Florida. After a while, it was very late and we said good night and signed off. And I knew that I had started something that I wasn't sure I wanted to stop—something thrillingly illicit that would keep me occupied. And no matter what, I knew I couldn't ever mention one word of it to Todd.

Over the next month or so, after I returned to New York and threw myself back into my life there—filling up every hour I could with plans and social engagements and e-mails and dinners and, of course, the usual eight shows a week of *Rent*—Andy and I e-mailed each other every day, sometimes more than once a day, and when we found each other online at the same time, we chatted. He even sent me a handwritten letter with his picture enclosed, which I carefully hid away. And we made contact via phone more than once, although that seemed too risky, so I kept our phone calls to a minimum. In all of our various modes of communicating, I would tell him about the difficulties I'd been having with Todd, about how little Todd had been able to comfort me throughout my mom's illness and in the aftermath of her death, and Andy would offer to treat me with more love and kindness and care than Todd. I pined for Andy and thought about him and fantasized about him and looked forward to each opening of my AOL mailbox to see if there was something new from him. It was the closest I had ever come to having a full-blown affair, and I grew accustomed to the sensation of carrying around this secret when I was with Todd or when Todd also signed on to AOL from his apartment while I chatted with Andy online from mine. I knew that what I was doing was out of bounds, that it was wrong, but I convinced myself that since no physical contact of any kind had taken place, or would be taking place, that since it was all just talk, it really wasn't such a big deal. And besides, since Todd wasn't giving me the kind of care that I needed and wanted from him, fuck it, I had to get it from someone, right? Talking to Andy felt safe; he didn't begrudge me anything, he wasn't threatened by the attention I was receiving from my fans, and he had an open ear when I told him stories about my mother and everything that had happened in the last few months.

During this time, though, I began to feel that my mother's death had occurred long ago, that it had become some remote event lodged in the outer recesses of my memory. I had come back from our vacation in LA with a vengeance, not missing any more shows, pouring myself into every performance, loving being onstage again, spending as much time as possible with my friends, sleeping very little, making sure I was rarely alone and quiet. And for the moment, at least, I was feeling free of the pressures that had dogged me in the long long wait for the moment of Mom's death. So with all of my newfound energy, I gave myself over to this virtual-reality affair I was having with a near-stranger three thousand miles away, intoxicated by our illicit e-mails and instant messages, and thrilled by the escape from the stresses of my relationship with Todd that Andy's desire afforded me.

Idina was the next one to leave the cast, so she could go off and record her first album, with Hollywood Records. While I wasn't as close to her as I was to Daphne, I hated to see her go; her nightly, explosive rendition of "Take Me or Leave Me" had brought me so much joy. I had the privilege of sitting onstage show after show and drinking in the ridiculously raucous and joyful ovation she and Fredi always received.

Soon after her departure, word came down that Jesse would be the next to go; he had gotten a recurring role on *Ally McBeal,* and there was sure to be more work, so his time had come. I deeply dreaded saying goodbye to him; not only was he one of my dressing room mates (Adam was the other), but he was also one of my best friends in the cast. The consistency and passion for his work that he had continuously displayed had carried me along on nights when I had been just emotionally spent, or physically exhausted, or both. I hated losing such a strong source of support, especially now, only a month and a half after Mom's death.

But I tried my best to ignore his impending departure, stuffing down my dread in the same place I was stuffing down my guilt about Andy and my lingering grief in the wake of Mom's death, and I just kept at my frenetic pace of the past few weeks. I even managed to schedule a trip home to Joliet, to surprise Rachel on her tenth birthday.

Technically, it was a trip to New Lenox, the next town over from Joliet where Anne lived. I purposely avoided Joliet on my way to Anne's house; I just wasn't up to driving down its familiar streets without also going home to see Mom.

I walked into Anne's house, and Rachel immediately burst out of her chair and into my arms, her excitement as infectious as ever.

"Anthoneeeeeeeeee!"

I laughed as I gave her a huge hug. "Happy birthday, Rachel," I said, kissing the top of her head. Anne grinned, a rare occurrence, as she watched us embrace.

I spent the day with Rachel, taking her shopping and to see the movie *Babe,* which we both loved, and all day I tried to gauge whether I could broach the subject of Mom's death. I was especially mindful of my approach in the wake of a conversation I'd had with Anne right after Mom's memorial.

We were standing in her kitchen, and Anne was telling me about the "gratitude book" she'd given to Rachel.

"She gets to write an entry every day about something she's grateful for," she said.

"That sounds very nice," I said.

"I'm asking her to write something about Mom in it, too, if she wants."

"That sounds good. I'd love to talk to her about all of that at some point."

Anne regarded me firmly. "That's my job," she said, her voice on edge. "I'm responsible for her now."

I was surprised by the intensity of her declaration. And even though I didn't entirely agree, I said, "Okay."

But as I drove home with Rachel after the movie, I couldn't resist asking, "How are you feeling about Mom?"

"I miss her," Rachel said.

"Yeah, me too."

Concerned about overstepping the boundary Anne had set for me, I left it at that, for the moment, anyway.

That night, in Anne's darkened, sleeping house, I found myself awake well after everyone else had turned in for the night. Too much silence had settled into the house, so I went online and was happy to find that Andy was on. I promptly wrote hello. And because there was something even more illicit about engaging in this activity in my sister's house, I was bolder than usual.

"I really wish you were here right now," I said.

"Really? Why?"

"'Cause there are so many things I would want to do to you right now." Part of me felt silly for talking this way, like I was suddenly in a cheeseball porn film, but I continued. "I really want you."

"I want you, too," he said. And as he said this, Todd signed on as well, startling me. I didn't panic when I saw his screen name appear, although I was starting to feel a little high from all of the adrenaline that was firing through me.

"How are you?" Todd asked. I typed to Andy, "Todd is on, hold on," and then I typed to Todd, "I'm fine. Rachel was happy and surprised. I'm just writing e-mails and stuff."

"To who?"

"Just some fan mail and stuff. Nothing too important." It was easy to type those words, which were far from the truth. Since I was already in so deep, what was one more little lie?

"And stuff?"

"It's a turn of phrase, Todd, jesus."

"Well, I'm going to bed. See you tomorrow." I was scheduled to fly home the next day so I could be there in time for my performance.

"Okay, honey, see you tomorrow. Love you." Again, it was easy to be sickly sweet to Todd while, unbeknownst to him, Andy was off to the side, waiting for me to come back to him.

"Love you, too," Todd said.

And as soon as he signed off, I went right back to typing with Andy. "That was a close one," I said. I was starting to relish the idea that if Todd wanted to be so fucking jealous and paranoid all the time, I'd give him something to be jealous and paranoid about.

"Yeah," he said. "I wish you were alone . . ."

"Me too . . ." I sighed as I typed and then got up quickly and closed my bedroom door. I was feeling jumpy and incredibly horny and more impulsive and reckless and driven to misbehave than I'd ever been, and before I had really formulated my thoughts, I wrote, "I want to do something with you right now."

"What do you mean?" he replied.

"I don't know . . ."

"Well, what can we do? We're not even in the same city."

"I know . . ." And then I had a heady idea. "Let's both sign off and get ourselves off at the same time, and then sign back on so we know we did it." There was no stopping me now, I had crossed a line, but somewhere in my mind I thought that what I had proposed would exempt us from cheating, since we weren't directly engaging each other in a sexual act.

"Wow," Andy said. "Okay, I think that would be hot. Yeah, let's do it."

"Okay," I said, feeling giddy and stupid and incredibly turned on. "I'll see you back here in five minutes."

And we both signed off. As I leaned back and closed my eyes and got myself off, I imagined Andy doing the same thing in his little apartment in La Jolla, and it was hot hot hot and I drove away thoughts that I had seriously fucked up now, that there was no way I could get away with this for long, that Todd had been right about me all along—I was full of shit, he was right. I stuffed away those thoughts and signed back on to find Andy waiting for me there.

"That was hot," he said.

"Yeah," I said.

"Too bad you weren't really here."

"Yeah," I said. "Too bad."

We said good night and I staved off the chunks of guilt that were threatening to dislodge themselves from the outer edges of my mind. In these past few weeks, I had been getting more and more adept at keeping my thoughts at bay, at keeping myself occupied with any-thing but the consequences of my recent experiences, and soon after I lay down on my sister's guest bed, I drifted off into an easy sleep.

The next time I saw Todd, after my show the following night, I could barely look him in the eye; it was much harder to shove away my guilt in his presence than it had been while I was by myself. We had sex, though, not so much because I wanted to, but because if we didn't he was probably going to be upset and question whether I still loved him and wanted him. And as we lay in the dark after we were finished, I stared at the ceiling, my hand distractedly resting on his, and I tried to sort out how I could still put what I had done with Andy into a guilt-free context. It had been nothing, really, after all, it had just been talk, and what he and I had done we had done in our separate homes, on our own time, and how was that any different than if I had just jerked off by myself at any other time? And as my thoughts chased themselves around while Todd slept next to me, my head eventually slowed its churning and I was finally able to get to sleep.

The next day I was at home, avoiding silence by answering e-mails (Andy wasn't around online, although I was hoping that he would be) when Todd signed on.

"I want to talk to you," he typed.

Already I could feel my throat tightening at the thought of another fight with him. "Okay," I answered.

"On the phone," he said. That was sort of new; we'd been known to have long fights online as much as in person or on the phone.

"Okay," I said. He quickly signed off, and I followed him.

I stared at the phone for several long moments before dialing his all-too-familiar seven digits.

"What is up with you?" he asked.

"What do you mean?" I asked.

"You've been very distant since you came back. What's going on?"

I didn't answer him for a long moment. My stomach started to burn.

"What's going ON?" he said, his voice rising. *"Say* something! You're really freaking me out!"

My heart was thudding. "I . . ."

"WHAT?!?"

I didn't know what words I could use to explain or defend what I had done, or what kind of insanity I might encounter on the other end of the phone no matter what I said.

"I *need* you to fucking *say* something!" His breath came fast and heavy. "I'm going to start panicking if you don't fucking *talk.*"

"Todd, I . . ."

"*WHAT?!?*" I could hear him as he swallowed, hard. "What happened? What *happened*?!?"

I stared straight ahead, barely moving, my voice hardly above a whisper. My head felt incredibly heavy. "I don't know how to say it . . ."

"Say WHAT?!?" Where were the words? What words could I use? "Did you fuck someone?" he shouted. "DID YOU FUCK SOMEONE?!?"

"*No!*" I managed. "I didn't fuck anyone."

"Then *what*?"

"I . . ." I began, then stopped again. Mercifully, Todd waited for me to continue. And somehow, I managed to say, "I just . . . jerked off with someone."

"What do you mean?" His voice was low and thick and horrible. "What does that *mean*?!?"

"He's in California, he's someone I met in California . . ."

"WHO?!?"

"He's in *Rent* there, I met him when I went down to La Jolla—"

"Oh my god," Todd said. "Oh, *fuck*."

I was beginning to cave into myself. "I'm sorry," I said.

"When was this?" he said.

"Just the other night," I said.

"*What* other night?!?"

"The other night, when I was home," I said.

"Oh, fuck. You're *sick*," Todd hissed. "You're fucking *sick*. In your sister's house? You fucking did this in your sister's *house*?!?"

My skull felt heavy, weighing my head down. "Yes," I said.

"You sick motherfucker. I can't fucking believe this. You *asshole*. You sick *asshole*."

"I'm sorry . . ."

"I don't know what to do," Todd said, his voice rising again.

"What do you mean?"

"I don't know what to do. I can't believe this, I can't fucking believe you *did* this to me, after *everything,* I can't fucking *believe* it."

"I'm sorry . . ."

"You fucking better be sorry," he growled. "Fucking sick *asshole.* "

I heaved a huge sigh. "I don't know what else to say . . ."

"I'll talk to you later, I can't talk to you right now, I can't fucking *BELIEVE* you!" he screamed and then hung up. I sat staring at the phone—it had all happened so quickly, it was out, the truth of what I had done was out, just like that, and now what would happen? Was that it? Had I fucked up so badly that it was over? He was right, what I had done was sick, it was sick and wrong and fucked up and stupid and sick. I began to rub furiously at my eyes, digging into them, trying to find somewhere to put my shame and guilt and rage and exhaustion, and as I was scouring my eyelids into my palms I realized I had seen Mom do this very thing over and over again, endlessly rub her eyes while sitting at the kitchen table, night after night, when she was upset or tired or just weary from laughter, and as I saw her in my mind doing this most familiar thing, I fought off a fresh hot wave of grief that was welling up out of my chest and throat, threatening to engulf me, and I stuffed it all back down, I trampled it, I crammed it away, because in that moment, if I had failed to overcome it, if I had lost myself to it, I really didn't know if I would ever recover.

Every conversation with Todd over the next day and a half followed the same pattern. I apologized over and over, and he called me sick and fucked and twisted over and over, and when I asked him what else I could say or do, he said he didn't know, and I knew then that there was no way out of this mess that I'd created, there was no turning back or erasing what had happened. It had happened—it had, it *had*—and our fights continued. And then one of our fights was happening at the Nederlander, in the alley by the wall with all of the signatures on it from our fans and friends and loved ones, and I was sitting there with my head in my hands, and Todd was there because it was the night of Jesse's last show and he wanted to be there to see that happen, and I so hated that Jesse was leaving, that so many of our friends were there to tell him goodbye, and here I was having this endless fight with my boyfriend, and the alley was full of people—cast members and friends and well-wishers—but there we were, Todd and I, fighting through it all again, but keeping our voices down as much as possible, and as Todd railed at me, I began to feel increasingly numb, almost dead really, just numb, just nothing, and his voice and his rage kept coming at me and coming at me and coming at me, and finally, after Todd had hammered at me once again how sick and fucked and twisted I was, I found myself saying into my lap, "I can't do this anymore."

Todd stopped. "What?"

I breathed deeply, staring at my hands, which were clenched into fists. "I can't do this anymore." Once again, my voice was tiny. I lifted my head and somehow managed to look at Todd. He stared wildly back at me.

"What does that mean?" he said.

"I can't do this anymore." It was all I could say. I wasn't even trying to say it; it was just coming out of me. "I can't. I can't do it anymore."

He suddenly stepped back, his face all twisted up, and he shouted at me, "Fuck you!" He backed away from me and said, "Fuck you!" again, and then he said, pointing at me, hurling his words at me, "Don't you fucking *talk* to me, don't you fucking *write* to me, don't you fucking *call* me, I never want to fucking *see* you again!" He turned and started to walk away, and the sight of him turning his back on me, of another person that I loved leaving me behind, of one more loss, was too much, everything that had happened was just too much—I had held it all at bay for weeks now, I had managed to just go and go and go and go and *go*—but in that moment, in that exact moment, as I saw Todd stride away from me, something inside of me cracked and fell away. I suddenly had no control over my body, and as I watched myself in slow motion, I leaped up and charged forward, and I pummeled Todd, I punched him in the back of the head, knocking him down, and I saw him turn to me, terror in his eyes, and I punched his head and his arms, and I dimly heard shouts behind me and I felt hands pulling me off him, and I heard Jesse's voice in my ear saying, "Anthony, Anthony, come on, come on now," and I heard Norbert, Adam's understudy, whisper, "Hey hey hey hey," and together they pulled me off Todd, who was now huddled on the concrete, his hands covering his head, and Norbert's and Jesse's hands were strong around my arms as they pulled me away from Todd, but I pressed into the ground with the full strength of my legs and I reached out and crawled with my hands and knees across the concrete, dragging these two men with me until I ripped free of them and charged back at Todd, assailing him with fresh blows to his back and his shoulders, saying, "Fuck you fuck you fuck you!" with each punch, and once again Jesse and Norbert were on me, and once again they pulled me off Todd, and this time he leaped up and dashed out of the alleyway, gasping for breath, and with the sight of him vanishing around the corner, I suddenly came back into my body.

"Oh god oh god oh god oh god," I said. I looked down at my hands, which were shaking uncontrollably and filthy. I was beginning to hyperventilate. I couldn't look at any of the faces of the people who were in that alleyway, all of the people who had witnessed what I had just done, and there was nowhere to go, there was no escape. I moved to the fire escape that was tucked in the corner of the alley, and as I raced up the clanging metal steps I heard Jesse call my name, but I couldn't look at him, I couldn't respond, and I was sobbing now, really sobbing, terrified of what I'd just done, the full weight of it crashing down, sure that I would never see Todd again, I may as well have killed him, and no, not another loss like this, not another one, no no no no no, how had I fucked everything up so much, how had I done this, how had I lost control of myself? I had completely lost control, I was not there, I was gone, somewhere else—what had I done, what had I become, how did that *happen?*—and I paced back and forth on the landing of the fire escape, horrified at the prospect of ever heading down and facing my friends and colleagues and whoever else had witnessed my insanity. And I stared at my hands, which would not stop their awful shaking; they were black with soot, and bloody, not from Todd, I knew that, but from scraping my hands along the ground as I had dragged Norbert and Jesse behind me. And I knew that this was the worst thing that I had ever done, the absolute worst, irreversible and horrible and shameful and awful and hateful and how would I ever recover from it? How would my life ever return to normal?

I dimly realized that I was terribly thirsty, and I rushed downstairs. Hiding my face, I opened the stage door and huddled in front of the water cooler, staring at the stream as it filled my cup. My hands were still shaking, and now my whole *body* was shaking, and I gulped all of the water down, refilled my cup, and felt a hand on my shoulder. I couldn't look at whose hand it was but I heard Adam's voice say, "Hey, are you okay?" I heard myself say, "No, I'm not," and I gulped more water down. I heard Adam say, "Jesse told me what happened," and I gulped more water down. I said, "Uh huh," and I heard Adam say, "You gonna be okay?" I said, "I don't know." And I still couldn't face him as I got up and walked upstairs toward my dressing room, my knees almost giving way with the force of their shaking, and there was Crystal, one of our stage managers, standing on the landing. I couldn't look at her as she said, "Anthony, I need to talk to you for a second." There was nothing reprimanding about how she said it, there was no malice—her voice was actually gentle—and I stopped and stared at the ground, my breath beginning to come back under control little by little. She said, "I need to know if you will be able to do the show tonight." And this hit me with enormous force, the knowledge that all of what I had done, all of this had happened on the night of Jesse's last show, and I almost began to hyperventilate again. I said, "I don't know, I don't know." She said a little more firmly but still gently, "Anthony, look at me." I swallowed and breathed and somehow raised my head and looked her in the eye. She regarded me very steadily, with compassion and patience, and said, "It's okay either way. I just need you to tell me so I can let everyone else know." And as she said it, she was clear and warm and strong, and as she awaited my answer, holding me in her kind gaze, my breathing finally normalized, and my heartbeat finally slowed. I knew then that what I had just done was not a crime to her, I knew that I wasn't disgusting and sick and horrible to her, I knew that everything was going to be all right. And I knew that I couldn't bear to miss doing this one last performance with Jesse. I took another deep breath, and said, "Yes, I can do the show."

"Okay," she said. "Thank you." She squeezed my shoulder and went downstairs. I knew that I had to go downstairs too, that I had to see if Todd was still around. I had to see if he was all right; I had to see if I had really hurt him.

Jesse was standing right outside the door, smoking, when I emerged into the alleyway. He put his hands on my shoulders and looked me right in the eye. "You okay?" he asked. He was asking me if *I* was okay?

"Yeah, I think so," I said, my voice still feeling far away. "Are you okay?"

"Yeah, I'm okay." And he smiled ruefully, shaking his head, taking a drag of his cigarette. "Man . . ." he said.

"I'm sorry," I said.

"Naw, man, it's okay, it's all right. What the hell happened to you?"

"I don't know," I said. How could I possibly begin to tell him?

"I mean, one second, I was standing here with Norbert, just talking and smoking, you know, and then the next thing I knew you turned into Mike Tyson." He kind of laughed as he said it.

"I know," I said. "I just . . . lost control," I said.

"No *shit*, man. I mean, you were a little scary there for a minute."

"I know," I said. "I'm sorry it had to happen tonight, of all nights, I mean it's your last show . . ."

"Naw, man, don't worry about that. It actually kind of helped me take my mind off it, you know?"

"Uh huh." And then I said, "Um, do you know where Todd is?"

"Uh, yeah, he's outside, talking to Cy."

Of course Cy would be here tonight, for Jesse's last show; she had become friends with all of us, and wouldn't have missed this occasion. And how lucky I was that she was here; what better person was there to tend to Todd at a moment like this than Cy? "Is he okay?" I asked.

"He's a little spooked, I think, but he's okay. I mean, it doesn't look like you hurt him too badly or anything."

"I want to see him," I said.

"Yeah, that's probably a good idea. I'll go get him." And as he walked off to get Todd, I looked around the alleyway, to see who else might have witnessed my meltdown, but I had no way of knowing who had and who hadn't. And then there was Todd walking toward me, looking young and scared but also open and strangely at peace. I reached out my hand and hugged him and held him close to me and said in his ear, "I'm sorry, I'm so sorry." He said quietly in my ear, "I know, I know, it's okay." And I knew that he meant it. I pulled back and looked him in the eye and said, "Are you okay?" and he said, "I think you banged yourself up more than me." He held my gaze, chewing his lip a little, but steadier than I'd seen him in a long time.

"I'm so sorry," I said again, holding his hands in mine, squeezing them, while he squeezed back. And after all the noise and fury and haranguing that he'd thrown my way over the last couple of days, after he'd unrelentingly railed at me for what I'd done with Andy, after all of that, and after months of fighting about so many things, and after today, after the worst possible thing I could have done to him was done, after all of it, I knew that right now, for the first time, I felt his forgiveness.

"I just couldn't see you go like that," I said. "I couldn't control myself, I'm sorry, but I couldn't see you go."

"I know," he said.

"I'm so sorry," I said.

"I know," he said. "It's okay. It's okay."

"I love you."

"I love you, too," he said. "Now go do your show."

"Okay." And he kissed me and turned and walked out, and I looked over to Cy, who had followed Todd in, and I said to her, "Thank you for helping him out there."

She reached out and grabbed my hand, her manner as steady and gracious as ever. "Are you okay?" she asked. People kept asking me if I was okay, and I was the attacker. It was so strange, this outpouring of concern for my welfare in the wake of what I'd done.

"Yeah," I said. "I don't know how that happened. But yeah, I'm okay."

"Well, honey, no one's that badly hurt, thankfully. These things happen. Sometimes people lose control. You know? And I hope you know that this didn't come from nowhere; you've gone through a tremendous amount lately. You've been under enormous pressure."

"Yeah, but still . . ."

"I'm not suggesting that you should go around doing this sort of thing all the time, my dear. I hope you know that."

"Of course."

"But I think he can understand where this came from. He's a very bright young man, you know. And he loves you very much."

"Yes, he does, I do know that."

"And there are no broken bones, only a few bruises, and in the end, you know, he's all right, and you're all right."

I sighed. "Yeah . . ." Then I said, "Thank you again for your help."

"It's the least I could do. He's fine. You'll be fine."

Crystal poked her head out the stage door. "It's half hour," she said.

"I've got to go in," I said to Cy.

"Have an amazing show."

"Okay." I regarded this remarkable woman who had given me so much support in this tumultuous year and a half, and I reached out and gave her a firm hug. "Thank you for everything," I said.

"Thank *you,*" she replied.

I made my way upstairs to my dressing room, and Adam was the next person to ask me whether I was okay. "I think you scared the crap out of a few people," he said, smiling. Jesse giggled.

"Whassup, Tyson?" he said.

Abashed, but grateful that my friends hadn't abandoned me after witnessing my insanity, I smiled in spite of myself and started getting into my costume.

Adam continued, "I wouldn't have known you had it in you like that."

"Neither would I," I said, regarding myself in the mirror as I pulled on my well-worn striped sweater. My eyes were a little puffy, but otherwise I looked none the worse for wear. Everything had happened in such a flash, only about twenty minutes ago, and it amazed me how quickly I had recovered, how easily I had been welcomed back into my family at the theatre.

"I mean you're not that big a guy," Adam said, "and Jesse and Norbert aren't small guys, and you got away from both of them."

"I know," I said.

"Well, he's not big," Jesse said to Adam, "but he's *strong* when he wants to be. And he wanted to be." He giggled again.

I turned to him and said, "Sorry again that it all went down like that tonight, when, you know . . ."

"Hey, man, I said don't worry about it. I've seen crazier shit than that in my life before now, believe me. But that was pretty crazy." He chuckled. "Hey, man, I'm just glad you're okay."

"Thanks." I gave him a big hug, which he gave right back, saying, "Have a great show," and before we both started blubbering we broke away and headed downstairs.

We had already all lived through so many charged performances of our show, and this night was no exception. Everyone else shared my opinion of Jesse's importance to our show, onstage and off, so during his love song with Angel, "I'll Cover You," the entire company and all of the stagehands gathered together in the wings and drank in this final rendition. Jesse's joy and love and generosity of spirit poured out of him, and I grinned through my tears, cheering along with everyone when he and Wilson reached the end.

The roughest moment, as usual, was the reprise of "I'll Cover You," and as we sang we all struggled to hold ourselves together. Todd had secured a seat in the front row, and when I joined the line at the edge of the stage, I glanced down, and he flashed his familiar "I love you" sign to me, and I raised my voice and sang with all of my friends. I sang for Jesse and Idina and Daphne and Jonathan and Ben Wackerman and, especially, I sang for my mother. I sang for all of them with my friends in this show that had transformed my life so fully and irrevocably. I sang my whole heart out.

After the show, I stopped off in the stage manager's office. Leaning against the door, exhausted from the intensity of the events before the show and from the performance itself, I said to Crystal, "I just wanted to thank you for talking to me before the show."

She regarded me with clear, strong eyes and said, "You're welcome."

"I really lost control of myself out there," I said.

"I know."

"And I don't think I would have been able to come back from that if you hadn't been so patient with me," I said. "Thank you for that."

"Well, I could identify," she said. "When I lost my father a few years ago, there was one night I found myself literally banging my head into a wall."

"Really?" I said.

"Yes, really." She put her hand on my shoulder. "You have got to get some help with this, Anthony. You've been holding yourself together, and we all appreciate how much you've been going through, but it seems like maybe you've been holding too much of it in, and you need to get it out, believe me, or you will keep exploding like that. And that won't do you any good at all. And I can only say this because I've been there."

I nodded, sighing a little. "You're right."

"So go get help," she said again. "Because you don't want something like that to happen again, okay?"

"Of course not."

She folded me in her arms in a firm, warm embrace. "You take good care of yourself, okay?"

"Okay."

And remarkably, there seemed to be no major ill consequence from my meltdown backstage at the Nederlander. Having lived through tornadoes back in Joliet, I recognized that the new peace that Todd and I were now experiencing was something like the rare tranquility that follows a violent storm. The truth of my infidelity was out, and the worst possible aftermath of that revelation had occurred, and yet in its wake, we had survived, a little the worse for wear, but stronger, too. It was as if Todd could relax now that his most vivid fears had been made real, and he had emerged more or less intact. But his surprising and graceful forgiveness and acceptance of me continued to move me, and I did my best to honor the opportunity he'd given me to make amends and redeem myself.

And I did take Crystal's advice, and started seeing a therapist on a regular basis, Robin, a kind and urbane lesbian who worked at Friends In Deed. Robin began to help me explore my family's long history of avoiding conflict, the effect that legacy had on me now, my need to avoid saying or doing the wrong thing, my reluctance to admit to myself or to Todd when I was attracted to other people, and my reluctance, at times, to set clearer boundaries for how I should be treated, and on and on.

And she listened as I shared stories of my mother, and she sat patiently as I wept at times, and our sessions became a safe haven. She began to help quiet down and smooth over the more jagged and noisy edges of my grief, so much so that soon I found that I was no longer as afraid as I had been of what I might say or do. And over time, I began to allow room for everything that was in me.

thawing

The morning sun glowed through the skylight of our bedroom, waking me up. I quietly got out of bed and padded across the floor, softly closing the door behind me, leaving Todd asleep, and I headed out the glass doors onto the verandah.

Our guesthouse sat at the edge of a three-hundred-foot cliff on the north shore of Maui, situated on a beautiful, remote outcropping. Where the coastline curved away to the left, whales came to spawn in the spring. We were on this vacation in October, so there wouldn't be any whales to see, but I loved imagining what they might look like.

I had expected Maui to be one giant tourist attraction, but I was delightfully surprised to discover how rugged and unspoiled and exotic much of it still was. I had never breathed in such fragrant and balmy sea air, or seen such an infinite variety of luminescent wildflowers, or spotted so many surprising, instantaneous rainbows.

Mom had been gone for almost five months now, and my relationship with Todd had survived, and even begun to flourish, in the wake of everything that had happened. My life in *Rent* had begun to shift: Jesse's departure had been followed soon after by Taye's, and then Fredi's, until only Wilson, Adam, and I were left of the original eight principals. I had started to grow accustomed to, and even fond of, the different rhythms of the talented people who had been brought in to replace my friends, but I knew that my time in the show was going to end soon. I was starting to miss too many people too much. I was starting to become too haunted by phantoms.

About a month prior to my trip to Maui, I had talked to Todd about wanting to take a vacation in time for Mom's birthday. I'd anticipated that it would be a difficult time for me, a pointed reminder of her absence, and I thought that if we could be somewhere beautiful and peaceful and remote, I might have a better chance of making it through with more ease. Todd had agreed that it was a good idea, and since his brother Lawrence lived on Maui and knew a gay couple that owned a lovely guesthouse there, we had made our plans and booked our tickets and now there we were.

And today was Mom's birthday. Fifty-six years ago she had been born to Dolores and Robert Baird of Elmira, New York. She would be followed by twelve others. She had raised three children of her own and one that wasn't her own by birth, but who had become her own. She had administered loving nursing care to countless children and juvenile delinquents and even murderers. She had taken every step she could to leave the people in her life at peace with her passing, and she had died with grace.

I thought of all of this as I sat on the verandah, gazing out at the tremendously blue and endless ocean, wishing she could have lasted longer, wishing she could have managed to make the journey to such a beautiful place as this before she died. The only regrets that my mother had expressed to me before her death were that she wished she had traveled more, and she wished that she had had more fun. While I truly believed that Cy was right, that everything that happened in life was exactly the way it should have happened, because it *did* happen, I also truly believed that Mom had been too young, that too much of her life had been taken away by her death at fifty-five. If she had made it through her illness I would have made sure that she traveled more; I would have made sure that she had more fun.

I heard the screen door open behind me, and Todd said, "How long have you been up?"

"Just a little while," I said, my voice thickened with tears.

"Oh, honey," Todd said, and sat down next to me and held my hand and rubbed my hair out of my face. This softness from him, which had been so rare at times, this loving touch, which I had not asked for but which I so desperately needed, melted me, and I sank into his arms.

"She's here, you know," he said, his voice so soothing. He kissed the top of my head. "She's right here."

"I know," I said, and I breathed, pressing my face into Todd's chest. "I know."

I stayed in the Broadway company of the show for another two months after our trip to Hawaii, finally leaving in January of 1998. I then joined the touring company for a couple of weeks during its run in Chicago so I could perform for my hometown crowd. That was where Anne and Rachel were finally able to see it. Happily, they loved it. Soon after that, I traveled to London with Jesse, Adam, and Wilson, where we opened the West End production.

I was going to be in London in May, on the first anniversary of Mom's death, and as the 22nd loomed ever closer, I felt an old, familiar, raw edge begin to creep its way back into my being. Todd was visiting me from New York at the time, and I sat him down one day.

"I just want you to know that I'm starting to feel a little raw," I said. This phrase had become part of our shorthand; I had become more adept at warning him of the days in which my grief was taking a larger toll than normal, although those days had become fewer and fewer over the last year.

"Okay," he said. "Don't worry, I'll be here."

It had been a remarkable turnaround; his new patience brought me tremendous relief. I still bore the brunt of his jealousy at times, and we still bickered and struggled through many moments, but overall, the peace that had followed my backstage explosion had remained.

I braced myself for a meltdown during the performance on the anniversary itself, but I made it through without incident. Even during the reprise of "I'll Cover You" and "Halloween" and "Goodbye Love," which had often been difficult to get through following Jonathan's death and during Mom's illness and after her death, I held steady. I waited for the grief that was lurking around the corner of my consciousness to overcome me, but it stayed at bay.

I was living in a flat on the south bank of the Thames, about a twenty-minute walk from the Shaftesbury Theatre, where *Rent* was playing, and that night, Todd met me at the theatre so we could take the walk together.

"How are you holding up?" he said.

"Fine, I guess." And I was, surprisingly so.

We walked along the narrow, quiet streets around Covent Garden, hardly saying anything. I sensed the beginnings of tightness in my chest, but I still felt strong.

And then, when we crossed over the Hungerford Footbridge and began to make our way along the Thames, something about the perfect beauty of the cool night air and the amber glow of the lights shining on Big Ben and Parliament and the unbearable knowledge that these were examples of the things my mother never got to experience and never would, prevented my legs from holding me up, and I barely managed to find a bench to sit on. And the tightness in my chest bloomed open into wracking sobs that wouldn't stop. And it was worse than a year ago, when I was in my mother's room with her dead body lying there, and I almost couldn't breathe for the heaving of my chest, and it was horrible that all this time had passed and she wasn't here but I was, living on and on, and there had been times in the past year when I had hardly thought about her, and how terrible was that, how *selfish*? I thought things were supposed to get easier as time went on, but this wasn't easier, this was harder, the truth of her absence was harder than ever to take. I was drowning now, and I gulped down air, and Cy was wrong, there was no way out of this, it would never end, how could I return to myself in the face of the truth that no matter how hard I tried to get on with my life, no matter how much I tried to honor her memory, no matter how much I talked about her or shared stories about her or dreamed about her, she was dead and gone, and forever, and would never be able to comfort me or talk to me or scold me or witness my life for the rest of my life.

I sat with my head buried in my hands, my face slick and hot, and Todd sat with me, resting his hand on my back. But none of it was breaking open and away, as so many of my crying fits in the wake of Mom's death had. Minutes and still more minutes wore on. Flashes ran through my mind of myself crying in front of my mother while she was in her sickbed, when she had so tenderly reached out her hand and stroked my hair and soothed me, and this image brought harder sobs, the knot in my throat making it impossible to breathe.

I could only imagine how twisted up and scarlet my howling face must have seemed to Todd or anyone who walked by, and without thinking I got up and stumbled to my building. I leaned against the wall in the elevator, unable to meet Todd's eyes, wishing it would stop, it would all stop, and after a long, long while, exhausted and spent and hollow, and for the first time not cleansed by my tears, I was able, finally, to quiet down and drift off to sleep.

Mercifully, that first anniversary's awful power has been absent in the ensuing six. As time has gone on, I still experience an ache, on some days more keenly than others, and will undoubtedly forever miss my mother's presence in my life. I always try to mark the anniversary in some way, sometimes by making a small toast or by sending up a thought, or, in one case, writing a letter to Mom.

•   •   •

In November 2001, in the wake of turning thirty, and in response to the urgent reminder of September 11th that nothing is certain and that life deserves to be as full of love and joy and as free of conflict and hardship as possible, Todd and I finally ended our long, tumultuous, loving—but at the core always difficult—relationship. Part of my motivation to end it came when he confessed that all during the time he'd questioned me about sleeping with other people, after all of the endless conversations in which I'd defended myself, he'd gone out and slept with many people himself, several of whom were mutual acquaintances, and some of whom he'd accused me of bedding. At first, this news brought with it a sense of clarity. Of course he had been neurotically jealous; he knew what he was capable of doing, so he would naturally suspect me of the same behavior. I was happy to have the truth out in the open, since it made so much sense of our past. But as time wore on, and I thought more and more about how much work he'd put into deceiving me and how much energy he'd invested in accusing me, and for so long, not to mention how much he'd put us at risk by sleeping around (although we both tested negative after his revelation), I found no way to reconcile our past with our future. Todd agreed, and our ending was more peaceful than much of our relationship.

He and I have both found new love in the wake of our breakup. Rodney's and my three-year anniversary has passed, and we are beginning the long process of adopting a child. Our child will have its share of cousins: my sister, Anne, and her husband, Ken, have given their son Brendan two little sisters, Carley and Lilly, in the years since Mom died. Happily, Anne and I have managed to communicate more openly over the years—although there is always more room to grow—and have continued to give each other spirited competition in Scrabble. She's done a fantastic job raising Rachel as well, who will soon graduate from high school and then pursue a career in law enforcement.

My brother Adam's children—so far—are of the literary, theatrical, and cinematic variety; he has published several novels and plays since Mom died (she was alive for the publication of his first two novels) and will soon start directing his second feature film. Because of our proximity to each other (we live several blocks apart in New York City) and our frequent artistic collaborations, he and I have grown much closer over the last several years. He has consistently provided a wonderful example of how to move on in the face of great loss by funneling his grief over Mom's death into many of his artistic works.

I had the privilege of performing in one of his plays, *Nocturne,* a few years ago, and I found great truth and comfort in these lines I got to say every night: "Grief does not expire like a candle or the beacon on a lighthouse. It simply changes temperature."

postscript:
homecoming

The frigid night air hovered at around 20 degrees Fahrenheit. Huge lights had been lofted into the sky on cranes, shining gorgeously onto Tompkins Square Park. A small crowd had gathered at the end of the block, huddling for warmth under a large tent on the corner of Seventh Street and Avenue B. I stood halfway down the block in the middle of Seventh Street and shivered, my breath pluming out before me. I looked up into the night sky and imagined that Jonathan was looking back down from wherever he was—if he was anywhere, that is—and if he was in fact looking down, that he was catching a glimpse of all of this.

Then Chris Columbus yelled, "Action!" and the turbulent guitars and pounding drums of "What You Own" blared out of the speaker being held in front of me, and a camera crew, seated in the back of an electric car, led me down the street, filming as I, hardly believing it was all really happening right then and there and for real and forever, began to sing out into the cold night air, in the middle of an East Village street, this song that I loved.

After many years of rumors and speculation and false starts, the film version of *Rent* was finally happening. Chris Columbus, with whom I'd made *Adventures in Babysitting* in 1987, had given many of us from the original cast the great gift of the opportunity to reprise our roles on film, and shooting had begun in New York City two days prior. We had already spent a couple of months rehearsing and recording in and around San Francisco, but this nighttime walk that I was taking down the middle of the street (a couple of blocks away from the apartment I'd lived in while I was performing in *Rent* at the New York Theatre Workshop and on Broadway) brought the reality of what was happening home more than anything I'd yet experienced while working on the film. I was in the real neighborhood where Mark and Roger lived, in the real city in which the story Jonathan had written all those years before was set, and I was doing it all more than ten years after performing in the original studio production.

Even though I had been singing some of these songs for over a decade, when I walked into the first day of rehearsals on San Francisco's Treasure Island three and a half months earlier, I couldn't wait to start working on them anew. And as I sang through them with my old friends from the cast and Tim Weil, our original musical director, who had happily been hired to work on the film with us, I realized that I would never grow tired of *Rent*'s music. I would always be grateful to Jonathan for having written such gorgeous songs, which continued to fulfill and reward and reveal themselves in the singing of them, all these years later.

I delighted in witnessing Tracie Thoms and Rosario Dawson struggle to contain their excitement as they felt for the first time the overwhelming power of the harmonies in "Seasons of Love" surround them. Tracie tore into her solo with power and soul, went toe to toe with Idina in "Take Me or Leave Me," and gave me good stuff to play off in "Tango: Maureen." Rosario slinked her way through "Light My

Candle," howled her way through "Out Tonight," and bared her heart wide open in "Without You." Since not all of the original cast could be a part of the film, we were blessed to have Tracie and Rosario with us.

I stood at the piano during rehearsals and listened as Tim led Jesse and Wilson through "I'll Cover You." Years before, in London, I had witnessed what I thought was their last rendition of this song, and here they were again, singing to one another with as much joy and love and connection as ever. I couldn't stop beaming.

I sat in the rehearsal room and was freshly devastated by the agonized and explosive wails of Adam's "One Song Glory," which I also thought I would never hear again.

I joyfully leaped onto the table as we rehearsed "La Vie Boheme," finding my groove again, rediscovering how spastic I could be, doing my best to lead the way as we danced and boogied and sang our tribute to all things bohemian.

And as the weeks of rehearsal, recording, and filming continued, I felt that I had come home.

As I write this, we have just finished shooting the film, and while I have only seen the first teaser trailer and a couple of brief scenes cut together, all indications are that the film will far exceed my hopes for its success. Members of the crew, many of whom had never heard of *Rent* before working on it, regularly went out of their way to say how extraordinary they thought the material was. Chris told us that he was making the most important film of his life. One of the crew members even told me he thought the film was headed for Oscar nominations. That may or may not come to pass.

Regardless, *Rent* has continued to profoundly alter and affect the quality of my life. And now my partner, Rodney, who never saw me play Mark Cohen and missed the initial wave of the show's success, will experience that for the first time. He will bear witness to this new chapter of *Rent* in my life, and share in whatever new gifts it brings our way.

I do wonder if Mom, or some essence of Mom, is aware of this latest turn of events. I know she would be thrilled. And on the night of the world premiere of the film, at the incredible Ziegfeld Theatre in New York City, as I'm watching myself onscreen in the darkness of the cinema, wishing she was there by my side, I will take comfort in this memory: standing on the stage of the Nederlander Theatre on opening night nine years ago, singing my heart out, and looking up to see the reflection of our hundreds of stage lights gleaming and shining off my mother's proud and loving face.

acknowledgments

This book was written over several years, in several cities, and required the patience and kindness and support of many.

For reading early chapters and offering invaluable insight and criticism, I thank Traci Wallack, Carrie Friedman, Laura Varoscak, Elizabeth "Butch" Walker, Melanie McBride, Melissa Anelli, Bill Jahnel, Laura Morris, Cybele Pascal, Shana Campbell-Jones, and Bruce C. Steele.

For meeting with a neophyte author like myself and encouraging me to believe I am a real writer, I thank David Black, Elaine Markson, Kip Kotzen, Beth Vesel, Mary Evans, and Jennifer Rudolph Walsh.

For offering safe, supportive spaces in which to write while I was staying in their homes, I thank David Román and Richard Meyer, Carolyn Lowen, Camryn Manheim, Patrick Fischler, and Felix Pire.

For inspiring me immeasurably throughout this process, I thank the best teacher I ever had, Sande Shurin.

For offering compassionate wisdom and loving-kindness when I needed it the most, I thank the staff of Friends In Deed, especially Cy

O'Neal, Jon Read, Robin Magid, and their colleague Sharon Kleinberg.

For offering me incredible opportunities for growth over the years, I thank the men and women—especially Karen Bihari and Sandy Robbins—with whom I volunteered and participated in Landmark Education's courses and programs. Collectively, they helped me locate within myself the courage to be true to who I am; they inspired me to expand my vision of what was possible for me in the world; and, most important, they urged me to then step out into the world and do everything in my power to make a difference where I could.

For providing more care to my mother during her illness than I was ever able to, I thank my family, especially my aunt Roberta and my sisters, Anne and Rachel.

For never giving up on me during this process, even when I couldn't see my way through it, I thank my agent, Irene Skolnick.

For leading the way in living a life as an accomplished writer and for becoming one of my closest friends, I thank my brother, Adam.

For opening up my heart and showing me new hope in my life, I thank my partner, Rodney To.

For sharing themselves so fully on and offstage (and now on and offscreen), I thank the casts and crews of all the various incarnations of Rent with whom I have had the privilege to work.

For giving this book his generous blessing, I thank Jonathan's father, Al Larson.

For seeing this book through to its completion with sensitivity, grace, and intelligence, I thank my editor, Terra Chalberg.

And finally, for asking me to write this book in the first place—thereby reawakening my long-dormant desire to be a writer—and embracing it even after my appointed task was long overdue, I thank Rob Weisbach, without whom this book truly would not have come into being.

about the author

ANTHONY RAPP has been acting professionally since he was nine years old. He's best known for originating the role of Mark Cohen in Jonathan Larson's Pulitzer Prize–winning landmark rock opera *Rent,* taking the show from off-Broadway to Broadway, Chicago, and London. He shared an OBIE Award with the rest of the original cast for his performance. He has appeared in numerous films, including *Adventures in Babysitting, Dazed and Confused,* the Oscar-winning *A Beautiful Mind,* and most recently, the film adaptation of *Rent.* In 2000, he released his debut album, *Look Around.* He lives in New York City with his partner, Rodney To, and their three cats, Emma, Sebastian, and Spike. This is his first book.